P9-AZV-735

SPRINGDALE PUBLIC LIBRARY
405 S. Pleasant
Springdale, AR 72764

WALK THROUGH WALLS

WALK THROUGH WALLS

A Memoir

MARINA ABRAMOVIĆ

WITH JAMES KAPLAN

CROWN ARCHETYPE
NEW YORK

SPRINGDALE PUBLIC LIBRARY
405 S. Pleasant
Springdale, AR 72764

Copyright © 2016 by Marina Abramović

All rights reserved.
Published in the United States by Crown Archetype,
an imprint of the Crown Publishing Group,
a division of Penguin Random House LLC, New York.
crownpublishing.com

CROWN ARCHETYPE and colophon is a registered trademark
of Penguin Random House LLC.

Library of Congress Cataloging-in-Publication Data is available upon request.

ISBN 978-1-101-90504-3
eBook ISBN 978-1-101-90505-0
Collector's Edition ISBN 978-0-8041-8980-4

PRINTED IN THE UNITED STATES OF AMERICA

Book design by Elizabeth Rendfleisch
Jacket design by Christopher Brand
Jacket photograph by Inez and Vinoodh
Photographs are courtesy of the author unless otherwise noted in
the photo credits on pages 369 and 370.

1 3 5 7 9 10 8 6 4 2

First Edition

I am dedicating this book
to
FRIENDS and ENEMIES

Acknowledgments

I could not walk through walls alone.

I would like first of all to express my deepest gratitude to James Kaplan. He listened to me for countless hours and helped me to tell my story. His desire to understand my life moved me to the core.

My heartfelt thanks goes to David Kuhn, who convinced me that it was time for my memoir and tirelessly guided me through the literary world, and to Nicole Tourtelot.

Thank you to my publisher, Molly Stern, for seeing the potential in my story with an open heart.

I am beyond grateful to my editor, Tricia Boczkowski, for her brilliant comments, her constant support, and her appreciation of my Slavic sense of humor.

It was a joy to work with the highly professional and dedicated team at Crown Archetype: David Drake, Penny Simon, Jesse Aylen, Julie Cepler, Matthew Martin, Christopher Brand, Elizabeth Rendfleisch, Robert Siek, Kevin Garcia, Aaron Blank, and Wade Lucas.

It is a blessing to work with the resilient and passionate people on my team at Abramović LLC: Giuliano Argenziano, Allison Brainard, Cathy Koutsavlis, Polly Mukai-Heidt, and Hugo Huerta; and at the Marina Abramović Institute: Serge Le Borgne, Thanos Argyropoulos, Billy Zhao, Paula Garcia, and Lynsey Peisinger.

I wish to thank my galleries for supporting the art that you read about in this book: Sean Kelly Gallery, New York; Lisson Gallery, London; Galleria Lia Rumma, Naples and Milan; Luciana Brito Galeria, São Paulo; Art Bärtschi & Cie, Geneva; Galerie Krinzinger, Vienna; and Galleri Brandstrup, Oslo.

I hope that in reading these lines, my brother, Velimir, his daughter, Ivana, and my three godchildren, Vladka, Antonio, and Nemo, will better understand certain choices and decisions I made in my life.

To Dave Gibbons for his invaluable spiritual advice in my personal and professional life, and to Rita Capasa for her friendship and sisterly love.

To the wonderful people who have been keeping me healthy for a long time and during the making of the book: Dr. David Orentreich, Dr. Linda Lancaster, Dr. Radha Gopalan, my personal trainer Mark Jenkinsm, and my massage therapist Sarah Faulkner.

There are so many people whose paths crossed with mine and are important to me. I wish I could have had space for all of them.

Finally, I hope that this book is inspirational and teaches everyone that there is no obstacle that you cannot overcome if you have the will and love for what you do.

—Boulbon, France, 2016

WALK THROUGH WALLS

1.

I was walking into the forest with my grandmother one morning. It was so beautiful and peaceful. I was only four years old, a tiny little one. And I saw something very strange—a straight line across the road. I was so curious that I went over to it; I just wanted to touch it. Then my grandmother screamed, so loud. I remember it so strongly. It was a huge snake.

That was the first moment in my life that I really felt fear—but I had no idea what I should be afraid of. Actually, it was my grandmother's voice that frightened me. And then the snake slithered away, fast.

It is incredible how fear is built into you, by your parents and others surrounding you. You're so innocent in the beginning; you don't know.

Me in Belgrade, 1951

I come from a dark place. Postwar Yugoslavia, the mid-1940s to the mid-'70s. A Communist dictatorship, Marshal Tito in charge. Perpetual shortages of everything, drabness everywhere. There is something about Communism and socialism—it's a kind of aesthetic based on pure ugliness. The Belgrade of my childhood didn't even have the monumentalism of Red Square in Moscow. Everything was somehow secondhand. As though the leaders had looked through the lens of someone else's Communism and built something less good and less functional and more fucked-up.

I always remember the communal spaces—they would be painted this dirty green color, and there were these naked bulbs that gave off a gray light that kind of shadowed the eyes. The combination of the light and the color of the walls made everyone's skin yellowish-greenish, like they were liver-sick. Whatever you did, there would be a feeling of oppression, and a little bit of depression.

Whole families lived in these massive, ugly apartment blocks. Young people could never get an apartment for themselves, so every flat would contain several generations—the grandmother and grandfather, the newlywed couple, and then their children. It created unavoidable complications, all these families jammed into very small places. The young couples had to go to the park or the cinema to have sex. And forget about ever trying to buy anything new or nice.

A joke from Communist times: A guy retires, and for having been such an exceptional worker, he is awarded, instead of a watch, a new car, and they tell him at the office he's very lucky—he'll get his car on such and such a date, in twenty years.

"Morning or afternoon?" the guy asks.

"What do you care?" the official asks him.

"I have the plumber coming the same day," the guy says.

My family didn't have to endure all this. My parents were war heroes—they fought against the Nazis with the Yugoslav partisans, Communists led by Tito—and so after the war they became important members of the Party, with important jobs. My father was appointed to Marshal Tito's elite guard; my mother directed an institute that supervised historic monuments and acquired artwork for public buildings. She was also the director of the Museum of Art and Revolution. Because of this, we had many privileges. We lived in a big apartment in the center of Belgrade—Makedonska Street, number 32. A large, old-fashioned 1920s building, with elegant ironwork and glass, like an apartment building in Paris. We had a whole floor, eight rooms for four people—my parents, my younger brother, and me—which was unheard of in those days. Four bedrooms, a dining room, a huge salon (our name for the living room), a kitchen, two bathrooms, and a maid's room. The salon had shelves full of books, a black grand piano, and paintings all over the walls. Because my mother was the director of the Museum of the Revolution, she could go to painters' studios and buy their canvases—paintings influenced by Cézanne and Bonnard and Vuillard, also many abstract works.

When I was young, I thought our flat was the height of luxury. Later I discovered it had once belonged to a wealthy Jewish family, and had been confiscated during the Nazi occupation. Later I also realized the paintings my mother put in our apartment were not very good. Looking back, I think—for these and other reasons—our home was really a horrible place.

My parents, Danica and Vojin Abramović, 1945

My mother, Danica, and my father, Vojin—known as Vojo— had a great romance during World War II. An amazing story—she was beautiful, he was handsome, and each saved the other's life. My mother was a major in the army, and she commanded a squad on the front lines that was responsible for finding wounded partisans and bringing them to safety. But once during a German advance she came down with typhus, and was lying unconscious among the badly wounded, with a high fever and completely covered by a blanket.

She could have easily died there if my father hadn't been such a lover of women. But when he saw her long hair sticking out from under the blanket, he simply had to lift it to take a look. And when he saw how beautiful she was, he carried her to safety in a nearby village, where the peasants nursed her back to health.

Six months later, she was back on the front lines, helping to bring injured soldiers back to the hospital. There she instantly recognized one of the badly wounded as the man who had rescued her. My father was just lying there, bleeding to death—there was no blood available for transfusions. But my mother discovered that she had the same blood type, and gave him her blood and saved his life.

Like a fairy tale. Then the war divided them once more.

But they found each other again, and when the war was over, they married. I was born the following year—November 30, 1946.

The night before I was born, my mother dreamed she gave birth to a giant snake. The next day, while she was leading a Party meeting, her water broke. She refused to interrupt the meeting until it was over: only then would she go to the hospital.

I was born prematurely—the birth was very difficult for my mother. The placenta didn't come out completely; she developed sepsis. Again she almost died; she had to stay in the hospital for almost a year. For a while after that, it was hard for her to continue working, or to raise me.

At first, the maid took care of me. I was in poor health and not eating well—I was just skin and bones. The maid had a son, the same age as me, to whom she fed all the food I couldn't eat; the boy became big and fat. When my grandmother Milica, my mother's mother, came to visit and saw how thin I was, she was horrified. She immediately took me home to live with her, and there I stayed for six years, until my brother was born. My parents only came to visit me on weekends. To me they were two strange people, showing up once a week and bringing me presents I didn't like.

They say that when I was small, I didn't like to walk. My grandmother would put me in a chair at the kitchen table while she went to the market, and I would be there in the same place when she came back. I don't know why I refused to walk, but I think it may have had something to do with being passed around from person to person. I felt displaced and I probably thought that if I walked, it meant I would have to go away again somewhere.

My parents' marriage was in trouble almost immediately, probably even before I was born. Their amazing love story and their good looks had brought them together—sex had brought them together—but so many things drove them apart. My mother came from a rich family and was an intellectual; she studied in Switzerland. I remember my grandmother saying that when my mother left home to join the partisans, she left behind sixty pairs of shoes, taking only one pair of old peasant shoes with her.

My father's family was poor, but they were military heroes. His father had been a decorated major in the army. My father had been imprisoned, even before the war, for having Communist ideas.

For my mother, Communism was an abstract idea, something she'd learned about at school in Switzerland while studying Marx and Engels. For her, becoming a partisan was an idealistic choice, even a fashionable one. But for my father, it was the only way, because he came from a poor family, and a family of warriors. He was the real Communist. Communism, he believed, was a way through which the class system could be changed.

My mother loved to go to the ballet, the opera, to classical music concerts. My father loved roasting suckling pigs in the kitchen and drinking with his old partisan pals. So they had almost nothing in common, and that led to a very unhappy marriage. They fought all the time.

And then there was my father's love of women, the thing that had drawn him to my mother in the first place.

From the beginning of their marriage, my father was constantly unfaithful. My mother of course hated it, and soon she came to hate him. Naturally I didn't know about any of this at first, while I was living with my grandmother. But when I was six, my brother, Velimir, was born and I was taken back to my parents' house to live. New parents, new house, and new brother, all at the same time. And almost immediately, my life got much worse.

I remember wanting to go back to my grandmother's house, because it had been such a secure place for me. It felt very tranquil. She had all these rituals in the morning and in the evening; there was a rhythm to the day. My grandmother was very religious, and her entire life revolved around the church. At six o'clock every morning, when the sun would rise, she'd light a candle to pray. And at six in the evening, she'd light another candle to pray again. I went to church with her every day until I was six and I learned about all the different saints. Her house was always filled with the smell of frankincense and freshly roasted coffee. She roasted the green coffee beans and then ground them by hand. I felt a deep sense of peace in her house.

When I started living with my parents again, I missed those rituals. My parents would just wake up in the morning and work all day and leave me with the maids. Plus, I was very jealous of my brother. Because he was a boy, the first son, he was immediately the favorite. This was the Balkan way. My father's parents had seventeen kids, but my father's mother only kept photographs around of her sons, never the daughters. My brother's birth was treated as a great event. I found out later that when I was born, my father didn't even tell anyone, but when Velimir came into the world, Vojo went out with friends, drinking, shooting pistols into the air, spending lots of money.

Worse still, my brother soon developed some form of childhood epilepsy—he would have these seizures, and everyone hovered around him, giving him even more attention. Once when no one was looking (I was six or seven), I tried to wash him and almost drowned him—I put him in the bath, and he went *plop*, under the water. If my grandmother hadn't taken him out, I would have been an only child.

Me with Aunt Ksenija, my grandmother Milica, and my brother, Velimir, 1953

I was punished, of course. I was punished frequently, for the slightest infraction, and the punishments were almost always physical—hitting and slapping. My mother and her sister Ksenija, who moved in with us temporarily, did the punishing, never my father. They hit me till I was black and blue; I had bruises all over. But sometimes they had other methods. There was a kind of hidden clothes closet in our apartment, a very deep and dark closet—the word in Serbo-Croatian is *plakar.* The door blended into the wall, and it had no doorknob; you just pushed it to open it. I was fascinated with this closet, and terrified of it. I was not allowed to go inside. Sometimes when I was bad, though—or when my mother or my aunt said I'd been bad—they would lock me in this closet.

I was so afraid of the dark. But this *plakar* was filled with ghosts, spiritual presences—luminous beings, shapeless and silent but not at all frightening. I would talk to them. It felt completely normal to me that they were there. They were simply part of my reality, my life. And the moment I turned on the light, they would vanish.

My father, as I said, was a very handsome man, with a strong, stern face and a thick, powerful-looking head of hair. A heroic face. In pictures of him from the war he is almost always riding a white horse. He fought with the 13th Montenegro Division, a group of guerillas that made lightning raids on the Germans; it took impossible courage. Many of his friends were killed alongside him.

Vojo on liberation day, Belgrade, 1944

His youngest brother had been captured by the Nazis and tortured to death. And my father's guerilla squad captured the soldier who had killed his brother and brought him to my father. And my father didn't shoot him. He said, "Nobody can bring my brother back to life," and just let him go. He was a warrior, and had profound ethics about fighting the war.

My father never punished me for anything, never beat me, and I came to love him for that. And though he was often absent with his military unit while my brother was still a baby, Vojo and I gradually became best friends. He was always doing nice things for me—I remember he used to take me to carnivals and buy me sweets.

When he took me out, it was rarely just the two of us; he was usually with one of his girlfriends. And the girlfriend would buy me wonderful presents, which I would bring back home, so happy, and I'd say, "Oh, the beautiful blond lady bought me all this," and my mother would throw the presents straight out of the window.

My father and me, 1950

My parents' marriage was like a war—I never saw them hug or kiss or express any affection toward each other. Maybe it was just an old habit from partisan days, but they both slept with loaded pistols on their bedside tables! I remember once, during a rare period when they were speaking to each other, my father came home for lunch and my mother said, "Do you want soup?" And when he said yes, she came up behind him and dumped the hot soup on his head. He screamed, pushed the table away, broke every dish in the room, and walked out. There was always this tension. They'd never talk. There was never a Christmas when anybody was happy.

We didn't have Christmas anyway; we were Communists. But my grandmother, who was very religious, would have Orthodox Christmas, on January 7. It was wonderful and terrible. Wonderful, because she took three days to prepare an elaborate celebration—special foods, decorations, everything. Yet she had to put black curtains on the windows, because in Yugoslavia in those days it was dangerous to celebrate Christmas. Spies would write the names of families getting together for the holiday; the government would reward them for turning people in. So my family would arrive at my grandmother's place one by one, and behind the black curtains we would have Christmas. My grandmother was the only one able to get my whole family together. That was beautiful.

And the traditions were beautiful. Every year, my grandmother would make a cheese pie, and she would bake a big silver coin into it. If you bit the silver coin—and didn't break a tooth—it meant you were lucky. You got to keep the coin until the next year. She would throw rice on us; whoever got the most rice on them would be the most prosperous in the coming year.

What was terrible was that my parents weren't speaking to each other, even though it was Christmas. And every present I got, every year, was something useful that I didn't like. Wool socks, or some book that I had to read, or flannel pajamas. The pajamas were always two sizes too big—my mother told me they would shrink after they were washed, but they never did.

I never played with dolls. I never wanted dolls. And I didn't like toys. I preferred to play with the shadows of passing cars on the wall or a ray of sun streaming through the window. The light would catch the dust particles as they traveled to the floor, and I would imagine that this dust contained little planets with different galactic peoples, aliens who came to visit us, traveling on the rays of the sun. And then there were the glowing beings in the *plakar*. My entire childhood was full of spirits and invisible beings. It was shadows, and dead people that I could see.

⌣

One of my biggest fears has always been of blood—my own blood. When I was small, when my mother and her sister slapped me, I got blue bruises all over; my nose would bleed constantly. Then, when I lost my first baby tooth, the bleeding didn't stop for three months. I had to sleep sitting up in bed so I wouldn't choke. Finally my parents took me to doctors to see what was wrong with me, and they found out I had a blood disorder—at first they thought it was leukemia. My mother and father put me in the hospital; I was there for almost a year. I was six. This was the happiest time of my childhood.

Everybody in my family was nice to me. They brought me good presents for a change. Everybody in the hospital was kind to me. It was paradise. The doctors continued to do tests, and they discovered that what I had wasn't leukemia, but something more mysterious—maybe some kind of psychosomatic reaction to my mother's and aunt's physical abuse. I was given all kinds of treatments, then I went back home and the slapping and beatings continued, maybe a little less frequently than before.

I was expected to endure this punishment without complaint. I think that, in a certain way, my mother was training me to be a soldier like her. She might have been an ambivalent Communist, but she was a tough one. True Communists had "walk through walls" determination—Spartan determination. "As for pain, I can stand pain," Danica said, in an interview I did with her late in her life. "Nobody has, and nobody ever will hear me scream." At the dentist's office, she insisted on *not* being given anesthesia when she had a tooth pulled.

I learned my self-discipline from her, and I was always afraid of her.

My mother was obsessed with order and cleanliness—in part this came from her military background; in another way, maybe she was reacting against the chaos of her marriage. She would wake me in the middle of the night if she thought I was sleeping messily, mussing up the sheets. To this day, I sleep on one side of the bed, perfectly still—when I get up in the morning I can just flip the covers back into place. When I sleep in hotel rooms, you don't even know I'm there.

I also learned that it had been my father who named me when I was born, and that he named me after a Russian soldier he'd been in

My mother during the visit of the
Bulgarian delegation, Belgrade, 1966

love with during the war; a grenade had blown her up in front of his
eyes. My mother resented this old attachment deeply—and, by association, I think she resented me, too.

Danica's fixation on order moved into my unconscious. I used to
have a recurring nightmare about symmetry—it was deeply disturbing. In this strange dream I was a general inspecting a huge line of
soldiers, all of them perfect. Then I would remove one button from
one soldier's uniform, and the entire order would collapse. Then I
would wake up in a total panic. I was so afraid to break the symmetry.

In another recurring dream, I would walk into the cabin of an airplane and find it empty—no passengers. And all the seat belts were
perfectly arranged; each set lying on its seat just so, except for one.
And this one disarranged seat belt threw me into a panic, as though it
was my fault. In this dream I was always the one who had done something to break the symmetry, and this was not allowed, and there was
some kind of high force that would punish me.

I used to think my birth destroyed the symmetry of my parents'
marriage—after I was born, after all, their relationship became vio-
lent and terrible. And my mother blamed me, all my life, for being
just like my father, the one who left. Cleanliness and symmetry were
my mother's obsessions, along with art.

I knew from the age of six or seven that I wanted to be an artist. My mother punished me for many things, but she encouraged me in this one way. Art was holy to her. So in our big apartment I not only had my own bedroom, but my own painting studio. And while the rest of the flat was stuffed with stuff, paintings and books and furniture, from a very early age I kept both my rooms *spartak*—Spartan. As empty as possible. In my bedroom, just the bed, one chair, and a table. In my studio, just the easel and my paints.

My first paintings were of my dreams. They were more real to me than the reality I was living in—I didn't like my reality. I remember waking up, and the memory of my dreams was so strong that I would write them down, and then I would paint them, in just two very particular colors, a deep green and a night blue. Never anything else.

I was very attracted to these two colors—I can't quite say why. For me, dreams were green and blue. I took some old curtains and made a long robe for myself in those precise colors, the colors of my dreams.

The clothes I made from curtains, 1960

It sounds like a life of privilege, and in a way it was—in a world of Communist drabness and deprivation, I lived in luxury. I never washed my own clothes. I never ironed. I never cooked. I never even had to clean my room. Everything was done for me. All that was asked of me was to study and be the best.

I had piano lessons and English lessons and French lessons. My mother was completely into French culture—everything French was good. I was very lucky, but in all this comfort, I was so lonely. The only freedom I had was freedom of expression. There would be money for painting, but there would not be money for clothes. There would be no money for anything that I really desired as a young girl growing up.

Yet if I wanted a book, I would get it. If I wanted to go to the theater, I would be given a ticket. If I wanted to listen to any classical music, the records would be provided to me. And all this culture was not just provided to me, but pushed on me. My mother would leave little notes on the table before she went to work, saying how many French sentences I should learn, what books I should read—everything was planned out for me.

On my mother's orders I had to read all of Proust from beginning to end, all of Camus, all of André Gide; my father wanted me to read all the Russians—but even under orders, I found my escape in books. Just as with my dreams, the reality of the books I read was stronger than the reality around me.

When I read a book, everything around me stopped existing. All the unhappiness in my family—my parents' bitter fights, my grandmother's sadness at having had everything taken away from her—disappeared. I merged with the characters.

Extreme narratives fascinated me. I loved reading about Rasputin, whom no bullet could kill—Communism mixed with mysticism was very much part of my DNA. And I'll never forget a strange story by Camus, "The Renegade." It told of a Christian missionary who went to convert a desert tribe and instead was converted by them. When he broke one of their rules, they cut his tongue out.

I was powerfully drawn to Kafka. I consumed *The Castle*—I actually felt I lived inside this book. Kafka had such an uncanny way of drawing you into this bureaucratic labyrinth that the protagonist, K., was struggling to negotiate. It was agonizing: there was no escape. I suffered along with K.

Reading Rilke, on the other hand, was like breathing in pure poetic oxygen. He spoke of life in a different way than I'd ever understood it before. His expressions of cosmic suffering and universal knowledge related to ideas I would find later in Zen Buddhist and Sufi writings. Coming upon them for the first time was intoxicating:

Earth, isn't this what you want: to arise within us,
invisible? Isn't it your dream
to be wholly invisible someday?—O Earth: invisible!
What, if not transformation, is your urgent command?

The only good present my mother ever got me was a book called *Letters: Summer 1926*, about the three-way correspondence between Rilke, the Russian poet Marina Tsvetayeva, and Boris Pasternak, the author of *Doctor Zhivago*. The three had never met, but they adored each other's work, and for four years they all wrote sonnets and sent them to one another. And through this correspondence, each of them fell passionately in love with the other two.

Can you imagine a lonely fifteen-year-old girl coming upon a story like this? (And the fact that Tsvetayeva and I shared a first name seemed cosmically significant.) Anyway, what happened next was that Tsvetayeva began to feel more deeply for Rilke than she felt for Pasternak, and wrote to him that she wanted to come to Germany to meet him. "You can't," he wrote back. "You can't meet me."

This only inflamed her passion. She kept writing, kept insisting she was coming to meet him—and then he wrote, "You can't meet me—I'm dying."

"I forbid you to die," she wrote back. But he died anyway, and the triangle was broken.

Tsvetayeva and Pasternak continued to write sonnets to each other, she in Moscow, he in Paris. Then, because she was married to a White Russian who'd been imprisoned by the Communists, she had to leave Russia. She went to the south of France, but then her money ran out and she had to go back to Russia. And she and Pasternak decided that, after four or five years of this passionate correspondence, she would stop in the Gare de Lyon in Paris on her way home, and they would actually meet for the first time.

Both of them were terribly nervous when they met at last. She had an old Russian suitcase with her, so overstuffed with her belongings that it was falling apart: seeing her struggle to close the bag, Pasternak ran off and got a piece of rope. He tied the suitcase shut.

Now they were just sitting there, barely able to speak—their writing had taken them so far that when they actually found themselves in each other's presence, the emotions were overpowering. Pasternak told her he was going to get a pack of cigarettes—and he went off again, and never came back. Tsvetayeva sat there, waiting and waiting, and finally it was time to board her train. So she took the suitcase fixed with the rope and went back to Russia.

She returned to Moscow. Her husband was in prison; she had no money. So she went to Odessa, and there, desperate to survive, she wrote a letter to the writers' club, asking if she could be their cleaning woman. They wrote back that her help was not needed. And so she took the same rope Pasternak had used to fix her broken suitcase, and hanged herself.

When I read a book like this, I would never leave the house until I finished. I would just go to the kitchen, eat, and come back to my room, read, go back to eat, come back to read. That was it. For days.

⌒

When I was twelve or so, my mother got a washing machine from Switzerland. This was a very big deal—we were one of the first families in Belgrade to get one. It arrived one morning, shiny and new and mysterious: we put it in the bathroom. My grandmother didn't trust this machine. She would do the laundry in it, then take it out and give it all to the maid to wash by hand one more time.

One morning I was home from school for the day, and I just sat in the bathroom staring at this fascinating new machine doing its job, agitating the clothes with a monotonous sound—*DUN-DUN-DUN-DUN.* I was mesmerized. The machine had an automatic wringer and two rubber rollers that turned slowly in opposite directions while the laundry churned in the washer's tub. I began to play with it, darting my finger between the rollers, then quickly pulling it out.

But then I didn't pull my hand out fast enough, and the rollers caught my finger and started pulling it in, squeezing it. The pain was excruciating; I screamed. My grandmother was in the kitchen—when she heard me she ran into the bathroom, but with her extremely limited understanding of technology, she didn't think to simply unplug the machine. Instead, she decided to run down to the street for help. In the meantime, the rollers had pulled in my hand.

We lived on the third floor, and my grandmother was a heavy woman, and running down three flights of stairs and climbing back up again took her some time. When she returned, she had a muscular young man with her; my whole forearm was caught between the slowly turning rollers.

The young man's understanding of technology was no more advanced than my grandmother's, and unplugging the washing machine didn't occur to him, either: he decided to use his muscles to save me. With all his strength, he pulled the two rollers apart—and got such an enormous electrical shock that he was thrown across the bathroom, where he lay unconscious. I, too, fell to the floor, my arm swollen and blue.

At this point, my mother returned, and quickly understood the situation. She called an ambulance for the young man and me, and then she slapped me hard in the face.

⌐

Learning the history of the partisans was very important in school when I was a child. We had to know the name of every battle in the war, and of every river and bridge the soldiers crossed. And of course, we had to learn about Stalin, Lenin, Marx, and Engels. Every public space in Belgrade had a huge photo of President Tito, with pictures of Marx and Engels to the left and right of him.

When you reached the age of seven in Yugoslavia, you became a "Pioneer" in the party. You were given a red scarf to wear around your neck, which you had to iron and always keep next to your bed. We learned to march and to sing the Communist songs and to believe in the future of our country and so on. I remember how proud I was to have this scarf and to be a Pioneer and a member of the Party. I was horrified when I discovered one day that my father, who always had very elaborate hair, was using my Pioneer scarf as a bandanna to train his coiffure.

Parades were very important, and all the children had to participate. We celebrated the first of May, because that was an international Communist holiday, and November 29, which was the day that Yugoslavia became a republic. All the children who were born on November 29 could go visit Tito and get candies. My mother told me I was born on the 29th, but every year I was never allowed to go for candy. She told me I was not well behaved enough for the privilege. It was another way of punishing me. A few years later, when I was ten, I found out I was born on November 30, not the 29th.

⌐

I got my first period at twelve, and it lasted more than ten days—lots of bleeding. The blood kept coming, just this red liquid seeping out of my body and never stopping. With my childhood memory of uncontrollable bleeding and hospitalization, I was so afraid. I thought I was dying.

It was the maid, Mara, rather than my mother, who explained to me what menstruation was. Mara was a kind, round woman, with a big bosom and full lips. And when she so warmly took me in her arms to tell me what was happening with my body, I suddenly had the strange urge to kiss her on the mouth. The kiss didn't quite happen—a very confusing moment, and the urge didn't return. But my body was suddenly full of confusing feelings. This, too, was when I began to masturbate, often, and always with deep feelings of shame.

With puberty also came my first migraines. My mother also suffered from them—once or twice a week she would come home early from work and shut herself in her bedroom, in the dark. My grandmother would put something cool on her head, slices of meat or potato or cucumber, and nobody could make a sound in the apartment. Danica, of course, never complained—this was her Spartan determination.

I couldn't believe how painful my own migraines were: my mother never talked about hers, and she never said a sympathetic word to me about mine. The attacks lasted a full twenty-four hours. I would lie in bed in agony, every once in a while running to the bathroom to vomit and shit simultaneously. The retching and shitting only made the pain worse. I trained myself to lie perfectly still in certain positions—my hand on my forehead, or my legs perfectly straight, or my head tilted a certain way—that seemed to alleviate the agony slightly. It was the beginning of my education in accepting and overcoming pain and fear.

Around the same time, I discovered divorce papers under the bedsheets in the cupboard. But my mother and father continued to live together—in hell—for three more years. Sleeping in the same room, the pistols by the bedside. The worst part was when my father would come home in the middle of the night, and my mother would go crazy, and they would start beating each other. Then she would run to my room and pull me out of bed and hold me in front of her like a shield, so that he would stop beating her. Never my brother, always me.

To this day I can't stand, ever, anybody raising their voice in anger.

My brother, Velimir, 1962

When someone does that, I just completely freeze. It's as if I've had an injection—I simply can't move. It's an automatic response. I can get angry myself, but to scream with anger takes me a long time. It takes an unbelievable amount of energy. I sometimes scream in performance pieces—it's one way to exorcise the demons. But that's not screaming *at* somebody.

My father kept being my friend, and I became more and more my mother's enemy. When I was fourteen, my mother became a Yugoslav delegate to UNESCO in Paris, and she would have to go there for months at a time. The first time she left, my father brought some big nails into the salon, got on a ladder, and drove the nails into the ceiling. Plaster fell down all over the place! From the nails he hung a swing for my brother and me, and we loved it. We were in heaven—it was total freedom. When my mother returned, she exploded. The swing was removed.

On my fourteenth birthday, my father gave me a pistol. It was a beautiful little gun, with an ivory handle and an engraved silver barrel. "This is a pistol to carry in an opera bag," he explained to me. I never knew whether he was joking or not. He wanted me to learn to shoot, so I took the pistol out to the woods and fired it a few times—then accidentally dropped it in deep snow. I never found it.

Also when I was fourteen, my father took me to a strip club. It was wildly inappropriate, but I asked no questions.

I wanted to have nylon stockings, a forbidden item as far as my mother was concerned: only prostitutes wore stockings like this. My father bought them for me. My mother threw them out the window. I know he was bribing me—to love him, to not tell my mother about his escapades—but my mother knew everything.

She never wanted my brother and me to bring friends home, because she was deathly afraid of germs. We were so shy that other kids would make fun of us. Once, though, my school had an exchange program with kids from Croatia. And I went to the home of this Croatian girl in Zagreb, and she had the most wonderful family. Her parents were loving with each other and with their children; at meals they all sat at the table, talked together, and laughed a lot. Then the girl came to stay with my family, and it was horrifying. We didn't talk. We didn't laugh. We didn't even sit together. I was so ashamed—of myself and my family, of the complete lack of love in my household—and that feeling of shame was like hell.

When I was fourteen, I invited a friend, a boy from school, to my apartment to play Russian roulette. No one was at home. We did it in the library, sitting opposite each other at the table. I took my father's revolver from his nightstand, took all the bullets out but one, spun the chamber, and gave the gun to my friend. He pressed the muzzle against his temple and pulled the trigger. We just heard it click. He passed the pistol to me. I put it to my temple and pulled the trigger. Again, we just heard a click. Then I pointed the gun at the bookshelf and pulled the trigger. A huge explosion, and the bullet flew across the room and straight into the spine of Dostoevsky's *The Idiot*. A minute later, I broke into a cold sweat and couldn't stop trembling.

My teenage years were desperately awkward and unhappy. In my mind, I was the ugliest kid in my school, extraordinarily ugly. I was thin and tall, and the kids called me Giraffe. I had to sit in the back of the class because I was so tall, but I couldn't see the board, so I got bad grades. Finally they figured out I needed glasses. We're not talking about normal glasses—these were the ugly kind that came from a Communist country, with thick lenses and heavy frames. So I would try to break them by putting them on the chair and sitting down on them. Or I would put the glasses in the window and "accidentally" close it.

My mother would never get me any clothes that other kids had. For instance, it was a time when petticoats were very fashionable—I would have died for one of those petticoats, but she wouldn't get me one. This wasn't because my parents didn't have money. There was money. They had more money than anybody else because they were

With my father, wearing my makeshift petticoat, 1962

partisans, they were Communists, they were Red Bourgeoisie. So in order to make it look like I was wearing a petticoat, I would wear six or seven skirts under my skirts. But it never looked right—the different layers of skirts would show, or the skirts would fall down.

And then there were the orthopedic shoes. Because my feet were flat, I had to wear special corrective shoes—and not just any corrective shoes, but horrible, socialistic ones: heavy yellow leather, up to the ankle. And it wasn't enough that the shoes were heavy and ugly; my mother went to the shoemaker and had him make two metal pieces that fit on the sole, like a horseshoe, so the shoes wouldn't wear out too fast. So they made a noise—*clip-clop*—when I walked.

Oh my God, I could be heard everywhere with these *clip-clop* shoes. I was afraid even to walk down the street. If somebody was walking in back of me, I would step into a doorway to let them pass—I was that ashamed. I especially remember one May Day parade when our school had the great honor to march in front of Tito himself. Our formation had to be perfect—for a month we practiced in the school courtyard to get it exactly right. On the morning of May 1, we gathered to start the parade, and almost as soon as we started marching, one of the metal pieces on the sole of my shoe came off, and I couldn't walk properly. I was immediately taken out of the parade. I cried with shame and anger.

So if you can imagine—I had skinny legs, orthopedic shoes, and ugly glasses. My mother cut my hair way above the ear and fixed it with a pin, and put me in heavy wool dresses. And I had a baby face with an impossibly big nose. My nose was grown-up but my face was not. I felt hideous.

I used to ask my mother if I could get my nose fixed, and every time I asked, she would slap my face. Then I made a secret plan.

Brigitte Bardot was the big star then, and for me, she was the ideal of sexiness and beauty. I thought that if I could just have a Brigitte Bardot nose everything would be fine. So I came up with this plan, which I thought was perfection. I cut out photos of Bardot from every angle—looking straight at the camera, from the left side, from the right side—to show her beautiful nose. And I put all the photos in my pocket.

My mother and father had this huge matrimonial bed made of wood. It was the morning, when my father liked to play chess in town and my mother liked going out to have coffee with her friends, so I was left alone in the house. I went to their bedroom and decided to spin around as fast as I could. I wanted to fall on the hard edge of the bed and break my nose so I could go to the hospital. I had the photos of Brigitte Bardot in my pocket, and I thought it would be a very small job for the doctors to just fix my nose to look like hers while I was there. In my mind, it was a perfect plan.

So I spun and spun and fell onto the bed, but I missed my nose. Instead I cut myself badly on the cheek. I lay there on the floor, bleeding, for a long time. Eventually my mother came home. She scanned the situation with her severe eyes, then flushed the photographs down the toilet and slapped my face. Thinking back, I'm so grateful that I didn't manage to break my nose, because I think my face with a Brigitte Bardot nose would be a disaster. Plus, she didn't age very well.

⌒

My birthdays were sad occasions, not happy ones. First of all, I never got the right present, and then my family was never really together. There was never any kind of joy. I remember on my sixteenth birthday I cried so much, because I realized for the first time that I was going to die. I felt so unloved, so abandoned by everybody. I listened to Mozart's "Piano Concerto No. 21" over and over—there was some motif in that music that made my soul bleed. And then at one point, I actually cut my wrist. There was so much blood that I thought I was dying. It turned out I'd cut deeply but missed the all-important radial arteries. My grandmother took me to the hospital, where I got four stitches; she never told my mother anything.

I used to write sad poems about death. But death was never talked about in my family, especially in front of my grandmother. We never discussed anything unpleasant in front of her. Years later, when the Bosnian war broke out, my brother went up on the roof of our grandmother's apartment building and started shaking her television antenna so she would think something was wrong with her TV—which was then taken away for "repair." For this reason (and also because she never left the house), she never found out about the war.

When I was seventeen, my mother and father threw a party to celebrate their anniversary: eighteen years of happy marriage. They had a dinner at our house and invited all their friends. Then, after everybody left, the drama started again.

My father went into the kitchen to clean up, which was strange, because he never did anything in the kitchen. For some inexplicable reason, he was in the kitchen and said to me: "Let's wash the champagne glasses. You dry."

So I took the towel and prepared to dry. But by accident he broke the first glass he washed, and at that moment, my mother entered the kitchen, saw the broken glass on the floor, and exploded. They had just spent several hours pretending to be happy, and she had built up all this anger and bitterness—rage. She saw the broken glass on the floor, and she started yelling at my father about everything: about how clumsy he was, and what a disaster their marriage was, and how many women he'd slept with. He just stood there. And I watched silently, holding this little towel in my hand.

She yelled and yelled, and my father said nothing. He didn't move. It felt like a Beckett play. After many minutes of her lamenting about all the shit in their marriage, she stopped, because he wasn't responding. Finally he said to her, "Are you finished?" When she said yes, he picked up the other champagne glasses and, one by one, smashed all eleven on the floor. "I cannot hear this eleven more times," he said and walked out of the house.

This was the beginning of the end. He left for good soon afterward. The night he left, he came into my bedroom to say good-bye, and told me, "I'm going now, and I'm not coming back, but we will still see each other." And he went to a hotel and he never came back.

The next day, I was crying so much that I had some kind of nervous breakdown. They had to bring the doctor over to give me something—I couldn't stop crying. I was out of my mind with grief because I'd always felt love and support from my father. I knew that with him gone, I would be even more alone.

But then my grandmother moved in.

⌒

The kitchen became the center of my world; everything happened in the kitchen. We had a maid, but my grandmother Milica never trusted her, so she would always come in first thing in the morning and take over. There was a wood-burning stove and a big table where I would sit with my grandmother and talk about my dreams. That was mainly what we did together. She was very interested in the meaning of dreams and read them as signs. If you had a dream that your teeth were falling out but you didn't have any pain, it meant that someone you knew was going to die. But if you had pain, that meant somebody in *your family* was going to die. Dreaming about blood meant you would get good news soon. If you dreamed of dying, it meant your life would be long.

My mother would go to work at seven fifteen A.M., and everybody relaxed when she left. And when she came back in the afternoon (two fifteen, on the dot) I'd feel like military control had been reestablished. I was always afraid that I had done something wrong, that she would see I'd moved a book from the left to the right, or the order of our home was somehow broken.

Sitting at our kitchen table once, my grandmother told me her story—she was so much more open with me, I think, than with anybody else.

My grandmother's mother came from a very rich family, and she fell in love with a servant. This was forbidden, of course, and she was expelled from the family. She went to live with the servant in his village, and they were dirt poor. She had seven children with him, and to make money, she washed clothes. She even went to her own family as a servant, to do their laundry. They gave her a little money, and sometimes some food. But there was very little food in my great-grandmother's house. My grandmother told me that her mother, out of pride, would always have four pots on the stove, but this was just for appearances, in case the neighbors stopped by. She was only boiling water because there was nothing to eat.

My grandmother was the youngest of the seven children, and very beautiful. And one day when she was fifteen, she was going to school when she became aware of a gentleman—he was walking with another man—looking at her. When she got home, her mother told her to make coffee because there was somebody who was interested in marrying her. This is how things were organized in those days.

For my grandmother's family, this gentleman's interest in her was a blessing—they didn't have anything, so once she was married there would be one less mouth to feed. Even better, the man was from the city, and also rich—but he was also much older: she was fifteen and he was thirty-five. She remembered making Turkish coffee for him that day, and bringing it to him, her first real chance to see the face of her husband-to-be. But when she served the coffee, she was too shy to look at him. He talked over the marriage plans with her parents, and then he left.

Three months later she was taken from her home to the place where the wedding was to happen, and then, at fifteen, she was married and living in this man's house. She was still a child, a virgin. No one had ever told her about sex.

She told me what happened the first night, when he actually tried to make love to her. She screamed bloody murder and ran to her husband's mother—they all lived together—and got into his mother's bed to hide, saying, "He wants to kill me, he wants to kill me!" And the mother held her in her arms all night, saying, "No, he doesn't want to kill you; this is not a killing; this is something different." It was three months before she actually lost her virginity.

My grandmother's husband had two brothers. One was a priest in the Orthodox Church, the other was in business with my grandfather. They were merchants. They imported spices and silk and other goods from the Middle East; they owned shops, houses, and land and were very wealthy.

My grandfather's brother the priest eventually became Patriarch of the Orthodox Church in Yugoslavia, the most powerful man in the country next to the king. And in the early 1930s, when the country was still a monarchy, Alexander, the king of Yugoslavia, asked the Patriarch to unite the Orthodox and Catholic churches, and the Patriarch refused.

The king invited the Patriarch and his two wealthy brothers to lunch to discuss the issue. They went to the lunch, but the Patriarch refused to change his mind. And the king had the three brothers served food that had crushed diamonds mixed into it. Over the next month, all three, the Patriarch and my grandfather and the other brother, died terrible deaths from intestinal bleeding. And so my grandmother was widowed at a very young age.

My grandmother and my mother had a strange relationship—a bad relationship. My grandmother was angry at my mother all the time, for so many reasons. Before the war, my grandmother, the rich widow, had to go to prison because her daughter, my mother, was such an outspoken Communist; she was forced to buy her way out of jail with the gold she'd put aside. Then after the war, when the Communists took over, my mother, to show her commitment to the Party, had to renounce all her worldly goods—and all the worldly goods of her mother. She actually made a list of my grandmother's possessions, and gave the list to the Communist Party, because she was such a loyal Communist. This was for the good of the country. So my grandmother lost her shops. She lost her land and her house. She lost everything. She felt deeply betrayed by her own daughter.

And now here she was, with my father gone, living with us. Difficult for her and my mother, but so important for me.

I still remember vividly several things about her. From the age of thirty on, she started setting aside the clothes she wanted to be buried in. Every ten years, as fashions changed, she would change her burial clothes as well. In the beginning it was an all-beige outfit. Then she got into polka dots. Next it was dark blue with thin stripes, and so on. She lived to the age of 103.

When I asked her what she remembered about the First and Second World Wars, she told me the following: "Germans are very correct. The Italians always look for a piano and want to make a party. But when the Russians come, everyone runs away because they rape all the women, young and old alike." I also remember that when my grandmother flew on a plane for the first time, she asked the stewardess not to seat her next to the window, because she'd just had her hair done and didn't want the wind to mess it up.

Like many people in our culture at that time, my grandmother was deeply superstitious. She believed that if when you left your house you saw a pregnant woman or a widow, you had to immediately pull a button off one of your garments and throw it away, or bad luck would befall you. But if a bird took a shit on you, it was considered the best luck of all.

When I had exams in school, my grandmother would pour a glass of water over me as I left the house so that I would do well. Sometimes in the middle of the winter, I would be walking to school and my whole back would be soaking wet!

Milica told fortunes with Turkish coffee grounds or with a handful of white kidney beans, which she'd throw into a pattern and then read the abstract images they created.

These signs and rituals were a kind of spirituality for me. They also connected me to my inner life and my dreams. Many years later, when I went to Brazil to study shamanism, the shamans looked at the same kinds of signs. If your left shoulder itches, it means something. Every single part of the body is connected with different signs that allow you to understand what's happening inside you—on a spiritual level, but also on a physical and mental level.

In my teenage years, though, all this was just beginning to dawn on me. And my gawky body was little else to me besides a source of embarrassment.

I was president of the chess club in my school—I was a good player. And my school won a competition, and I was chosen to receive the award onstage. My mother didn't want to get me a new dress for the ceremony, so there I was onstage in my orthopedic shoes and fake petticoat. And the official gave me the award—five new chessboards—and as I was carrying them offstage, my big shoe got caught on something and I fell down, the boards flying every which way. Everybody laughed. After that they couldn't get me out of the house for days. No more chess.

Deep shame, maximum self-consciousness. When I was young it was impossible for me to talk to people. Now I can stand in front of three thousand people without any notes, any preconception of what I'm going to say, even without visual material, and I can look at everyone in the audience and talk for two hours easily.

What happened?

Art happened.

When I was fourteen, I asked my father for a set of oil paints. He bought them for me, and also arranged for a painting lesson from an old partisan friend of his, an artist named Filo Filipović. Filipović, who was part of a group called Informel, painted what he called abstract landscapes. He arrived in my little studio carrying paints, canvas, and some other materials, and he gave me my first painting lesson.

He cut out a piece of canvas and put it on the floor. He opened a can of glue and threw the liquid on the canvas; he added a little bit of sand, some yellow pigment, some red pigment, and some black. Then he poured about half a liter of gasoline on it, lit a match, and everything exploded. "This is a sunset," he told me. And then he left.

This made a big impression on me. I waited until the charred mess had dried, and then very carefully pinned it to the wall. Then my family and I left for vacation. When I came back, the August sun had dried everything up. The color was gone and the sand had fallen off. There was nothing left but a pile of ashes and sand on the floor. The sunset didn't exist anymore.

Later on, I understood why this experience was so important. It taught me that the process was more important than the result, just as the performance means more to me than the object. I saw the process of making it and then the process of its unmaking. There was no duration or stability to it. It was pure process. Later on I read—and loved—the Yves Klein quote: "My paintings are but the ashes of my art."

I kept painting in my studio at home. But then one day I was lying on the grass, just staring up at the cloudless sky, when I saw twelve military jets fly over, leaving white trails behind them. I watched in fascination as the trails slowly disappeared and the sky once more became a perfect blue. All at once it occurred to me—why paint? Why should I limit myself to two dimensions when I could make art from anything at all: fire, water, the human body? Anything! There was something like a click in my mind—I realized that being an artist meant having immense freedom. If I wanted to create something from dust or rubbish, I could do it. It was an unbelievably freeing feeling, especially for someone coming from a home where there was almost no freedom.

I went to the military base in Belgrade and asked if they could send up a dozen planes. My plan was to give them directions about which way to fly so that their jet trails would make patterns in the sky. The men at the base called my father and said, "Please come and get your daughter out of here. She has no idea how expensive it is to fly jets for her to make drawings in the sky."

I didn't stop painting all at once, though. When I was seventeen, I began preparing to go to the Art Academy in Belgrade—you had to go to night school and take drawing classes, to prepare a portfolio to present for admission. I remember all my friends saying, "Why do you even bother? You don't need to do anything—your mother can just make one phone call and get you in." That made me so angry, but really I was just embarrassed. What they were saying was true. It made me more determined than ever to establish my own identity.

The night-school classes were in life drawing, and there were nude models, female and male. And I had never seen a nude man. I remember once the model was a gypsy—he was a small man, but his phallus hung to his knees. I could not look at him! So I drew everything except the phallus. Every time the professor would come around and look at my drawing, he would say, "This is an unfinished drawing."

Once, when I was eleven or twelve, I was sitting on the couch reading a book that I really liked and eating chocolate—my rare moment of happiness was complete. I was sitting there reading and eating, thoroughly relaxed, my legs splayed across the couch cushion. And out of nowhere, my mother came into the room and slapped my face so hard that it made my nose bleed. I said, "Why?" She said, "Close your legs when you're sitting on the couch."

Me in Rovinj, Istria, 1961

My mother had a very strange attitude about sex. She was very worried that I would lose my virginity before marriage. If I got a phone call and it was a male voice, she would say, "What do you want with my daughter?" and slam the phone down. She even opened all my mail. She told me sex was dirty and that it was only good if you wanted to have a child. I was terrified of sex because I didn't want to have children, which to me felt like it would be a terrible trap. And all I ever wanted was to be free. When I got to art school, everybody in my class had already lost their virginity. Other people went to parties and things, but my mother always demanded that I be home by ten o'clock—even when I was in my twenties—so I didn't go. I'd never had a boyfriend and I thought something was seriously wrong with me. And now when I look at photographs, I think I looked fine, but back then I felt terribly ugly.

I had one kiss when I was fourteen that I don't count. We were on the Croatian seaside and the boy was called Bruno. It wasn't even a kiss on the mouth—just a light kiss on the cheek. But my mother saw us and she took me by the hair and dragged me away from him. My first real kiss was later. I had a friend, Beba, who was very beautiful and all the boys were always around her. So she would have all these requests for dates, and most of the time she couldn't attend to all of them, so she would send me instead. Once she had a date with someone I knew who lived in the building just across the street from me, but she couldn't go, so she sent me to the cinema where they were supposed to meet to tell him she couldn't make it. So I went to the cinema and found him and said, "I'm so sorry, but she cannot come." And he said, "But I have two tickets for the cinema. Do you want to come?" So we saw the movie, and then afterward we went outside in the snow and drank the vodka that he had brought with him. We ended up lying down in the snow and he kissed me. That was my first real kiss. I liked him, but I didn't sleep with him. His name was Predrag Stojanović.

I didn't want to lose my virginity to somebody I liked, because I

My first love, 1962

didn't want to risk falling in love with the first person I had sex with. I wanted to do it with somebody I didn't care about.

I knew that when a girl slept with a guy for the first time, she was usually in love with him, and that the guy would always leave afterward, and the girl would suffer. I didn't want any of that to happen to me, so I made a plan: I would look for some guy who was having a lot of sex—who was kind of known for that—and I'd just use him to lose my virginity. Then I would be normal like everybody else. But it had to be on a Sunday, and it had to be ten A.M., so that I could tell my mother I was going to a movie matinee, since she wouldn't let me go to the cinema in the evening. So I went to the academy and looked around and spotted this one guy who was into partying and drinking. Perfect. I knew that he loved music, so I went up to him and said, "I have the new Perry Como record. Do you want to listen to it sometime? I can't lend it to you but we can listen to it together." (I actually only listened to classical music at the time, and I'd borrowed the record from a friend specifically for that purpose. Of rock 'n' roll I knew next to nothing.)

So the guy said, "Okay. When?" And I said, "How about Sunday?"

He said, "Yes. What time?" I said, "Ten in the morning." He said, "Are you crazy?" So I said, "Okay. Eleven?"

To prepare, I bought Albanian cognac. It's the worst, cheapest alcohol you can imagine—they make it in the morning and drink it in the evening. That was the joke, anyway. Albanians went to Yugoslavia in those days to buy white bread, because they only had very bad brown bread. Not like healthy brown bread that you can get in the United States, but bread that was brown because it was made from bad wheat. It had an almost sandy taste. They would take one piece of white bread between two pieces of their brown bread and eat it like a cheese sandwich.

So you can imagine what Albanian cognac, which was made from this bad bread, tasted like. I didn't even drink, but I thought I should bring it to use as a kind of anesthetic.

I went to his house around eleven o'clock and knocked on the door. Nobody answered. I knocked some more, and finally he came to the door, but he was half asleep, like he'd gone to a party the night before and had come home late. And he said, "Oh . . . you're here. Okay. I'm going to take a shower. You make some coffee."

While he took a shower, I made some coffee and I put a huge amount of Albanian cognac in it. So we drank the coffee, and I put the Perry Como on the record player, and we sat on the couch, and I literally jumped on top of him. We were hardly undressed when we had sex, and I screamed. He knew then that I was a virgin, and he got so angry that he threw me out of his house. It took me another year to do it properly, and I did it with Predrag Stojanović, who became my first love. But I was proud of myself for getting it out of the way.

I was twenty-four years old. Still living at home with my mother, still required to be home by ten P.M. every night. Still controlled by her completely.

2.

My father had tried many times to teach me to swim—in a pool, in the shallow water of a lake—but nothing worked. I was just too scared of the water, especially being in water over my head. He finally lost patience. One summer day when we were at the seaside, he took me out in a little rowboat, far offshore, and threw me into the water like a dog. I was six.

I panicked. The last thing I saw before I sank beneath the Adriatic was my father rowing away from me, his back to me, not even glancing over his shoulder. Then I was underwater and sinking—down, down, down, my arms flailing, salt water pouring into my mouth.

But as I drowned, I couldn't stop thinking about my father rowing away, never turning his head to look at me. And it made me angry, more than angry—it made me furious. I stopped inhaling water, and somehow my flailing arms and my kicking legs lifted me back to the surface. Where I swam to the rowboat.

Vojo must've heard me, because he still never looked—he just reached over and grabbed my arm and pulled me into the boat.

And that is how the partisans taught their children to swim.

I got into the Academy of Fine Arts, and I continued to paint. During this time, my relatives would ask me to make paintings for them, and they would buy them from me. I would get orders to create different kinds of still-life compositions, like a vase of tulips, a pot of sunflowers, a fish with a lemon, or an open window with the curtains blowing and a full moon. I would do whatever they wanted and I would sign these paintings with a huge MARINA on the bottom, in blue.

Painting in my studio, Belgrade, 1968

Eventually, my mother bought back many of these paintings from our relatives and put them on her walls. She was proud of the pictures, but I was so ashamed. Today, various galleries around the world that I work with will occasionally hear from someone saying, "I have an original painting signed by Marina Abramović!" But I want to die when I see these canvases, because I did them for money, and with no feeling. I consciously made them very kitschy, and dashed them off in fifteen minutes. When my mother died, I took all the paintings she had, about ten of them, and put them in storage. I have to figure out what to do with them. Maybe I'll burn them. Or—because I've finally learned to expose what I'm most ashamed of—show them to the world in all their kitschy glory.

At the Academy, I painted in an academic style: nudes and still lifes and portraits and landscapes. But I also began to have new ideas. For instance, I became fascinated with traffic accidents, and my first big inspiration was to make paintings of them. I collected newspaper photographs of car and truck wrecks; I also took advantage of my father's police contacts and I would go to the stationhouse and ask if any big crashes had happened. Then I would go to the scene and take photographs or make sketches. But I found it difficult to translate the violence and immediacy of these disasters into paint on canvas.

In 1965, though, when I was nineteen, I did a kind of breakthrough painting: it was a small picture called *Three Secrets*. This very simple canvas shows three pieces of fabric—one red, one green, one white—draped over three objects. The picture felt important to me because instead of presenting an easily digestible image, it made the viewer a participant in the artistic experience. It demanded that imagination take place. It allowed for uncertainty and mystery. It opened a door for me, into the *plakar* of my unconscious.

Then came 1968.

After World War II, Tito's Yugoslavia had split with the Soviet Union and declared itself an independent Communist state, un-aligned with either the East or the West. Our heroic victory over the Nazis was a great point of pride, as was our independence.

But in fact Tito wasn't so independent: rather, he was very clever about playing the Soviets and the Chinese against the West, and accepting favors from both sides. He claimed his doctrine of "self-management," which allowed workers to decide on the results of their labor, was truer to Marx's teachings than the Stalinist brand of Com-munism. Yet Tito had built a cult of personality in Yugoslavia, and his single-party government had become riddled with corruption, with officials from the top down gathering wealth, possessions, and privilege while the working class lived lives of colorless gloom.

Nineteen sixty-eight was a terrible year, a time of unrest around the world. In the United States, Martin Luther King Jr. and Bobby Kennedy were assassinated; even Andy Warhol was shot and almost died. In America, France, the Czech Republic, and Yugoslavia, stu-dents seeking freedom were at the forefront of the political upheavals.

In Belgrade that year, there was a swelling disillusionment with the Communist Party—we suddenly felt the whole thing had been for show. We didn't have freedom or democracy.

At that time, I was still very close to my father, and I learned something surprising: though Tito had appointed Vojo to his elite guard after the war, he had demoted him to a lesser military unit in 1948. The postwar years were a period of extreme anti-Soviet feeling in Yugoslavia, and my father just had too many friends who were Soviet sympathizers. Many people went to prison during that time; my father barely escaped this fate. Vojo felt personally betrayed by Tito, but always believed that a truer version of Communism would emerge in time. Twenty years later, he had given up this hope.

My father kneeling next to Tito during an annual
partisan meeting, Belgrade, 1965

He had never talked about any of this with me. (Suddenly I saw the symbolism in his using my Pioneer scarf as a head-rag.) My father was broken by disillusionment. He took all the photographs of himself and Tito together and cut Tito out, leaving only himself. He was particularly upset that everyone in the government who'd been in line for leadership was pushed out over time, so as Tito grew old—by now he was already in his mid-seventies—and had to give up his rule, there would be nobody to take his place.

In June 1968, everybody I knew in Belgrade supported the student demonstrations. Students paraded through the city and occupied university buildings. Posters were hung all over the campus, with slogans like DOWN WITH THE RED BOURGEOISIE, and SHOW A BUREAUCRAT THAT HE IS INCAPABLE AND HE WILL QUICKLY SHOW YOU WHAT HE IS CAPABLE OF. Riot police filled the streets, then sealed off the campus. As president of the Communist Party at the art academy, I was part of the group occupying our building. We slept there; we held loud and passionate all-night meetings. I was literally prepared to die for the cause, and I thought everybody felt the same way.

My father did something that impressed me profoundly. Handsome in his raincoat and necktie, his hair piled up majestically, he stood in the middle of Marx and Engels Square and gave a passionate speech renouncing his membership in the Communist Party and denouncing Yugoslavia's Red Bourgeoisie and all it stood for. At the climax of his oration he threw his party membership card into the crowd—an amazing gesture. Everyone applauded wildly. I was so proud of him.

And my mother completely disapproved of all forms of protest at the time, both his and mine.

My father speaking in Marx and Engels Square during student demonstrations, Belgrade, 1968

The next day, a soldier brought my father's card back to him. Vojo would need the card, the guy said, if he wanted to keep collecting his pension.

The students put together a petition of a dozen points that we wanted the government to accept, saying that if they didn't agree to all of them, we would go to the barricades. We demanded freedom of the press and freedom of expression; we called for full employment, a higher minimum wage, and democratic reforms to the League of Communists. "Privilege in our society must be liquidated," we proclaimed. "Cultural relations must be such that commercialization is rendered impossible and that conditions are created so that cultural and creative facilities are open to all," we demanded.

What we had in mind with this last demand was getting a student cultural center. The location we wanted was a building on Marshal Tito Avenue where the secret police would go to play chess, and the wives of the secret police, in their silk scarves, would do needlework, gossip, and watch films. A very impressive building—it looked like a castle—with the Communist star on the roof and huge portraits of Tito and Lenin in the foyer.

We kept waiting for Tito to respond to our petition. Finally, on the morning of June 10, it was announced: he was going to speak at three that afternoon. At ten that morning there was a meeting of all the university representatives. I went into this meeting thinking that if the government didn't accept every point in our petition, we were going to see the demonstrations through to the end. That meant barricades, gunfire, serious confrontation with the police, and even death for some of us. Instead, all that the others at the meeting could talk about was the party we would have after Tito's speech! They were discussing who would sing, and what food we were going to order. I said, "But how can we plan for a party if we don't even know what he's going to say?" Everybody looked at me like I was a complete idiot. They said, "Don't be so naive. It doesn't matter what he says. It's all over." And I said, "What do you mean?" I couldn't believe it.

They were prepared to accept whatever he offered, even if he offered nothing. That meant the whole thing had just been a sham, a hollow exercise. I felt so betrayed.

I went back to the art academy and waited. At three P.M., Tito gave a rousing and very clever speech. He praised the students' political engagement (which he managed to link to his doctrine of self-management). He doubled the minimum wage (from $12 to $24 a month). And he accepted four of the points on our petition—including giving us the student cultural center we wanted.

The councils of the student government, which had been prepared to accept any scrap Tito tossed them, were thrilled. The students ended the occupation of university buildings and, as fireworks filled the night sky, paraded in triumph across Belgrade. Feeling anything but triumphant, I threw my Party membership card into a fire and watched as it burned to a crisp.

A week later, I saw my father on the street, kissing the beautiful young blond woman who would become his second wife. He pretended not to notice me. I didn't see him again for ten years.

After the demonstrations, five fellow students at the academy and I began to get together, in an informal way but on a regular basis, to talk about art—and to complain about the art we were being taught. All of them except me were guys: Era, Neša, Zoran, Raša, and Gera were their names. We met at the academy (despite Tito's concession, the secret police and their wives were reluctant to vacate their social center right away), and we drank coffee and more coffee, and fueled by the coffee, we talked and talked, often into the night, with all the passion and intensity of youth.

This was one of the times in my life when I was truly happy. I would wake up in the morning, go to my studio and paint, then meet with these guys and talk, then go home—always by ten P.M.—then get up the next day and do it again.

Group 70 at the Student Cultural Center, Belgrade, 1970;
from left: Raša Todosijević, Zoran Popović, me, Gera Urkom,
Era Milivojević, and Neša Paripović

What the six of us were talking about, obsessively, was a way past painting: a way to put life itself into art.

My car-crash paintings continued to frustrate me. For a while, on very large, five-foot-square canvases, I started painting clouds. Not realistic clouds, but something like symbols of clouds—like heavy peanut shapes hovering over monochromatic fields. Sometimes in these clouds there appeared a body: the nude body of a big old lady who used to model at the academy, always seen from behind. Sometimes she would transform into the landscape. This went with a daydream I used to have as a girl—that the entire universe, everything we know, is nothing but a pebble in the heel of the shoe of a cosmic fat lady.

In the West, along with the revolutions in politics and popular music, art was changing dramatically. In the 1960s, a new avant-garde was starting to reject the old idea of art as commodity, as paintings and sculptures that could be collected, and new ideas of conceptual and performance art were beginning to catch on. Some of these ideas filtered into Yugoslavia. My little group of six talked about the Conceptualists in the United States (where people like Lawrence Weiner and Joseph Kosuth were making pieces in which words were as important as objects); the Arte Povera movement in Italy, which was turning everyday objects into art; and the anti-commercial, anti-art Fluxus movement in Germany, whose stars were the provocative performance and Happening artists Joseph Beuys, Charlotte Moorman, and Nam June Paik. There was a Slovenian group called OHO that rejected art as an activity separate from life: any part of life at all, they believed, could be art. They were doing performance art as early as 1969: In Ljubljana, an artist named David Nez did a piece called *Cosmology*, where he lay inside a circle on the floor, with a lightbulb suspended just over his stomach, and tried to breathe in tune with the universe. Some members of OHO came to Belgrade to speak about their beliefs; I stood up in the auditorium and praised them.

Their example inspired me. In 1969 I proposed to the Belgrade Youth Center my first idea for a performance piece of my own. It involved the public, and it was called *Come Wash with Me*. My idea was to install laundry sinks around the gallery of the Youth Center. When the visitors came in, they would take off their clothes and I would wash, dry, and iron them. When I returned their clothes, the gallery visitors could get dressed again and leave, literally and metaphorically clean. The Youth Center rejected my idea.

The following year, I proposed another performance to them: I would stand in front of an audience in my regular clothes, then gradually change into the kind of clothes my mother always bought me: long skirt, heavy stockings, orthopedic shoes, ugly polka-dot blouse. Then I would put a pistol with one bullet in the chamber to my head and pull the trigger. "This performance has two possible endings," my proposal said. "And if I live my life will have a new beginning."

Once again I was rejected.

In my last year at the academy, I fell in love with one of the guys in my group. Neša was thirty years old, with fine, sandy hair, flying eyebrows, and strange, sharp, dramatic features—he reminded me of a character in an Ingmar Bergman film. He was very talented; his mind worked in odd ways. He had something different than anybody else I knew. For an arts festival in the hillside town of Groznjan, in Istria, Neša suspended a monochrome red canvas across the town square at sunrise: he called it *Red Square*. For me, his ideas were the sexiest thing about him. We began spending time together, but I still had to be home every night at ten—not much of a basis for a relationship.

I graduated the academy in the spring of 1970, with a grade of 9.25 out of 10. My diploma entitled me "to the professional title of academic painter, and thus all rights associated with this title." It was a strange and mixed compliment (and to the end of her days, my mother drove me crazy by addressing her letters to me: "Marina Abramović, Academic Painter"); still, it was an encouragement to keep painting, at least for a little while.

Soon after graduating I went to Zagreb, in Croatia, to do post-diploma study in the master workshop of the painter Krsto Hegedušić. It was a great honor to be selected for his class: he never had more than eight students at a time. Hegedušić was an old man, very famous for his genre paintings of peasants and strongly delineated landscapes of fields of crops—kind of a Yugoslav Thomas Hart Benton. Not exactly a natural match with me! Although I also remembered that Jackson Pollock had studied with Benton, and that had turned out well. And I liked Hegedušić very much. He said two things that I've always remembered. First, that if you get so good at drawing with your right hand that you can even make a beautiful sketch with your eyes closed, you should immediately change to your left hand to avoid repeating yourself. And second, don't flatter yourself that you have any ideas. If you're a good artist, Hegedušić said, you might have one good idea; if you're a genius, you might have two, period. And he was right.

For me the best thing about Zagreb was that it was the first time I had been away from home. It was very exciting to be out from under my mother's thumb. But I was also away from Neša, who began writing me letters wondering if we should still be together if we were in two different places. My emotions about him were very mixed.

Still, in the meantime I was free. I rented a little room, with a small, shared kitchen across the corridor. A few friends of mine from the academy were also in Zagreb, including a Croatian girl I knew, Srebrenka, who was studying to be an art critic. She was a very gloomy person—so gloomy that she was always telling us she was going to commit suicide. She said it so often that we all sort of got fed up: "Just do it! Leave us alone," we told her.

Srebrenka lived down at the end of my street. One morning I was supposed to get together with her for coffee, but it was raining like hell all day, so I never went. And that rainy afternoon, she actually did it: she committed suicide. But—when we Slavs do things, we do them big!—she committed not just single but quadruple suicide: She turned on the gas in the oven, cut her wrists, took sleeping pills, and hanged herself.

At her funeral, all her friends felt the same—the mood was angry. We'd all been fed up with her threatening suicide all the time, and we were all so mad at the waste of her life. She'd been so young, so beautiful. But there was also guilt. I thought, *My God, if I'd seen her that morning, maybe she wouldn't have done it.*

The funeral was at eleven in the morning; again it was raining, off and on. It was strange weather—sometimes the sun peeked out for a few seconds, then it went away. When I came home, it was pouring again. At around five in the afternoon, I lay on my bed, exhausted from the long day. My bedroom was in half light. I closed my eyes, and when I opened them, I saw Srebrenka, as clear as day, sitting at the end of my bed, looking at me with a triumphant smile on her face, as if to say, "I finally did it."

I freaked out. I jumped up, turned on the lights. Srebrenka had vanished. But for the next few days, whenever I crossed the corridor to the kitchen, just before I turned on the light, I would feel, very gently, a hand close over my hand. And then it went away.

I didn't know then and I don't know now who or what creates this invisible world, but I do know that it can be entirely visible. I became convinced that when we die, the physical body dies, but its energy doesn't disappear—it just takes different forms. I came to believe in the idea of parallel realities. I think that the reality we see now is a certain frequency, and that we're all on the same frequency, so we're visible to each other, but that it's possible to change frequencies. To enter a different reality. And I think that there are hundreds of these realities.

I no longer felt comfortable in my Zagreb bedroom. One day shortly after Srebrenka's death, there was a storm and one of the panes in the window broke and fell onto my bed—and I was so depressed, so lost, that I didn't even bother to clean the pieces of glass from the sheets. I just lay down and fell into a deep sleep, and when I woke in the morning, I was bleeding. It was time to go back to Belgrade.

At long last the secret police and their wives left, and we finally got our student cultural center—the SKC. And the SKC got a miraculous director, a young woman named Dunja Blažević. Dunja was an art historian, and her father was president of the Croatian parliament, which meant she had the privilege to travel the world looking at art. She'd taken full advantage of her position—she'd really been around, and she was extremely open-minded and informed. Just before the center opened, Dunja had attended the first *documenta*, an avant-garde art exhibition in Germany under the aegis of a brilliant Swiss curator, Harald Szeemann. Szeemann really raised the profile of conceptual and performance art. Dunja took it all in. When she came back to Belgrade, she was inspired and excited, and she proposed the SKC's first exhibition, which she called *Drangularium*—literally, "trinketarium," or "Little Things."

The purpose of the show was to let artists exhibit everyday objects that were somehow significant to them, rather than artworks, per se: the idea came from Arte Povera in Italy. Around thirty artists, including me, were invited to participate.

It was an amazing exhibition. Gera, one of the guys from my group of six, showed an old green blanket, full of holes, that he used in his studio. Instead of being significant, he wrote in the catalogue, it was the most meaningless object he could think of. A friend of mine, Evgenija, brought in the door to her studio—"a practical object with which I am in contact every day through the doorknob," she wrote. Raša, another guy in my group, brought in his beautiful girlfriend and sat her on a chair beside a blue nightstand with a bottle on it. "I have no rational excuse for the objects I have exhibited," he wrote. "I do not wish them to be interpreted as symbolic." But to us he admitted the real reason for his choice: "I always have sex with my girlfriend before I go to work," he said.

My exhibit related to the cloud paintings I had been doing. I brought in a peanut in its shell and fixed it to the wall with a straight pin. The peanut stuck out just far enough from the wall to cast a tiny shadow. I called the piece *Cloud With Its Shadow*. As soon as I saw that little shadow, I realized two-dimensional art truly was a thing of the past for me—that piece opened a whole different dimension. And that show opened new worlds for many people.

⌣

While I was in Zagreb, I went to see a famous clairvoyant. He was a Russian Jewish man with the ability to look at the grounds from a cup of Turkish coffee and tell you your future. There was a six-month waiting list just to see him, but I really wanted to go, because I had heard so many stories about him, and I wanted to know my destiny. And finally, somebody cancelled or something, and I got a call, and I went to see him.

My appointment was at six in the morning! Not only that, but the clairvoyant lived in the new part of Zagreb—I had to take three buses to get there. Finally I got to his apartment; I rang the bell and he opened the door. He was a very skinny, tall old man, maybe in his fifties or sixties. I was so young—anyone over forty-five looked old to me. Very silently, all business, he brought me to a table and poured two cups of Turkish coffee.

I drank my cup. Then he took my grounds and mixed them in with his. There was a Russian newspaper on the table. He turned his cup over onto the newspaper, and we waited in silence. Then he set the cup upright again and looked at the grounds on the newspaper. Then he sat back and rolled his eyes back in his head so that only the whites were visible.

He was quite a sight—kind of scary. And as he sat there with his eyes rolled back, he told me many things. He said that I would have success only late in my life; that I would live next to a big ocean; that I would move from Belgrade. He told me that I would first go to one country, which would be important to me at the beginning of my career; that I would get an unexpected invitation to return to Belgrade; that I would be offered a job that I should accept. He told me that one person was going to help me greatly, that this person would have a terrible tragedy in his life, and his name would be Boris. He told me that I had to look for a man in my life who would love me more than I loved him—then and only then would I find happiness. But he said that actually my biggest success would come to me when I was alone, because men would create obstacles in my life.

A couple of years later, after attending the Edinburgh Festival on my first trip outside Yugoslavia as an artist, I found myself living in London, working menial jobs and desperate for money. One day my mother telephoned me from Belgrade to tell me she had applied on my behalf for a teaching position at the art academy in Novi Sad. Usually, I would've told my mother no—I was always rebelling in those days, constantly trying to escape her influence—but this time I was really in a tough spot. My mother told me there were a few people in line for the job, that I was on the short list, but I needed to come back to be interviewed.

Danica arranged for a ticket, and I flew back to Yugoslavia. I landed in Zagreb first, then changed planes for the short flight to Belgrade. The Zagreb-Belgrade plane was almost empty. Flying made me nervous, and I was smoking in those days, so I sat in the smoking section. I took out a cigarette—then I realized I didn't have a lighter. Suddenly a man appeared and lit my cigarette for me. (I used to hold my cigarette with my thumb and forefinger, palm up: very sophisticated.)

The guy sat next to me, and we started talking—just chitchat at first. I told him I was coming from London for a meeting in Belgrade. He said that he, too, was going to a meeting in Belgrade. Then he said a little more, and I realized he was on the arts commission that oversaw the job I was applying for. I suddenly had a flashback to my session with the Russian clairvoyant. Then he lit another cigarette for me. I said, "Thank you, Boris."

We hadn't introduced ourselves—he instantly turned pale. "How do you know my name?" he asked.

"I also know that you have had a terrible tragedy in your life," I said.

He started shaking. "Who are you?" he asked. "How do you know these things?"

Leaving out the fact that we were heading to the same meeting, I told him about my session with the clairvoyant, and he told me his story. He had been married, he said, to a young wife whom he loved very much. She became pregnant. But—he only found this out later—she was having an affair with his best friend. And one day his wife and the friend were driving together, and they were both killed in a car wreck.

After our encounter on the plane, I went to my interview with the commission—where Boris was very surprised to see me walk into the room! I got the job, and never saw him again.

⌒

I couldn't imagine moving from my little Zagreb life of freedom back to my mother's apartment, where there was no freedom, where I couldn't leave home after ten. I'd had enough. The whole time I was away, Neša had kept writing me with his anguished questions—so finally I decided to do something about them. "Why don't we get married?" I said.

It was like a pact between him and me: Let's marry, so I can be free. So we got married, in October 1971. But my mother didn't change anyway. Not only did she not come to the wedding, but she didn't allow Neša to move into the apartment with me. She said, "A man will never come and sleep in this house," so he never came to sleep in my house. (Well, now and then he snuck in in the middle of the night, but there was no sleeping then! And he always had to sneak back out before the sun rose.) We didn't have the money to get a place of our own, so we lived apart, he with his parents, I with my mother and grandmother. Still having to be home every night by ten. A very strange arrangement, and not a pleasant one.

Neša's parents, who were very poor, lived in a tiny flat in Belgrade: just one bedroom for his mother and father, one small room for Neša, and a kitchen. His mother was very religious, and his father was a laborer of some kind. The father came down with uremia—blood in his urine—and he was sick for a long time, and in great pain. The only position he could be even slightly comfortable in was sitting on the bed, hunched over, with a pillow pressed to his midsection. In the middle of the room was a table with a lit candle and a Bible. Whenever anyone came to visit, Neša's mother would say, "Oh, come and sit with him a little bit."

One day I was visiting Neša, and his mother was in the kitchen making lunch, and they both said, as usual, "Sit a little bit with him." So I went into the bedroom and sat on the chair next to the table with the candle, and I started reading the Bible. There was nothing else to do. Neša's father would never look at anyone—in his pain, he just sat and stared into space. But at one point, he turned and looked at me for a long, long time. It was incredible—I had never had this kind of contact with him. He looked and looked at me, and then very slowly, he let go of the pillow that he was holding to his stomach, and very gently, he fell onto the pillow behind him, with a small smile on his face, as if he had seen something that I couldn't see. Then he slowly closed his eyes and let out a long breath, and after a moment I realized he was dead.

It was the first time I had ever seen someone die, and it was one of the most beautiful deaths I have ever seen. That moment was so peaceful and so special—it was as though he felt comfortable enough to die in my presence. I knew that if his wife had been in the room, it would've been hell: Slavic women make a grand display in these circumstances. She would have screamed, she would have beaten her breast. I think the poor man just wanted some peace.

I was so mesmerized by this moment that for a long, long time I didn't move from the table—I just wanted to give him this time. Then I stood up very slowly, went to the kitchen, and said, "I think your father is dying." Neša's mother rushed in, saw that her husband was gone, and went nuts. She kept screaming at me: "How could you not call me, why didn't you call me?"

She was an impossible woman anyway. Anytime Neša would go somewhere, she would always tell him she would die before he came back—there was this constant emotional blackmail. On the rare occasions when we'd saved enough to go on a holiday, she would say, "Oh, you kids have a good time, but when you come back I will not be here." And of course she lived a long, long life.

A strange story about Neša and me. There was a strong attraction between us, and I always wanted to make love, but he could not finish the act. It was very frustrating for both of us. But then I somehow got pregnant from this inadequate lovemaking. I had an abortion—the first of three I would have in my life. I never wanted to have children. This was an absolute with me, for so many reasons.

Clockwise from top left: Raša Dragoljub Todosijević, Zoran Popović, my first husband, Neša Paripović, and me, Belgrade, 1967

But then, the moment Neša learned that I was pregnant, every-thing changed—he became instantly potent. It was amazing! And still we continued our frustrating life together, yet not really together.

I constantly thought about freedom—from my mother, from Bel-grade, from two-dimensional art. One path to freedom was money. I had never had any money of my own. Even though I never lacked for anything, I lived under a tyranny of support. From my childhood on, schoolbooks were bought for me. Clothing was bought for me. Shoes for the summer, shoes for the winter. Coats. Everything Danica chose for me was practical and durable, and I hated all of it.

At the academy, students could apply for summer work restoring frescoes and mosaics in the basilicas on the Adriatic coast. I did that job for a couple of summers; I loved being by the seaside, the sun and salt on my skin. And then there was less pleasant work in Belgrade, cleaning office buildings and setting up trade fairs—building stands and painting floors and walls. I was glad to do all of it. Because I was still living at home, I could pocket all the money I made and buy the things I really liked: books, records, and even clothes.

I bought something else, too, on credit: a one-room cottage in Grožnjan, the artist-colony town in Istria. A place to go during the summer. A tiny gesture of independence.

But mostly I was in my mother's apartment. There I was, almost twenty-five, a married woman, living apart from my husband. That flat was such a strange place—it was packed with all the fancy bric-a-brac of a very materialistic Communist lady.

I was in constant rebellion against everything, and most of all my mother. One day, to protect myself from her, I smeared the contents of three hundred cans of brown shoe polish all over the walls, win-dows, and doors of my room and studio. It looked as if the room was covered in shit; the smell was unbearable. My plan worked perfectly. She opened the door, screamed, and never entered again.

The more my mother filled the apartment with her insane collec-tion of stuff, the more *spartak* I kept my rooms. There was one excep-tion, my contribution to the flat's general clutter: my mailbox. I built a huge wooden postbox, painted it black, and put a sign (designed by my friend Zoran) on it. CENTER FOR AMPLIFIED ART, the sign read. Zoran also designed a letterhead for me, and a Center for Amplified Art logo for the stationery.

I don't quite know where I came up with that name, but it meant something profound to me. In my mother's apartment, in the midst of Belgrade, in Communist Yugoslavia, it felt very important to make contact with the outside world: the art world. I wrote to galleries everywhere—in France, Germany, England, Italy, Spain, the United States—asking for catalogues and art books, and they started coming, piles of them, stacking up inside my giant mailbox. I read every one of them, hungrily taking in all the advances in the art world, dreaming of the time when I would be part of them.

⌒

There was a lot of excitement after *Drangularium*, and a new show quickly followed at SKC: it was called "Objects and Projects." For this exhibition I created a work called *Freeing the Horizon*. I reproduced ordinary picture postcards of various streets and monuments in Belgrade, photographically erasing the monuments themselves and most of the surrounding buildings. For instance, in a postcard of the grand Old Palace of the Obrenović Dynasty, I whited out the palace itself, leaving only the grass in front, a couple of cars, a few people strolling by.

The effect was eerie, but it expressed my strong wish for freedom from the suffocation I felt living in that city, under the control of my mother and the Communist regime. Oddly enough, during the Kosovo war in the late 1990s, some of the very buildings I had erased photographically were destroyed by American bombs.

The more I thought about it, the more I realized how unlimited art could be. Around this time, I was also becoming fascinated by sound. And I had an inspiration: I wanted to take a sound-effects recording of a bridge collapse to an actual bridge and play the recording every three minutes—every three minutes, though the structure was clearly intact, you'd hear the gigantic crashing sound of the whole thing falling down. Visually, the bridge still existed, but acoustically it was disappearing. Yet I had to get permission from the municipal authorities to mount this piece, and permission was not granted. They told me the bridge could actually collapse from the strong sound vibrations.

But just a month after "Objects and Projects," there was another, even more minimal, show at the Student Cultural Center, and for it I made my first sound pieces. In a tree outside the gallery I installed a big speaker that played a continuous loop of birds singing, as if we were in the middle of a tropical forest and not gloomy Belgrade. And inside the gallery, inside three cardboard boxes, I put tape machines playing other sounds of nature: wind blowing, surf crashing, sheep bleating.

At that same show, something happened, quite spontaneously, that would turn me toward my future. One of the most talented guys in my group of six, Era, had created a piece for the exhibition by simply covering a big mirror in the gallery with transparent packing tape, subverting the normal use of a mirror by forcing visitors to see their reflected images in a distorted way. One day, in the late afternoon, I felt tired and lay down on a low table in the gallery. And suddenly, Era had an inspiration: he decided to wrap me with his tape. I went along with it, lying there, arms at my side, my whole body except for my head completely mummified. Some of the onlookers were fascinated; some, repelled. But nobody was bored.

The next year, I did more sound pieces for other shows in Belgrade: in one of them (called *War*), installed in the entrance of the Museum of Contemporary Art, visitors walked down a narrow corridor formed by two sheets of plywood to the deafening roar of recorded machine-gun fire. I was using sound as if it were a broom cleaning the minds of visitors before they entered the museum. Once they were inside, the aftermath of total silence allowed them to appreciate the art around them in a new way.

And I finally got to do my falling-bridge piece, not on a bridge, but just outside the SKC, where a speaker hidden in a tree blasted out the

SPRINGDALE PUBLIC LIBRARY
405 S. Pleasant
Springdale, AR 72764

Era Milivojević taping me to a bench at the Student Cultural Center, Belgrade, 1971

sounds of demolition, giving the unsettling illusion that the entire structure was crashing down.

A couple of months later, I created a more playful piece inside the lounge of the SKC: a continuous recorded loop playing the same airport announcement over and over: "Please, all passengers on airline JAT are requested to proceed immediately to Gate 265. [At the time, there were only three gates at the Belgrade Airport.] The plane is leaving for New York, Bangkok, Honolulu, Tokyo, and Hong Kong." Everyone sitting in the lounge—whether they were drinking coffee, waiting to see a movie, or just reading a newspaper—became the passengers for this imaginary trip.

The irony was that at that point in my life, I had barely gone anywhere outside Belgrade.

At the end of 1972, a curator from Scotland, Richard Demarco, visited Belgrade looking for fresh ideas for the next Edinburgh Festival. Our government escort took him around to see all the officially sanctioned painters; Demarco of course was bored out of his wits. The night before he was going to leave, though, somebody whispered in his ear about the SKC, then got word to my little group that Demarco wanted to meet us. We went to his hotel room to tell him about our work and show him photographs of it; he was very interested in all of us. He sent the government a letter inviting us to participate in the next festival, but the government turned him down, saying that this kind of art could not represent Yugoslavian culture. Finally he told us that if we could make our own way to Scotland, he would put us up. I was glad I had been saving my money.

In the summer of 1973 we all went to Edinburgh—except Era, the guy who had wrapped me in packing tape. It was strange: in my mind, he was so talented and interesting; he reminded me of a Slavic Marcel Duchamp. But when I asked him, "Why aren't you coming with us?" he said, "I came from a little village to Belgrade—this was already a big step. You are going from Belgrade to Edinburgh, but I already made my Edinburgh by coming to Belgrade." He never left, and he never really made it.

It's interesting with art. Some people have the ability—and the energy—not just to make the work, but to make sure it's put in exactly the right place, at the right moment. Some artists realize they have to spend as much time as it took them to get an idea in finding the way to show it, and the infrastructure to support it. And some artists just don't have that energy, and have to be taken care of, by art lovers or collectors or the gallery system. During the controversial performance artist Vito Acconci's early career, for example, the art dealer Ileana Sonnabend paid him $500 a month, which took care of his rent and everything else. He didn't sell his work—he didn't have to. This regular stipend just allowed him to produce steadily. In Belgrade in the early 1970s we had no such support systems, and so poor Era just fell by the wayside.

We arrived in Edinburgh. I stayed with a family there, friends of Demarco, and planned my first performance. Joseph Beuys was there, the charismatic star of the festival (it was his first art trip out of Germany), wearing his trademark white shirt and vest and gray fedora and giving social sculpture performance lectures of six or seven hours, with notes and diagrams on a chalkboard. A lot of international artists were there, including the American conceptual artist Tom Marioni, the Polish theater director Tadeusz Kantor, and also Hermann Nitsch and several other members of Wiener Aktionismus (Viennese Actionism), a group whose wild performances had made them notorious. (One of them, Günter Brus, was sentenced to prison after a piece in which he simultaneously masturbated, spread feces over his body, and sang the Austrian national anthem.) It was a high-powered crowd; on a certain level I was terrified. It was my first trip to the West as an artist. I felt like a very small fish in a very big pond.

But there was also a part of me that didn't care about any of that. My mother and father had many faults; but they were both very brave and strong people, and they passed along much of that strength and courage to me. Some big part of me is thrilled by the unknown, by the idea of taking risks. When it comes to doing risky things, I don't care. I just go for it.

Me, Joseph Beuys, and Dunja Blažević, the director of the SKC, 1974

That doesn't mean I'm fearless. Quite the opposite. The idea of death terrifies me. When there is turbulence on an airplane, I shake with fear. I start composing my last will and testament. But when it comes to my work, I cast caution to the winds.

That is how I felt about *Rhythm 10*, the piece I planned to perform at Edinburgh. *Rhythm 10* was absolutely crazy. It was based on a drinking game played by Russian and Yugoslav peasants: You spread your fingers out on a wooden bar or table and stab down a sharp knife, fast, in the spaces between your fingers. Every time you miss and cut yourself, you have to take another drink. The drunker you get, the more likely you are to stab yourself. Like Russian roulette, it is a game of bravery and foolishness and despair and darkness—the perfect Slavic game.

Beforehand, I was so nervous that I was scared I'd get one of my incapacitating whole-body migraines. I could hardly breathe from the idea that I was going to do this. But I was also serious about what I was about to do, 100 percent committed. I was so serious about everything then! Yet I think I needed this gravity. Much later on, I read a statement of Bruce Nauman's: "Art is a matter of life and death." It sounds melodramatic, but it's so true. This was exactly how it was for me, even at the beginning. Art was life and death. There was nothing else. It was so serious, and so necessary.

My variation on the game involved not one but ten knives, and sound, and a new idea: turning accidents into the plan for a piece of performance art. On the floor of the gymnasium of Melville College— one of the sites of the festival—I unrolled a big sheet of heavy white paper. On this paper I arranged ten knives of various sizes and two tape recorders. Then, with a big crowd watching—including Joseph Beuys at the front, in his little gray fedora—I knelt down on the paper and turned on one of the tape recorders.

I had been terrified beforehand, but the second I began, my fear evaporated. The space I occupied was safe.

Rat-tat-tat-tat-tat—I stabbed the knife down between the fingers of my left hand, as fast as I could. And of course because I was going so fast, every once in a while I would miss, just slightly, and nick myself. Each time I cut myself, I would groan with pain— the tape recorder would pick it up—and I would switch to the next knife.

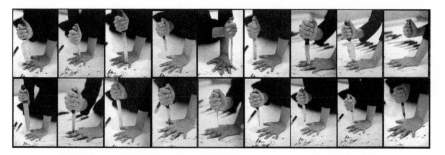

Rhythm 10 (performance, 1 hour), Museo d'Arte Contemporanea, Villa Borghese, Rome, 1973

Pretty soon I had gone through all ten knives, and the white paper was stained very impressively with my blood. The crowd stared, dead silent. And a very strange feeling came over me, something I had never dreamed of: It was as if electricity was running through my body, and the audience and I had become one. A single organism. The sense of danger in the room had united the onlookers and me in that moment: the here and now, and nowhere else.

That thing that each of us lives with, that you are your own little self privately—once you step into the performance space, you are acting from a higher self, and *it's not you anymore*. It's not the you that you know. It's something else. There on the gymnasium floor of Melville College in Edinburgh, Scotland, it was as if I had become, at the same time, a receiver and transmitter of huge, Tesla-like energy. The fear was gone, the pain was gone. I had become a Marina whom I didn't know yet.

The moment I cut myself with the tenth knife, I switched the first tape recorder from record to playback, turned the second machine on, recording, and began all over again with knife number one. Only this time, as the first tape machine played back the sounds of the knifepoint thudding rhythmically and my groans of pain, I tried quite deliberately to nick myself in precise unison with my previous accidents. As it turned out, I was good at this—I only missed twice. And the second tape machine was recording both the playback and my next round of the knife game.

Nikola Tesla reading a book, with his equipment for producing
high-frequency alternating currents, 1901

When I'd gone through the ten knives once more, I rewound the second tape recorder, played the double soundtrack of both performances, then stood up and left. Listening to the wild applause from the audience, I knew I'd succeeded in creating an unprecedented unity of time present and time past with random errors.

I had experienced absolute freedom—I had felt that my body was without boundaries, limitless; that pain didn't matter, that nothing mattered at all—and it intoxicated me. I was drunk from the overwhelming energy that I'd received. That was the moment I knew that I had found my medium. No painting, no object that I could make, could ever give me that kind of feeling, and it was a feeling I knew I would have to seek out, again and again and again.

3.

Once upon a time there was a beautiful little blond girl, so pretty and so cute. And she was sitting looking into a pond when she saw a goldfish. She reached into the water and caught it! And the goldfish said, "Let me free, and if you tell me three wishes, I will fulfill them." So the little girl let the fish free.

"What is your first wish?" the goldfish asked. The girl said, "My first wish is to have very, very long arms, almost touching the ground." "No problem," the fish said. And just like that, the little girl had long, long arms, nearly touching the ground. "What is your second wish?" the goldfish asked. "My second wish," the girl said, "is for my nose to be so big that it would hang almost halfway to my chest." The fish said, "Easily done," and it was done.

"What is your third wish?" the goldfish asked. "I want big ears, like elephant ears, covering half of my face," the girl said. The fish replied, "Presto!" And lo and behold, the beautiful little girl was transformed into a monster, with long arms, giant nose, and big, floppy ears.

"I know it's not my business," the fish said, before swimming away, "but can you tell me why you wanted to look like this?" The little girl said, "Beauty is temporary. Ugliness lasts forever."

Once I was a postwoman. Not for very long, though.

None of us had wanted to go back to Belgrade when the festival was over, but in order to stay in Edinburgh, we had to find work. So I got a job as a mail lady. I was excited about my new job, but after a few exhausting days of walking around the city, often lost and not speaking the language very well, I decided to only deliver the envelopes with nice handwritten addresses and throw out everything else—especially the bills. My supervisor asked me to return my uniform. That was that for postal work.

Then Demarco asked me if I knew anything about interior design. "Of course," I said. Of course I knew nothing.

He took me to an architectural firm and introduced me to one of the principals. "We are designing a dining room for a luxury cruise ship," the guy said. "Can you give us your input?"

I reported for work the next morning. The first thing I did was to take a pile of white paper and draw a closely spaced grid on each sheet. It was painstaking work with a ruler and pencil, and it took me all week. At the end of the week, the architect said, "Can you show me what you're thinking?" I showed him all the sheets I had so carefully prepared. He looked at me and took me to a supply closet. There, on a shelf, were reams and reams of preprinted graph paper. At least he was amused instead of angry at this clueless Slavic chick from the middle of nowhere, but that job didn't last very long, either.

Soon afterward the five of us moved to London, where I worked on an assembly line in a toy factory, manufacturing the Newton's cradle—the toy with the shiny metal balls swinging back and forth. I was such a fast assembler that my supervisor was impressed—so impressed that he kept hitting on me. I was bored and frustrated: I was an artist, and there seemed to be no way for me to do art in London.

At the very least, I thought, I could *look* at art. And so I spent many pleasant afternoons visiting London galleries. My favorite was Lisson Gallery, which featured cutting-edge contemporary pieces in several media. I vividly remember an exhibition of very conceptual work by a group that called itself Art & Language. And I remember the young man sitting at the gallery's front desk, to whom I was too shy to talk or show my work. As it turned out, this was Lisson's founder, Nicholas Logsdail—who, forty years later, became my gallerist in London.

This was when my mother found me a job without asking me, and once again Belgrade pulled me back. I'd stayed away as long as I could, yet in order to really leave, I had to return first.

I began teaching at the Novi Sad Academy, but—thanks to my growing notoriety and no doubt thanks to Danica's influence as well—my course load was small (I taught only one day a week) and my salary high. This gave me the freedom to save my money and pursue performance art seriously. In those days, it never crossed my mind that I could make a living from my performances. I simply had ideas, and felt that I had to realize them no matter what.

In late 1973 I went to Rome as part of an exhibition called "Contemporanea," curated by the Italian critic Achille Bonito Oliva. There I met such important performance artists as Joan Jonas, Charlemagne Palestine, Simone Forti, and Luigi Ontani, and the key Arte Povera figures Marisa and Mario Merz, Jannis Kounellis, Luciano Fabro, Giovanni Anselmo, and Giuseppe Penone. It was heady company. But as my horizons broadened and I understood how conceptualism was taking hold, I yearned to make my own art more visceral. That meant using the body—my body. In Rome I performed *Rhythm 10* once more, this time with twenty knives and even more blood than before. Once again I got a big reaction from the audience. My mind was ablaze—it felt as though the possibilities for performance art were infinite.

One of the artists I met in Rome was a Brazilian, a couple of years older than me, named Antonio Dias. I was fascinated with his work, which lay in a strange and wonderful territory between straightforward painting and conceptual art. One piece consisted simply of a record player, a 45rpm record, and a banana. While the record was playing, he put the banana on it, creating an interesting distortion of sight and sound.

In 1974 Beuys came to the April meeting of the SKC, and I spent a lot of time with him. My mind was on fire and fire was on my mind, as part of a new piece I was thinking about. But when I told Beuys about it, he sounded a note of caution. "Be very careful with fire," he warned me. But *careful* was not part of my vocabulary in those days. The piece I had in mind would be called *Rhythm 5*.

The "5" in the title stood for a five-pointed star—for two stars, really. There was the large five-pointed wooden star I planned to build in the courtyard of the SKC, and there were the starfishlike extremities of my body as I would lie inside it: my head and my outstretched arms and legs.

The star was actually a double star of wooden rails, one star inside the other, the outer one some fifteen feet from point to point, the inner just slightly larger than my body. In between the two star outlines I would lay wood shavings soaked in 100 liters of gasoline. Then I would set this highly flammable material ablaze and lie inside the inner star, my arms and legs outspread.

Why a star? It was the symbol of Communism, the repressive force under which I had grown up, the thing I was trying to escape—but it was so many other things, too: a pentagram, an icon worshiped and mystified by ancient religions and cults, a shape possessing enormous symbolic power. I was trying to understand the deeper meaning of these symbols by using them in my work.

Beuys, along with many others, was in the audience at the SKC the night I performed *Rhythm 5*. I set the wood chips ablaze, then I walked around the perimeter of the star a few times. I cut my fingernails and tossed the clippings into the fire. Then I took a scissors to my hair—which was down to my shoulders at the time—and cut it all off. I tossed my hair into the fire, too. Then I lay inside the inner star, stretching out my arms and legs to conform to its shape.

There was dead silence—all you could hear in the courtyard was the crackling of the flames. That was the last thing I remembered. Once the fire touched my leg and I didn't react, the audience quickly realized I had lost consciousness: the flames had consumed all the oxygen around my head. Someone picked me up and carried me to safety, but instead of being a fiasco, the piece had been a strange kind of hit. It wasn't just my act of bravery and foolishness: the audience had been transfixed by the symbolic spectacle of the blazing star and the woman within.

Rhythm 5 (performance, 1.5 hours), Student Cultural Center, Belgrade, 1974

In *Rhythm 5* I had gotten so angry that I'd lost control. In my next pieces, I asked myself how to use my body in and out of consciousness without interrupting the performance.

For *Rhythm 2*, which I performed at the Museum of Contemporary Art in Zagreb a few months later, I got two pills from the hospital: one that forces catatonics to move, and one that quiets down schizophrenics. I sat at a little table in front of the audience and took pill number one. In a couple of minutes my body was jerking around involuntarily, almost falling out of my chair. I was aware of what was happening to me, but there was nothing I could do to stop it.

Then, when that pill wore off, I took the second one. This time I went into a kind of passive trance, sitting there with a big smile on my face, aware of nothing. And this pill took five hours to wear off.

In Yugoslavia and in the rest of Europe, word was spreading in the art world about this reckless young woman. Later that year I went to Galleria Diagramma in Milan to perform *Rhythm 4*. In this piece I was naked, alone in a white room and crouched above a powerful industrial fan. As a video camera sent my image to the audience in the next room, I pressed my face against the hurricane blowing out of the fan, trying to take as much air into my lungs as possible. In a couple of minutes, the great torrent of air filling my insides caused me to lose consciousness. I had anticipated this, but as with *Rhythm 2*, the point of the piece had been to show me in two different states, consciousness and unconsciousness. I knew that I was experiencing new ways of using my body as material. The problem was that as with *Rhythm 5*,

I was perceived to be in danger. And while in the earlier piece the danger had been real, and this time it was only perceived, the Milan gallery staff, fearing for my well-being, rushed in and "rescued" me. It wasn't needed, it wasn't intended, but it all became part of the piece.

Rhythm 4 (performance, 45 minutes), Galleria Diagramma, Milan, 1974

I had wanted attention for my work, but much of the attention I got in Belgrade was negative. My hometown newspapers ridiculed me viciously. What I was doing had nothing to do with art, they wrote. I was nothing but an exhibitionist and a masochist, they said. I belonged in a mental hospital, they claimed.

The photographs of me naked in Galleria Diagramma were especially scandalous.

This reaction to my work led me to plan my most daring piece to date. What if instead of doing something to myself, I let the public decide what to do to me?

The invitation came from Studio Morra in Naples: Come and perform whatever you want. It was early 1975. With the scandalized reactions of the Belgrade press fresh in my mind, I planned a piece in which the audience would provide the action. I would merely be the object, the receptacle.

My plan was to go to the gallery and just stand there, in black trousers and a black T-shirt, behind a table containing seventy-two objects: A hammer. A saw. A feather. A fork. A bottle of perfume. A bowler hat. An ax. A rose. A bell. Scissors. Needles. A pen. Honey. A lamb bone. A carving knife. A mirror. A newspaper. A shawl. Pins. Lipstick. Sugar. A Polaroid camera. Various other things. And a pistol, and one bullet lying next to it.

When a big crowd had gathered at eight P.M., they found these instructions on the table:

RHYTHM 0

Instructions.
> There are 72 objects on the table that one can use on me as desired.

Performance.
> I am the object.
> During this period I take full responsibility.
> Duration: 6 hours (8pm - 2am)
> 1974
> Studio Morra, Naples.

If someone wanted to put the bullet into the pistol and use it, I was ready for the consequences. I said to myself, *Okay, let's see what happens.*

For the first three hours, not much happened—the audience was being shy with me. I just stood there, staring into the distance, not looking at anything or anybody; now and then, someone would hand me the rose, or drape the shawl over my shoulders, or kiss me.

Then, slowly at first and then quickly, things began to happen. It was very interesting: for the most part, the women in the gallery would tell the men what to do to me, rather than do it themselves (although later on, when someone stuck a pin into me, one woman wiped the tears from my eyes). For the most part, these were just normal members of the Italian art establishment and their wives. Ultimately I think the reason I wasn't raped was that the wives were there.

As evening turned into late night, a certain air of sexuality arose in the room. This came not from me but from the audience. We were in southern Italy, where the Catholic Church was so powerful, and there was this strong Madonna/whore dichotomy in attitudes toward women.

After three hours, one man cut my shirt apart with the scissors and took it off. People manipulated me into various poses. If they turned my head down, I kept it down; if they turned it up, I kept it that way. I was a puppet—entirely passive. Bare-breasted, I stood there, and someone put the bowler hat on my head. With the lipstick, someone else wrote IO SONO LIBERO—"I am free"—on the mirror and stuck it in my hand. Someone else took the lipstick and wrote END across my forehead. A guy took Polaroids of me and stuck them in my hand, like playing cards.

Things got more intense. A couple of people picked me up and carried me around. They put me on the table, spread my legs, stuck the knife in the table close to my crotch.

Someone stuck pins into me. Someone else slowly poured a glass of water over my head. Someone cut my neck with the knife and sucked the blood. I still have the scar.

There was one man—a very small man—who just stood very close to me, breathing heavily. This man scared me. Nobody else, nothing else, did. But he did. After a while, he put the bullet in the pistol and put the pistol in my right hand. He moved the pistol toward my neck and touched the trigger. There was a murmur in the crowd, and someone grabbed him. A scuffle broke out.

Some of the audience obviously wanted to protect me; others wanted the performance to continue. This being southern Italy, voices were raised; tempers flared. The little man was hustled out of the gallery and the piece continued. In fact, the audience became more and more active, as if in a trance.

And then, at two A.M., the gallerist came and told me the six hours

Rhythm 0 (performance, 6 hours), Studio Morra, Naples, 1974

were up. I stopped staring and looked directly at the audience. "The performance is over," the gallerist said. "Thank you."

I looked like hell. I was half naked and bleeding; my hair was wet. And a strange thing happened: at this moment, the people who were still there suddenly became afraid of me. As I walked toward them, they ran out of the gallery.

The gallerist drove me back to my hotel and I went to my room alone—feeling more alone than I'd felt for a long time. I was exhausted, but my mind wouldn't stop buzzing, replaying scenes from the wild evening. The pain that had been absent when I received the pinpricks and the cut to my neck now throbbed. The fear of that little man wouldn't leave me. Eventually I fell into a kind of half sleep. In the morning I looked in the mirror, and a whole clump of my hair had turned gray. In that moment, I realized that the public can kill you.

The next day, the gallery received dozens of phone calls from peo-

Rhythm 0 (performance, 6 hours), Studio Morra, Naples, 1974

ple who had participated in the show. They were terribly sorry, they said; they didn't really understand what had happened while they were there—they didn't know what had come over them.

What had happened while they were there, quite simply, was performance. And the essence of performance is that the audience and the performer make the piece together. I wanted to test the limits of how far the public would go if I didn't do anything at all. This was a brand-new concept to the people who came to Studio Morra that night, and it was perfectly natural that those who attended felt worked up about it, both during the performance and afterward.

Human beings are afraid of very simple things: we fear suffering, we fear mortality. What I was doing in *Rhythm 0*—as in all my other performances—was staging these fears for the audience: using their energy to push my body as far as possible. In the process, I liberated myself from my fears. And as this happened, I became a mirror for the audience—if I could do it, they could do it, too.

⌒

Another Yugoslav joke:

Why do girls from good families go to bed at five P.M.?

To be home by ten P.M.

At the spring salon of Belgrade's Museum of Contemporary Art, I proudly exhibited photographs of all my *Rhythm* pieces, including *Rhythm 0.* After the opening, a group of my friends went out to dinner, but I knew I couldn't go with them if I was to make it home in time for my ten o'clock curfew. So, like the obedient daughter I was, I went home. The apartment was dark, which made me happy—it meant my mother had gone to sleep and I wouldn't have to deal with her. Then I turned on the light and saw her.

My mother was sitting at the dining room table in her work uniform: double-breasted suit with a brooch on her lapel, her hair in a chignon. Her face was contorted with rage. Why? During the opening, somebody had called her and said, "Your daughter is hanging naked in the museum."

She screamed at me. How could I produce such disgusting work? she asked. How could I humiliate our family this way? I was no better than a prostitute, she spat. Then she picked up a heavy glass ashtray from the dining room table. "I gave you life, and now I will take it away!" she yelled, and flung the ashtray at my head.

In a millisecond, two thoughts flickered simultaneously through my mind: first, that my mother's exclamation was a direct quote from Gogol's *Taras Bulba* (*Leave it to her to create the ultimate drama*, I thought); and second, that if the ashtray killed me or seriously injured me, she would go to prison. How lovely that would be!

Then again, I had no wish to risk death or brain damage. At the last instant I moved my head, and the ashtray smashed the pane of glass in the door behind me.

Neša, on the other hand, was quietly proud of me, but he was too nervous to watch me perform in Belgrade, and too poor in any case to accompany me on my travels. We still tried to grab moments together—in the cinema, in the park, and still sometimes in my mother's apartment in the middle of the night—yet we were growing apart. I loved his work, I liked his spirit, I liked being with him. But at the same time I was dying. I was young, and I was extremely sexual. Neša and I were on different wavelengths this way. I remember having to take long, cold showers just to cool down.

In the summer of 1975 I went to Vienna after a gallerist there, Ursula Krinzinger, invited me to participate in a performance by Hermann Nitsch. Nitsch was a burly, bearded Austrian, one of the Viennese Actionists but also filled with dark fascinations all his own: his *Orgien Mysterien Theater* (*Orgiastic Mystery Theater*), begun in the early 1960s, was a series of strange, bloody spectacles involving many performers, frequently nude. The performances, which had the air of unholy religious rituals, frequently depicted slaughter, sacrifice, and crucifixion.

That summer Nitsch staged a performance in a castle outside Vienna called Prinzendorf. The piece was to last twenty-four hours. There were sixty participants, including me; most of the others were men. Some were naked, some dressed all in white. I was placed on a wooden stretcher, naked and blindfolded, and the stretcher was leaned against a concrete wall. As gloomy music played, Nitsch poured sheep blood and organs—eyes and liver—over my belly and between my legs. Things got stranger from there.

After this had gone on for twelve hours I took off my blindfold and walked away. Not that I couldn't take it physically. I just didn't want to be part of it anymore—I understood it was not my thing. It was the enormous amount of animals' blood, and the fact that we had to drink it, and that it all took place in a chapel in the castle—it felt like a kind of Black Mass or bacchanal. It seemed so negative to me. But at bottom it was just not my story. Not conceptually or in any other way.

Still, I hung around through the night just to see how it would all play out. The next morning there was quite a spectacle to behold: all the participants, covered with blood and dirt, were led out to a meadow where perfect tables with white tablecloths had been set out and a little orchestra played Viennese waltzes while liveried waiters served everybody soup for breakfast. That image was pretty good, I have to say. But again, it was Nitsch's thing, not mine.

While I was in Austria, I met a Swiss artist called Thomas Lips. He was a slim man with long curly hair, and very beautiful in a way that was both masculine and feminine—his androgyny fascinated me. Although I had never been drawn to women sexually, I was powerfully attracted to him, and we had a brief fling. (Years later, I ran into him in Switzerland. He had—to my great surprise—become a lawyer.)

Travel always had a kind of aphrodisiac effect on me. But this latest liaison, coming on the heels of the dark Nitsch extravaganza, somehow melded with that piece in my mind and got under my skin. That fall, Ursula Krinzinger invited me back to Austria, to her gallery in Innsbruck this time, where I staged a new performance, which I called *Thomas Lips*. The instructions read:

MARINA ABRAMOVIĆ

THOMAS LIPS

Performance.

    I slowly eat 1 kilo of honey with a silver spoon.

    I slowly drink 1 liter of red wine out of a crystal glass.

    I break the glass with my right hand.

    I cut a five-pointed star on my stomach with a razor blade.

    I violently whip myself until I no longer feel any pain.

    I lay down on a cross made of ice blocks.

    The heat of a suspended heater pointed at my stomach causes the cut star to bleed.

    The rest of my body behind to freeze.

    I remain on the ice cross for 30 minutes until the public interrupts the piece by removing the ice blocks from underneath me.

Duration: 2 hours

1975

Krinzinger Gallery, Innsbruck.

As I whipped myself, my blood flew everywhere. The pain was excruciating at first. And then it vanished. The pain was like a wall I had walked through and come out on the other side.

After a few minutes I lay on my back on blocks of ice that had been laid on the floor in the form of a cross. A heater was lowered from the ceiling on wires. It hung just above my stomach, warming the star I had cut so it continued to bleed. Meanwhile the entire back of my body was freezing on the ice cross. While lying on the cross, I felt my skin stick to the surface of the ice. I tried to breathe as slowly as possible and not to move at all.

I lay there for a half hour. Krinzinger was well known for showing extreme work, by the Viennese Actionists and others: the people who came to her gallery were sophisticated. Soon, though, *Thomas Lips* proved too much even for them. Valie Export, an Austrian performance artist in the audience, jumped up and, with a couple of other onlookers, covered me with coats and pulled me off the ice. I had to be taken to the hospital—not for the wounds on my belly, but for a deep cut on my hand I'd suffered when I broke the wineglass. It needed six stitches. Because of all the other intense sensations stirred up in me by the performance, I hadn't even noticed the cut was there.

⌒

On my twenty-ninth birthday, November 30, 1975, a letter arrived in the big wooden mailbox in my mother's apartment. It was an invitation from a gallery in Amsterdam called de Appel, asking me to do a performance for a Dutch TV show, *Beeldspraak* (*Picture Speech*). It was the third time that a gallery had invited me to perform, but this was not a common thing in those days. Then as now, money drove the art world, and performance art wasn't something that could be sold. But de Appel was run by a woman named Wies Smals, and Wies was

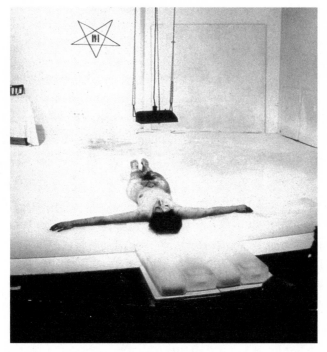

Thomas Lips (performance, 2 hours), Krinzinger Gallery, Innsbruck, 1975

a kind of visionary. She was the first gallerist in Europe to invite art-ists like Vito Acconci, Gina Pane, Chris Burden, and James Lee Byars to give performances. And she was subsidized by the Dutch govern-ment (as was the television show), so money was not an issue.

The gallery sent me a plane ticket and I flew to Amsterdam in early December. Wies met me at the airport with a German artist who called himself Ulay. He would be my guide while I was in town, she told me; he would also help me set up *Thomas Lips*, which I had decided to perform for the TV cameras. I stared at him: he didn't look like anyone else I'd ever met.

Ulay (his real name, I found out, was Frank Uwe Laysiepen, but he never used it) was in his early thirties, tall and skinny with long, flowing hair that he tied up in back with a pair of chopsticks—a fact that was immediately interesting to me, because I did my hair ex-actly the same way. But the other interesting thing was that the two halves of his face were different. The left side was shaved smooth and powdered, with a plucked eyebrow and light rouge on the lips; the right side was stubbly and a little greasy, with a normal eyebrow and no makeup. If you saw either side in profile, you would get a completely different impression—masculine on one side, feminine on the other.

He'd been living in Amsterdam since the late 1960s, Ulay told me, and he took photographs, usually with a Polaroid camera and often of himself. For the self-portraits he emphasized the female side of his face with a long half wig and heavy makeup, including false eyelashes and bright red lipstick. The masculine side he just left alone. I was immediately reminded of Thomas Lips.

But the connections, I would soon find, went on from there.

After I performed *Thomas Lips* at de Appel, Ulay cared very tenderly for my wounds, applying antiseptic and putting on bandages. We smiled at each other. Then we went out to a Turkish restaurant with Wies, a few other people from the gallery, and the TV crew. I felt relaxed and comfortable with everybody. I said how nice it had been that Wies's invitation had arrived on my birthday—practically the first time, I told everybody, that anything good had ever happened to me on that day.

"When is your birthday?" Ulay asked.

"November thirtieth," I said.

"That can't be your birthday," he said. "That's my birthday."

"No way," I said.

He took out his pocket diary and showed me that the page for November 30 was torn out. "I do that every year on my birthday," Ulay said.

I just stared at his little book. Because I hated my birthday so much, I would always rip that page out of my datebook. Now I took out my pocket diary and opened it. The same page was torn out. "Me too," I said.

Ulay stared back. That night we went back to his place, and we stayed in bed for the next ten days.

Our intense sexual chemistry was only a beginning. The fact that we shared a birthday was more than coincidence. From the start, we breathed the same air; our hearts beat as one. We would finish each other's sentences, each knowing exactly what the other had in mind, even in our sleep: we had conversations in dreams and half dreams, then woke up and continued them. If I hurt my finger on the left side, he would hurt his finger on the right side.

This man was everything I wanted, and I knew he felt the same about me.

During those first days, we made cards for each other—there was no special occasion; the only occasion was that we were falling deeply in love. Mine to him read, in French, *Pour mon cher chien Russe*— "For my dear Russian dog"—because to me Ulay resembled nothing so much as a beautiful Borzoi, long and lean and elegant. His card to me read, in German, *Für meine liebe kleine Teufel*—"For my dear little devil." Which was amazing: Ulay had no way of knowing that when I was small, my mother used to dress me in a devil costume to go to children's parties.

Me, top right, dressed as a devil, Belgrade, 1950

Of course her intention was nowhere near as loving as his.

Also early on, he found, in a medical museum, an old, eerie photograph of the skeletons of conjoined twins: this, too, we made into a card, the perfect symbol of our physical and spiritual merging.

Around the same time I got the invitation to Amsterdam, I'd also been invited to participate in an arts festival in Copenhagen. I went for a few days, reluctantly leaving my new lover but promising to be back soon. At the Charlottenborg Festival I performed a new piece. In it I sat naked before the audience, a metal brush in one hand, a metal comb in the other. For a solid hour, I brushed my hair as hard as I could, to the point of pain, yanking out clumps of hair, scratching my face, all the while repeating over and over, "Art must be beautiful, artist must be beautiful." A videographer documented the performance: it was the first video I ever made.

Art Must Be Beautiful, Artist Must Be Beautiful (performance, 1 hour), Charlottenborg Art Festival, Copenhagen, 1975

The piece was profoundly ironic. Yugoslavia had made me so fed up with the aesthetic presumption that art must be beautiful. Friends of my family would have paintings that matched the carpet and the furniture—I thought all this decorativeness was bullshit. When it came to art, I only cared about content: what a work *meant*. The whole point of *Art Must Be Beautiful, Artist Must Be Beautiful* was to destroy that image of beauty. Because I had come to believe that art must be disturbing, art must ask questions, art must predict the future. If art is just political, it becomes like newspaper. It can be used once, and the next day it's yesterday's news. Only layers of meaning can give long life to art—that way, society takes what it needs from the work over time.

⌒

I returned to Amsterdam for a few more beautiful days with Ulay, then I went back to Belgrade. I was floating on a cloud, so in love that I could not even breathe. I steered clear of Neša—whenever he called, I always managed to be busy. I told him nothing about Amsterdam. I shut myself in my room, lying on the bed with the telephone like a teenager, making long, long calls to Ulay in the Netherlands. He tape-recorded every call, with my knowledge. I think we both felt from the outset that there was something historical about our relationship; we wanted to memorialize it. Even during our brief time together in Amsterdam, we had already begun to chronicle everything we did, almost obsessively. We'd taken dozens of Polaroids of each other. (For a couple of years, Ulay had been under contract with Polaroid: they gave him cameras and film and, now and then, expense money to travel and photograph what he saw. He was truly a Polaroid child.)

We talked and talked on the phone—and when the first phone bill came, my mother hit the ceiling. She literally locked the telephone in a cupboard. From then on, Ulay and I had to communicate by letter.

I was deeply in love, but also in a state of confusion. There was another clairvoyant I wanted to consult, a very famous guy who called himself Aca Student, but he was so booked up I couldn't get in to see him.

I felt more isolated than ever in Belgrade, which seemed more and more like a small town to me. A small town in a small country. A few people—the tiny knot of people around the SKC—had ideas, but nobody outside the Cultural Center wanted to listen to them. Our audiences were never more than twenty or thirty people at a time. The government controlled art, and the government's only interest in art was to decorate offices and party members' apartments.

The more Ulay and I corresponded, the more we realized how impossible it was to stay apart. We planned a secret rendezvous in Prague, exactly halfway between Amsterdam and Belgrade. I told my mother and Neša I was going to attend some meetings at the film academy there and flew off, breathless with excitement.

Before I left I went to a bookbinder and had a special scrapbook made, with blank pages and a red-brown canvas cover, our names printed on it in gold, like a Communist passport. During our glorious week in Prague (we stayed in the Hotel Paris), we filled the book with mementos: train and bus and museum tickets; menus, maps, and brochures. We were starting to build a history together. And by the time I returned to Belgrade, we had decided to live together.

⌒

That spring I performed a new piece at the SKC. In *Freeing the Voice*, I lay on a mattress on the floor, dressed all in black, my head hanging off the edge of the mattress, and screamed at the top of my lungs, shrieking out all my frustration with everything: Belgrade, Yugoslavia, my mother, my entrapment. I screamed until my voice was gone—three hours later.

Freeing myself would take a little longer. In the meantime I kept teaching, and saving my money.

Around the same time, an Italian art magazine put a photograph of me on its cover. It was an image from my performance in Milan the previous year: there I was, naked and kneeling over the industrial fan, in *Rhythm 4*. At the academy in Novi Sad, this quickly became a major scandal. I heard mutterings: the faculty were planning a secret meeting, during which, after discussing the budget and other banal

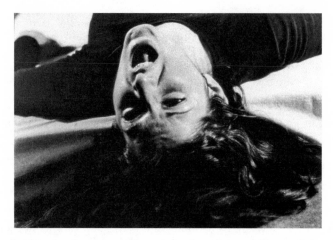

Freeing the Voice (performance, 3 hours), Student Cultural Center, Belgrade, 1975

matters, they would vote to fire me. Rather than give them the satisfaction, I resigned.

I'd already decided to leave Belgrade for good. My escape would
have to be secret—I couldn't tell Neša, and my mother mustn't find
out or she would come up with some way to pull me back. I bought a
one-way second-class train ticket to Amsterdam, and stuffed into one
bag as much photo documentation of my work as I could fit: if I'd taken
any extra clothing, Danica would have figured out what I was doing.

And it was the strangest thing—the night before I was to leave, I
got a call from Aca Student, the clairvoyant. He finally had an opening for me.

I went to his apartment. Like the guy in Zagreb, he drank a cup
of Turkish coffee, then poured the grounds onto a sheet of newspaper
and peered at them. After a minute he shook his head and frowned.
"You absolutely should not go," he told me. "This is going to be a
disaster. This man is going to crush you. You must stay here." This
wasn't what I expected at all—he was freaking me out. "No," I said.
"No." I stood up and backed out the door. I ran down the stairs. The
next morning, my brother and our friend Tomislav Gotovac, a filmmaker, took me to the train station. I got on the train to Amsterdam
with my second-class ticket and never looked back.

4.

In my teens, before my father left us, I would often have lunch with him at the polytechnic institute, where he was a lecturer on war strategy and tactics. One day his lecture ran long, and I went to the amphitheater to wait for him to finish. I opened the door in the back of the auditorium, and as he saw me coming down the aisle, he said, "And this is my daughter." When he said this, the entire amphitheater full of students—all of them boys—looked at me and started laughing like hell.

It was like a bad dream: I was so self-conscious in those days, so insecure about my looks. I turned bright red and ran away. And I never understood why this had happened.

Many years later, a friend of mine said, "I remember the first time I ever saw you. It was when I was taking your father's course at the university, and you entered the amphitheater, and your father said, 'This is my daughter'—that was when I saw you for the first time." I said, "Okay, can you tell me why you all laughed?" He said, "Your father was talking about war wounds, and saying that sometimes they can look very light but have terrible consequences in life, and sometimes they can look disastrous but it's okay, you can live with them. He said, 'Take me, for instance. During the war, a grenade exploded near me and a fragment destroyed one of my balls. But you should see what kind of daughter I made.' At that moment you walked in, and he said, 'This is my daughter.'"

I never knew that my father had only one ball.

Besides my single suitcase I had next to nothing when I arrived in Amsterdam, just a few nearly worthless dinars I'd brought with me from Yugoslavia. Ulay, on the other hand, had a lot of baggage.

If my childhood had been materially comfortable but emotionally desolate, his early years had been even harder. He was born in Solingen in the middle of the war; soon afterward, as Hitler desperately mobilized thousands of older men and young boys, Ulay's father, who was over fifty already, was drafted and sent to fight in the Nazi siege of Stalingrad. It would be a long time before he returned.

In the meantime, the Allies began to win the war on the western front, and the Russians threatened Germany from the east. In a panic, Ulay's mother took her baby and fled toward what she thought was unoccupied Polish territory. But she wound up in a village full of Russian soldiers, where she was gang-raped. As this was happening, baby Ulay crawled away—and fell into a field latrine, a hole full of shit. A Russian, maybe even one of the soldiers who had raped his mother, spotted the partially submerged infant and pulled him out.

Ulay's father returned after the German defeat, very sick. Before the war he'd had a cutlery factory, but an American bomb had destroyed it. After the war, Ulay's parents struggled to make ends meet, and his father never really recovered from his illness: he died when Ulay was fourteen. Not long before his death, he advised his son never to join the army if he could help it.

Ulay took his father's advice to heart. As a young man, he trained as an engineer, then married a German woman, with whom he had a son. But when his draft notice came, Ulay fled the country, leaving his wife and child behind, drifting to Amsterdam—where he impregnated yet another woman.

He told me most of this history; I would learn the rest gradually. And as crazy as I was about this man, as I breathed with his breathing and ached with his aches, underneath it all I felt a tiny seed of ambivalence. I felt I could never have children with Ulay because he always abandoned them. But somehow, at the same time, I believed our working relationship would last forever.

Ulay's Amsterdam apartment was spare and modern, but filled with a certain amount of history. In New York a couple of years before, he'd met a gorgeous young Nicaraguan woman, a diplomat's daughter named Bianca. He'd taken hundreds of pictures of her, and the Polaroids of the woman who later became Mick Jagger's wife hung all over the apartment.

And then there was Paula.

She was a KLM stewardess; her husband was a pilot. They were separated from each other for long periods, and apparently enjoyed an open marriage. It later turned out that Paula had been paying the rent on Ulay's nice modern flat in New Amsterdam; her name was on the lease. It also turned out that they'd had a very passionate relationship. Understandably enough, I guess, he never wanted to talk about her. I also think I didn't want to know too much about her.

Apparently, though, he didn't handle the break-up very well. When I arrived, two telegrams to Ulay were sitting on the kitchen counter. One was from me, from Belgrade: "I can't wait until I see you," it read. The other was from Paula: "I never want to see you again."

⌒

Some couples buy pots and pans when they move in together. Ulay and I began planning how to make art together.

There were certain similarities to the work we'd done as individuals: solitude, pain, pushing limits. Ulay's Polaroids of that period often showed him piercing his own flesh in various bloody ways. In one work, he tattooed one of his aphorisms on his arm: ULTIMA RATIO (meaning final argument or last resort, referring to force). Then he cut a square hunk of flesh containing the tattoo out of his arm, slicing so deeply that the muscle and tendon were visible. He framed and preserved the tattooed flesh in formaldehyde. For another image, he held a bloodstained paper towel over a self-inflicted razor wound in his belly. A series of shots showed him slicing his fingertips with a box cutter and painting the white tiles of a bathroom with his own blood. Then there was the little jeweled brooch, in the shape of an airplane, that he pinned to his bare chest. I realized later that this symbolized his longing for Paula. In the Polaroid, he posed with his head cocked like Jesus dying on the cross; a red trickle, like the blood from the spear wound in Christ's side, ran from the airplane pin down Ulay's flesh.

I had been invited to perform at the Venice Biennale that summer, and when I arrived in Amsterdam I told Ulay that I wanted him to perform with me. First, though, we had to figure out what to do.

We bought a big roll of white paper, unrolled it, and taped a ten-foot-long sheet onto the clean white wall of the apartment. On this mega notepad, we began jotting down ideas about the kind of performance we wanted to make: there were phrases, sketches, doodles. In the midst of this process, inspiration struck when somebody gave Ulay—of all things—a Newton's cradle, the same item I'd worked on assembling at the factory in London. He was fascinated by the back-and-forth swinging of the shiny metal balls, the little *clack* they made when they collided, the perfect transfer of energy.

"What if we did that?" he said.

I immediately understood what he was talking about: a performance where the two of us would collide and bounce off each other. But obviously we weren't made of metal, and there was no way a collision between us would be neat and crisp.

And that was a beautiful thing.

Ulay/Marina Abramović, *Relation in Space* (performance, 58 minutes),
XXXVIII Biennale, Giudecca, Venice, 1976

We were naked, standing twenty meters apart. We were in a warehouse on the island of Giudecca, just across the lagoon from Venice. A couple hundred people were watching. Slowly at first, Ulay and I began to run toward each other. The first time, we just brushed past each other as we met; on each successive run, though, we moved faster and faster and made harder contact—until finally Ulay was crashing into me. Once or twice he knocked me over. We had placed microphones near the collision point, to pick up the sounds of flesh slapping flesh.

Part of the reason we were nude was to produce the simple sound of two naked bodies colliding. There was a music to this sound, a rhythm.

But there were other reasons, too. For one thing, we wanted to create a work that was as minimalist as possible, and nothing is more minimal than the nude body in an empty space. Our statement for the piece read, simply: "Two bodies repeatedly pass, touching each other. After gaining a higher speed, they collide."

But for another thing, we were in love, we had an intense relationship—and the audience couldn't help sensing this relationship. But of course there was also much they didn't know about it, much that each audience member projected onto us as we continued to do this performance. Who were we? Why were we colliding? Was there hostility in the collision? Was there love, or mercy?

When it was over, we felt triumphant. (We also both hurt like hell from our bodily collisions.) We decided to take a few days off at my cottage in Grožnjan, which was just across the Gulf of Trieste from Venice. One morning we were in bed when I heard keys rattling in the front door downstairs. "Oh my God," I said. "It's Neša."

My husband, now so distant from me, hadn't seen me in months at this point. All he knew was that I was traveling for my art, to Amsterdam and Venice. And he had no idea of Ulay's existence.

I threw on some clothes and went down to meet him. And then we went to a café and, after having been with my new love for eight months, I told my husband the truth.

We divorced. In a Communist country it was very simple: it was just a matter of going to the notary and signing two pieces of paper. There was nothing to share, no communal property. Not a spoon, not a fork—nothing.

Neša realized I had to go my way, and in order to go my way I had to leave the country. I simply could not be there anymore. And he understood.

⁓

It was our birthday, the day Ulay and I shared: November 30, 1976. I was turning thirty, he was turning thirty-three, and we decided to do a birthday performance for our twenty Amsterdam friends. We called the performance *Talking About Similarity*.

We had lived together for almost a year, and we had come to feel that in many ways we were the same person, thinking the same thoughts. Now it was time to test that hypothesis.

We held the performance in the studio of a friend, the photographer Jaap de Graaf. We set up chairs, like in a classroom; Ulay sat in front, facing the audience. There was a tape recorder to play sound, and a video camera to record the performance. As soon as our friends had sat down, Ulay opened his mouth wide and I turned on the tape recorder, which played the sound of a dental suction device. He sat that way for twenty minutes, then I turned off the tape recorder and Ulay closed his mouth. He then took out a heavy needle, the kind used to sew leather, attached to some thick white thread, and he sewed his lips shut.

This didn't happen quickly. First he had to penetrate the skin below his lower lip—not easy—and then the skin above his upper lip. Also not easy. Then he pulled the thread tight and tied a knot. And then he and I changed places: Ulay sat down among the audience, and I sat in the chair he had just occupied.

"Now," I told our friends, "you will ask me questions and I will answer as Ulay."

"Does he feel pain?" one guy asked.

"Excuse me?" I said.

"Does he feel pain?" the guy asked again.

"Could you repeat the question?"

"Does he feel pain?"

I was making him ask it again and again because in more than one way it was the wrong question. First, I had told our friends I would be answering as Ulay; therefore, the correct way to put it would have been, *Do you feel pain?*

But also, and more important, pain was not the issue. The piece wasn't about pain, I told the guy; it was about decision: Ulay deciding to sew his mouth closed and me deciding to think for him, speak for him. I had learned in *Rhythm 10* and *Thomas Lips* that pain was something like a sacred door to another state of consciousness. When you reached that door, then another side opened. Ulay had learned this, too—even before we met.

A woman spoke up. "Why are you talking when Ulay is silent?" she asked.

It didn't matter which of us talked and which was silent, I told her. The concept was what mattered.

Was the piece about love? someone else asked. Or was it about trust?

The piece, I said, was simply about one person trusting another person to speak for him—it was about love *and* trust.

And with that, Ulay turned off the video camera. We had a small reception after the performance, with food and drink; Ulay kept his lips sewn and sipped some wine through a straw. He was that committed to the continuity of our piece.

We'd lived together for a year; we were so close. I just wanted to make love with Ulay all the time—it was a constant physical need. Sometimes I felt I was burning from it. At the same time, there were some things that came between us. Amsterdam itself, for one. Ulay loved the city's freewheeling ways, its relaxed attitudes toward sex and drugs. Before we got together, he'd dabbled with drugs; he'd been a habitué of the city's transvestite scene, a fruitful subject for his Polaroids. And though he didn't use drugs anymore, he still drank, and he had dozens of friends he loved to drink with. He would get up in the morning and go to one of his favorite bars, Monaco, and just stay there all day. I was very, very jealous of this other life of his. Sometimes, out of sheer frustration and loneliness, I would go along with him, and have an espresso while he drank and drank. It was so boring.

I had never been interested in drugs or alcohol. It wasn't a moral decision; they just didn't do anything for me. The things I saw and thought in the normal course of my life were strange enough without clouding my mind.

But Ulay's drinking worried me, because I was in love with him and he was doing nothing with his life when he sat around these bars all day. I felt I was wasting my time, too. We had done these pieces together; I knew there was so much more we could do. I kept making the case to him—not nagging him, not criticizing him, but reminding him in the most loving way that there were worlds we could conquer together. Then one day he tapped his fingers down on the table and looked me in the eye. "You're right," he said.

From that moment, he stopped drinking. This was a guy, after all, who was capable of doing amazing things with his body. Now he would do them along with me.

We decided to change our lives totally. We didn't want to be tied down to an apartment, paying rent. And Amsterdam itself wasn't doing us any favors. So with some money from Polaroid and some money from the Dutch government, we bought a cheap used truck—an old Citroën police van with ribbed sides and a high roof— and hit the road. We would become a traveling troupe of two.

We didn't take much with us. A mattress, a stove, a filing cabinet, a typewriter, and a box for our clothes. Ulay painted the van matte black—it gave the vehicle a nice, utilitarian look, also slightly sinister. And we wrote a manifesto for our new life on the road:

ART VITAL

No fixed living place.	Mobile energy.
Permanent movement.	No rehearsal.
Direct contact.	No predicted end.
Local relation.	No repetition.
Self-selection.	Extended vulnerability.
Passing limitations.	Exposure to chance.
Taking risks.	Primary reactions.

This would be our life for the next three years.

At the beginning of 1977 we drove to the Art Academy in Dusseldorf to perform a new piece that built on *Relation in Space.* In *Interruption in Space* we were naked, running toward each other once again, only this time instead of meeting in the middle, we each ran into one side of a thick wooden wall. The audience saw us both; each of us only saw the wall between us.

When we were invited to do a performance, we always dealt with one of two kinds of spaces: given and chosen. In this case, we were given a space with a wall in the middle of the room. This was the architecture we had to deal with. In our performance, we were investigating our different attitudes to the obstacle between us. As before, we ran faster and faster toward the middle, colliding with the wall ever more violently. A microphone inside the barrier amplified the sound of flesh hitting wood.

The audience saw separation, but in our lives we were closer each day. Our hair was exactly the same length; often we tied it back in just the same way. We were becoming a kind of melded personality. Sometimes we called each other "Glue." Together, we were Super Glue.

We were happy—so happy that it's hard to describe. I felt we were really the happiest people in the world. We had next to nothing, almost no money, and we were going wherever the wind blew us. The de Appel gallery had tacked up a shoebox next to their window to collect our mail. And once a week we would call them from a payphone, and they would open our letters and tell us where we'd been asked to perform next: then we would drive there. Some weeks nobody asked. That was our life.

We were so poor. Sometimes there was food, sometimes there wasn't. I remember going to petrol stations with an empty mineral-water bottle to buy gasoline for the van—that was all we could afford. Sometimes, out of sheer pity, the gas station guy would look at our little bottle and fill it for free. In Switzerland that winter, the car doors froze shut with us inside: we had to breathe on the door handles to warm them up. Crazy.

The Citroën van we lived in for five years
during *Art Vital/Detour*, 1977

We stopped in Belgrade, to perform at the April meeting of the SKC. We had a big crowd, thanks to my notoriety in Yugoslavia. We called the piece we did *Breathing In, Breathing Out*. We stuck cigarette filters in our nostrils to block the air, and we taped little microphones to our throats. We kneeled down facing each other. I blew all the air out of my lungs and Ulay breathed in all the air he could. Then we clamped our mouths together and he blew his air into my mouth. Then I blew the air back to him.

As our mouths stayed fixed together, as the sound of our breathing (and then our gasping) was amplified throughout the cultural center, we exchanged, again and again, that one lungful of air—which became less and less oxygen and more and more carbon dioxide as it was exhaled time after time. After nineteen minutes, there was no oxygen left: we stopped just before losing consciousness.

My mother hadn't attended the performance. She couldn't help embracing me when we visited her, but there was something withdrawn about her—I was the prodigal child returning. I had done many shameful things. She was pleasant enough with Ulay, but I could tell it freaked her out that he was German. It didn't matter that he'd been a baby during the war: his father had fought at Stalingrad. His birth certificate had a swastika on it. She told all her friends and neighbors that he was Dutch.

With my father it was a different matter. I hadn't seen him for almost ten years now, since the day I'd seen him kissing his young woman, Vesna, on the street. That last moment, when he saw me but was so ashamed that he wouldn't acknowledge me, was deeply painful for me. And it appeared I'd been dreaming about him constantly. In the van, Ulay would often wake me in the middle of the night and tell me I'd been crying in my sleep and saying my father's name over and over: *Vojin, Vojin.*

"Why are you crying?" Ulay would ask me. "What's the dream?"

I didn't know what to tell him, only that I was suffering.

"Listen," Ulay said. "You have to write to him. Write to your father. Sit down and write the goddamn letter."

So I did. *I don't care if you love Vesna,* I wrote. *The only thing that's important to me is that I love you. I'm happy for you. I want to see you.*

I sent him the letter and he never answered.

That had been over a year before.

So now we were in Belgrade and I was desperate to see Vojin. But what if he rejected me again? I told Ulay how frightened I was.

"I don't care," he said. "I want you to see your father. We're going to see your father."

I was brave in my art, but the truth was (and still is) that I went through hell before every one of my performances. Sheer terror. I would go to the bathroom twenty times. And then the moment I stepped into the work, it was something else entirely.

So I reminded myself of this, and Ulay and I went to Vojin's house, unannounced.

He was still living with Vesna. It was morning, and we literally just went to the front door and knocked. She opened the door and broke into a huge grin. "Oh my God!" she said. "This is such a great thing." She touched my face. "You know," she said, "that letter you wrote to him—he reads it every day, full of tears. He's in pieces from that letter."

"Then why did he never answer?"

She shook her head. "You know your father," she said.

So we entered, and he was overjoyed to see me. He immediately sent somebody to make a suckling pig. All the neighbors came to celebrate my arrival. There was a feast, many toasts with rakia, the super-strong Balkan brandy. The whole scene was like one of Emir Kusturica's movies about Serbia—dark and ironic, but also warm and full of heart.

And my father loved Ulay. When he heard that Ulay's father had fought at Stalingrad, it only elevated father and son in his opinion. Vojin totally accepted Ulay—he even gave him a present that night: a pair of binoculars that had belonged to an S.S. general, probably someone he had killed personally. Ulay and my father bonded, and it was wonderful to see.

The next morning we went to the Belgrade dog pound and got a puppy. It was Ulay's idea. I had aborted his child the previous autumn, in Amsterdam, and I had no intention of ever starting a family—I

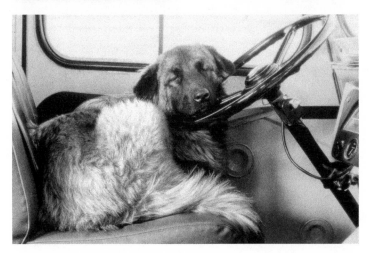

Domestic life in the van with Ulay and our dog Alba, 1977–78

simply could not reconcile fully being an artist with being a mother, too. And there in the Belgrade pound was an Albanian shepherd nursing her litter. I picked the smallest one, the runt. She was just a little ball of fluff. "What should I call her?" I asked Ulay. "Does she have a name?" I asked the attendant.

"Alba," he said.

Alba was beautiful; I loved her and she loved me in return. Nothing gave me greater pleasure than taking her for walks, being outdoors, sharing the delight of nature with her. And now that we had Alba, we were like a family.

Another phone booth, somewhere in Europe: an assistant at de Appel said an invitation had arrived in our box asking us to participate in the International Performance Week, in Bologna. A lot of important artists were going to be there—Acconci, Beuys, Burden; Gina Pane, Charlemagne Palestine, Laurie Anderson; Ben d'Armagnac, Katharina Sieverding, and Nam June Paik. We wanted to come up with a major new piece.

It was June 1977. We drove up to the Galleria Comunale d'Arte Moderna ten days early, on our last drop of gas. We parked in front and went to talk to the museum director about a place to stay. (We could always sleep in the van, but sometimes it was nice to have bathroom facilities.) He said we could bunk in their janitor's closet. Perfect. We set to work on planning our performance. The result was *Imponderabilia*.

In developing the work, we thought about a simple fact: if there were no artists, there would be no museums. From this idea we decided to make a poetic gesture—the artists would literally become the door to the museum.

Ulay built two tall vertical cases in the museum entrance, making it substantially narrower. Our performance would be to stand in this reduced opening, naked and facing each other, like doorposts or classical caryatids. Thus everyone coming in would have to turn sideways to get past us, and everyone would have to make a decision as he or she slid by: face the naked man, or the naked woman?

Ulay/Marina Abramović, *Imponderabilia* (performance, 90 minutes),
Galleria Comunale d'Arte Moderna, Bologna, 1977

On the wall of the gallery we posted an explanatory text: "Imponderable. Such imponderable human factors as one's aesthetic sensitivity. The overriding importance of imponderables determining human conduct."

We hadn't considered the all-too-ponderable consequences of human conduct when it came to money.

All the artists were supposed to be paid in advance for their participation, 750,000 lire—the equivalent of about $350. That was a fortune for us. We could live for weeks on that. And we literally didn't have a penny. So every day leading up to the performance, we went to the museum office and said, "Can we get our money?" All the other artists were doing this, too. And every day (it was Italy) there was an excuse: There was a strike. The office manager's cousin was in the hospital. The secretary had just left. Somebody forgot to bring in the key to the safe.

The day of the performance arrived. The public was lined up outside, waiting to get in; we were naked, ready to stand in the entrance, and we still hadn't been paid. We were desperate. We knew that if they promised to mail us our money, we would never get it. So Ulay, completely naked, got on the elevator, went up to the fourth floor, opened the office door and said, "Where's my money?" He was standing in front of the secretary, who was sitting at the table alone. As soon as she managed to contain her astonishment, she took the key (which had always been there, by the way), went to the safe, and handed Ulay a pile of banknotes.

Now he had 750,000 lire, he was naked, and he had to go perform immediately. Where to put our precious money? He had an idea. In the garbage pail he found a plastic bag and a rubber band. He put the banknotes in the bag, sealed it with the rubber band, and went into the public restroom. In Italy in those days, the toilets had tanks mounted on the wall. He opened the cover of one of the tanks and put the bag in, floating on the surface. Then he took the elevator downstairs, got in the doorway facing me, and the public began to file in.

We purposely stared blankly as we faced each other. So little did I know—as the people slipped by, some facing Ulay and some facing me, all with interesting expressions on their faces as they made their difficult choice—that he was worried the whole time about what might happen to our pay if someone flushed the toilet!

The performance was intended to last six hours. But after three hours, two handsome police officers came in (both chose to face me rather than Ulay). A couple of minutes later they returned with two members of the museum staff—and asked for our passports. Ulay and I looked at each other. "I don't have mine on me," he said.

The policemen told us that under the city laws of Bologna our performance was deemed obscene. We would have to stop immediately.

Fortunately our 750,000 lire were still floating in the toilet tank.

We were the only artists who got paid, incidentally.

⌒

We drove to Kassel, in West Germany, to participate in *documenta*, the once-every-five-years avant-garde arts exhibition. When we arrived we discovered that—for whatever reason—we weren't on the list of performers. We decided to go ahead anyway. Our latest idea, *Expansion in Space*, was still another variation on *Relation in Space* and *Interruption in Space*—only this time, instead of running toward each other, we would stand back to back, naked, then sprint in opposite directions, each colliding with a matching obstacle, a heavy wooden column four meters high. Then we would trot backward to the starting point and begin all over again.

The performance took place in an underground parking garage, and we had our biggest audience ever by far, over a thousand people. And *Expansion in Space* had a big, mythic feeling, something like Sisyphus rolling the big rock up the hill. Ulay had built the columns himself, and designed them to weigh precisely double our body weights—twice 75 kilos in my case, twice 82 kilos in his case. Each weighed well over 300 pounds. They could be moved when we ran into them, but only slightly. Sometimes they wouldn't move at all. They were hollow, with microphones attached to an amplification system inside, so they gave off a big *thud* with each collision. The audience watched raptly as we started simultaneously and ran into our respective columns, again and again, with a resounding impact but very limited results. Still, despite the fact that Ulay weighed more than me and was stronger than me, his column got stuck. No matter how hard he slammed against it, it wouldn't budge.

Then, abruptly, he stepped away from the performance.

At first I didn't realize that Ulay had stopped. Really, it was no big deal at this point in our career: in our previous piece, *Interruption in Space*, I had walked away when I reached my limit—it was just part of the performance. Now (unbeknownst to me) he was standing off to the side in the garage, having put some clothes on, watching me continue.

Then my column wouldn't move, either.

I kept backing up farther, to give myself more of a running start, and maybe enough additional force to budge the obstacle. Then, all at once, I realized that my back was no longer making contact with

Ulay's. I understood he had walked away. *Okay,* I thought, *maybe if I back up all the way into his space for my running start, I'll* really *get some momentum.*

Suddenly it worked. I ran the extra distance, and my column moved. The crowd cheered. But as I continued backing up and slamming into the column, over and over, the mood changed. Now I was in an altered state: the performance had become frenetic. The spectacle of this naked woman smashing into this heavy object, again and again, disturbed some of the onlookers. *"Halt, halt!"* they yelled, in German. "Stop, stop!" Others were still cheering lustily—it was like a football match.

Ulay/Marina Abramović, *Expansion in Space* (performance, 32 minutes), documenta 6, Kassel, 1977

Just then, at the back of the crowd (I found out later), the performance artist Charlotte Moorman, probably exhausted by the piece she'd just done with Nam June Paik, dropped to the floor in a faint. Ulay was busy trying to help her when something truly crazy happened. Some drunk guy in the audience jumped in front of my column with a broken beer bottle in his hand, the jagged rim pointed at me, and dared me to run into it. Strange or disturbed people, I'd found, had a way of being drawn to performance art. Fortunately the artist Scott Burton, who'd been watching, shoved the guy out of the way at the last second, and I kept running into my column—I was determined to succeed—until it actually moved a couple of inches more. Audiences at art performances usually refrained from applause, since performance was supposed to be unrehearsed, and more in the moment than theater. But after all this drama, when I finally stepped aside, a thousand people applauded.

That night, after the performance, we returned to the van to find that we had been robbed: our tape recorder and Ulay's camera were gone, along with some clothes and blankets. Alba, who was supposed to be our watchdog, was happily playing with one of my T-shirts in the empty vehicle.

At the Cologne Art Fair that fall we did a new piece called *Light/ Dark*. Clothed this time, and in jeans and identical white T-shirts, with our hair pulled back in identical buns, we knelt facing each other and took turns slapping each other in the face. After each slap the slapper would slap his or her knee, giving the performance a steady one-two rhythm.

Ulay/Marina Abramović, *Light/Dark* (performance, 20 minutes),
Internationale Kunstmesse, Cologne, 1977

We started slow and picked up the pace. It looked very personal, but in fact the piece had nothing to do with our relationship or the usual significance of face-slapping: it was about using the body as a musical instrument. We'd stated beforehand that the performance would end when one of us flinched—but that never happened. Instead, we simply stopped spontaneously after twenty minutes, when we couldn't slap each other any faster. At this point we were so close that it was as if there were a psychic link between us.

At the beginning of 1978, our wanderings took us to Sardinia. We stayed there for two months, working on a farm near the village of Orgosolo, milking their goats and sheep. It was cold on the high plains in the center of the island: at night we would make love to stay warm. This was what we had instead of television. Every morning at five A.M. we would milk two hundred sheep, then help the farmers make pecorino cheese (which I can still make). In exchange they would give us bread, sausage, and cheese.

They also gave us wool, wool that was smelly from sheep shit. I knitted sweater after sweater from this wool. These pullovers were

Me knitting in our van, 1977

always too big and funny looking and hot; they also tended to give you a rash if you wore them next to bare skin.

We had no money, but I felt we were rich: the pleasure of having some pecorino cheese, a few garden-grown tomatoes, and a liter of olive oil; of making love in the car, with Alba just sleeping quietly in the corner, was beyond wealth. There is no price for that. It was so impossibly beautiful—all three of us breathing the same rhythm, the days going by. . . .

As beautiful as it was, though, there was a worm in the apple.

5.

A big circus came to a little town. They put up a tent on the square and all of the town came to see the show. There were lions, tigers, elephants, and acrobats. At one point, a magician appeared on the stage. He asked the audience for a volunteer. One mother took her little boy by the hand, brought him on stage to the magician, and then went back to her seat. The magician put the child into a coffin and closed the lid. He waived his hands and said the magic words "abracadabra." He opened the lid and the coffin was empty. The public held their breath. The magician covered it again, said the magic words, and opened the coffin. The child came out and happily went back to his mother. Nobody, not even the mother, noticed that he was not the same child.

In Graz, Austria, in the spring of 1978, Ulay and I performed a new piece called *Incision—Incision in Space* was its full name—at Galerie H-Humanic. The piece was a departure for us in more ways than one. In it, he was naked and I was clothed; he was active and I was passive. Instead of being a participant, I was apparently just an onlooker.

The way it worked was as follows: A giant elastic was attached to the gallery wall at two points, about fifteen feet apart. With the elastic looped around his midsection, Ulay ran away from the wall, straining the band to its limit, at which point the rubber would just snap him back to his starting point. Then he would make another run, and be snapped back again, over and over and over. It was as though he was trying to escape something, except that the unbreakable elastic made escape impossible. Even the expression on his face was agonized: with his classic nude physique, he was like a Greek demigod struggling to break the bonds of a cruel fate. Meanwhile I stood off to the side in a man's shirt and an ugly pair of beige trousers, my shoulders slumped, gazing blankly at nothing, seemingly indifferent.

We knew how the piece would affect an audience: it was infuriating. While Ulay was naked and struggling and suffering, I was clothed and uncaring.

Except that we had a surprise planned.

About fifteen minutes in, out of nowhere, a man in a black ninja suit strolled out of the audience, and with a flying, double-legged karate kick, knocked me to the floor. The audience gasped as the attacker nonchalantly strolled out of the gallery. I just lay there for a moment, the wind seemingly knocked out of me. Would anyone come to my aid? A minute, then another, ticked by. But nobody would help me— they all hated me for standing by so uselessly. Why should they do anything for me? Finally, with all my effort, I got up and returned to the same position, impassive once more, as Ulay continued as though nothing had happened.

Ulay/Marina Abramović, *Incision* (performance, 30 minutes),
Galerie H-Humanic, Graz, Austria, 1978

When the performance was over, we had a discussion with the audience about the piece. When they heard that we'd planned the karate attack, they were incredulous at first, then angry, then furious. They felt we'd toyed with their sympathies—and they were exactly right. We had just wanted to test the willingness—or the unwilling-ness—of the public to participate. Still, I could never get over the fact that no one would lift a finger to help me.

Our performances had many meanings for the audiences who witnessed them, but they also held significance for Ulay and me. Sometimes these meanings went beyond what we consciously un-derstood. And at this distance of many years, I wonder: In *Incision*, were we acting out a conflict that had begun to bubble up between us? In *Expansion in Space*, was there something symbolic about the fact that Ulay walked away and I kept pushing the column? We were a team, we were like one person: UlayandMarina. Glue. But at the same time, people—gallerists, audiences—were more and more see-ing me as our public face. It wasn't a role I sought out: in fact, it was one that was starting to bring me a good deal of unhappiness in my private life.

⌒

In 1978, the Brooklyn Museum invited us to participate in a group show, the European Performance Series, and we packed up Alba in a cage and flew to New York. It was my first time in the city, and I was fascinated by it, especially downtown in Soho where we were staying.

When we performed *Imponderabilia* in Bologna the previous year, we had met an American critic and writer named Edit DeAk. Edit was of Hungarian ancestry and she was quite a character. I was so impressed by her: for one thing, she had a bigger nose than me. She had the biggest nose I ever saw in my life. It was huge. She pub-lished a downtown magazine called *Art-Rite*, which was avant-garde: homemade-looking and printed on cheap newsprint, it was given away for free on the streets of Soho, which was a very different place in 1978 than it is today.

New York was in financial trouble in those days, and the city was much grittier; Soho was one of the grittiest parts of Manhattan, totally uncommercialized and filled with giant artists' lofts that had no heat or hot water and were rented for next to nothing. Edit lived in one of these, on Wooster Street, and Ulay and I stayed with her for a couple of weeks. It was an amazing few weeks.

It was the height of punk, the time of the Mudd Club, W, CBGB, of the Ramones and Blondie and Lydia Lunch and the Talking Heads. Seeing and hearing these people play simply blew my mind. Edit was friends with the Ramones, and the Ramones were crazy about Alba— they put her in a video!

There were agencies then that would pay you to transport a car from New York to California: we decided it would be a good way to see America. So with Ulay at the wheel and Alba in the back seat, we headed west.

Chicago, Denver, Salt Lake City, Las Vegas—it seemed to me that this amazing country was infinitely large and infinitely fascinating. So many cheap and interchangeable motels, such gigantic meals in such bright and shiny restaurants. In Vegas it was so hot that we got Alba her own (cheap) air-conditioned motel room! And then we went to play in the casino. I loved the casinos in Vegas, without windows or clocks—at the roulette wheel or a slot machine, all sense of time vanished, or at least became something else entirely, just like in one of our performances. I got addicted to the slot machine. Ulay literally had to pull me away.

We delivered the car in San Diego, and for $900 we bought a big old Cadillac and drove it to Mexico. It was the perfect car to drive to Mexico—and of course we broke down in the middle of the desert. After the car got towed back to San Diego and the guy we'd bought it from had it repaired, we made the huge drive back to New York and tried to sell it. The Ramones were briefly interested, as was a guy who ran a garage on Houston Street, but a small detail got in the way: it turned out we didn't actually have the title to the vehicle. In the end we just parked it on a side street in Soho, with the key in the ignition, and flew back to Amsterdam.

⌒

A few months later, Edit came to Europe, bringing an urn containing the ashes of a cousin, which she wanted to bury in Hungary. First, though, she joined Ulay and me as we drove to an art fair in Cologne. A few other people accompanied us, including the filmmaker Jack Smith, who was very eccentric, very tall, very strange, very gay. The only music he ever listened to was the Andrews Sisters, and he had a complete obsession with Howard Hughes. And Baghdad. He also traveled with a stuffed gorilla in a red suitcase. Once he got in an argument with Edit about money, and the next morning we woke up to find the gorilla sitting in front of the mirror with a knife stuck in its back with Jack's red suitcases sitting packed by its side. Later that day he tried to strangle his assistant. I tried to stay away from him after that.

That November 30, we did a birthday performance, called *Three*, at a gallery in Wiesbaden. The third element in the piece was a four-foot-long python. The idea was that Ulay and I would both crawl around the gallery floor and each try to attract the snake. It was an interesting piece for me, because ever since the walk in the woods with my grandmother when I was four, I'd been terrified of snakes.

Once a performance began, however, I always passed through that portal where pain and fear transformed into something else. This time was no exception. As we each did all kinds of things to try to draw the python near—plucked a vibrating piano wire, blew across the mouth of a bottle—the reptile crawled ever closer to me. It stuck out its tongue. I stuck mine out, too, only an inch away. And there we were, face to face, the python and I. It was like something out of the Bible. The piece only ended (after four hours and fifteen minutes) when the snake decided to leave.

Ulay/Marina Abramović, *Three* (performance, 4 hours, 15 minutes),
Harlekin Art, Wiesbaden, 1978

A pattern was beginning to form, and I won't deny my part in making it happen—or maybe letting it happen. In our artistic partnership we were trying to leave ego behind, to leave masculinity and femininity behind, and meld into a third unity, which to me seemed like the highest form of art. At the same time, in our domestic life (if you can call living out of a van domestic), Ulay assumed the classic masculine role: he was the provider, the hunter-gatherer. He did all the driving, handled the money; I did the cooking and washing and knitted the sweaters.

But just as whatever it was that attracted the snake in *Three*, or led most of the public to turn to me in *Imponderabilia*, or drew the audience's attention (even though it was negative) in *Incision*, I was emerging as the dominant figure in the media. When our performances were written about in art magazines, I was almost always mentioned first. When the eminent Italian critic and philosopher Gillo Dorfles wrote a piece about *Relation in Space*, he left out Ulay entirely. The piece upset me so much that I hid it from Ulay.

I loved him. I didn't want him hurt. Yet though he didn't say anything about all this at first, he didn't like it a bit.

In 1979 I got an invitation to attend an artists' conference on Pohnpei, a tiny island in the middle of the Pacific, part of Micronesia. The invitation came from Tom Marioni, a conceptual artist who worked for Crown Point Press, in Oakland, California. I had met Tom when I performed in Edinburgh, and then later at one of the SKC April meetings in Belgrade. He knew my early work, and because of this, the invitation came to me, rather than Ulay and me together.

I felt terrible about this. I really wanted to do things together at that point. So I lied to him. I said they had invited both of us, but because their budget was limited, they had told us to toss a coin. At many of the important moments in my life, when a choice is involved, I have tossed a coin: that way, your energy is no longer involved; the decision becomes a kind of cosmic one rather than your own. When it came to this coin toss, I was fully prepared to lose—in fact, I wanted to lose. Then Ulay flipped the coin, and I called heads, and it came up heads.

And I went to Pohnpei.

This was an important trip for me. Twelve artists in all were there, including several I admired—Laurie Anderson, John Cage, Chris Burden, Brice Marden, Joan Jonas, and Pat Steir—and I formed some new friendships with John and Joan and Pat, and especially with Laurie, whom I'd first met in Bologna when Ulay and I performed *Imponderabilia*. Her reputation had preceded her. I remember reading about a piece she did on ice skates in Genoa, standing on a block of ice and playing the violin while the ice slowly melted beneath her. I thought that was so great.

Laurie and I took a canoe out to a little island, where there was a hut with some kind of ritual going on inside. The king of the island, who wore jeans and a huge cross on a chain around his neck, invited us to the ceremony with the rest of the tribe, who were all half-naked and wearing straw ornaments. Dinner was dog meat served on palm leaves. Laurie and I looked at each other. "No, thank you," we said.

"Maybe you would like to take some to your friends," the king said.

We felt we couldn't refuse. They gave us a couple of armfuls of smelly, bloody dog meat wrapped in palm leaves and we took it back in the canoe. Everyone (especially Cage, who was vegetarian) was repulsed when they saw it. The natives had also given us some tree bark to chew: the sap, they said, had magical powers. For twenty-four hours after I chewed it, I could hear everything—my heart beating, my blood flowing, grass growing. When we got back to New York, Laurie wrote a song about the whole experience.

Each artist in the program got twelve minutes to make a presentation and talk about any subject he or she wanted to the natives of the island: the organizers planned to record all the talks and issue them on a 12-inch LP called *Word of Mouth*. I started my talk by reciting a seemingly random series of numbers: "8, 12, 1,975; 12, 12, 1,975; 17, 1, 1,976; 17, 3, 1,976 . . ."

Then I spoke about the new idea Ulay and I had conceived, of melding our male and female identities into a third entity:

> Our interest is symmetry between male and female *principe*. With our relation work we cause a third existence which carries vital energy. This third energy existence caused by us does not depend on us any longer but has its own quality, which we call "that self." Three as a number means nothing else but "that self." Immaterially transmitted energy causes energy as a dialogue, from us to the sensibility and mind of an eye witness who becomes an accomplice. We chose the body as the only material which can make such an energy dialogue possible.

To me it made total sense.

I continued: "And now one very important thing I want to say." Then I began giving a speech in a made-up language. And some of the natives spontaneously applauded because some of the sounds I made sounded like actual words from their own language. At the end I pushed the play button on a tape machine and out came the voice of Ulay, speaking a message he'd recorded before I left: "Who creates limits?"

It was a very important statement about our performances—but now that I think of it, it was probably also his protest at being left behind.

⌒

Between money from our performances and grants from the Dutch government, we had a little more to live on. And so we moved out of the van and into a new place—a low-ceilinged loft in a warehouse building near the Amsterdam harbor. There were several of these buildings by the docks: they'd once been used to store spices. Now they were rented by artists.

Along with several new friends, we leased the entire third floor of Zoutkeetsgracht 116/118. It was a singular place, occupied by singular people. The floor plan consisted of four rooms—we used these as the bedrooms—surrounding a middle space, which served as a living area/kitchen. We fashioned a shower by attaching a hose to the kitchen faucet: you bathed standing in a bucket in the middle of the floor and spraying yourself with the hose. The building's elevator ran right through the center of the room—sometimes people going to another floor stopped on ours by mistake while someone was taking a shower.

And that was only the beginning of the strangeness.

About a year earlier, we'd stopped by de Appel and in looking through our shoebox-mailbox, we found a video, marked MANIAC PRO-DUCTIONS, SWEDEN. Just that—no one's name, no telephone number or return address. In those days videos were very rare, so our interest was immediately piqued. We watched it. It consisted of short performance pieces, each more amazing than the last. We watched the video again, then forgot about it.

Soon after we rented the spice loft, we were once again visiting the gallery when the door opened and the most improbable trio walked in: a tiny dark-haired man, a very tall and big-nosed guy with long hair like a rock star, and a girl in a white nightgown with a toilet seat around her neck. They were Edmondo Zanolini, Michael Laub, and a fifteen-year-old girl named Brigitte—an Italian, a Belgian, and a Swede—and they were the performance-art trio who called themselves Maniac Productions.

They gave themselves this name because, among other things, they would enlist people from their own families to do strange things. For instance, Edmondo's grandfather was a pyromaniac. And since he was also a bit senile, he was very dangerous—he had set his house on fire a number of times. His family was very careful to keep matches out of his reach at all times, except when Maniac Productions was performing. Then Edmondo would invite his grandfather to the theater and give him a big box of matches; the grandfather would wander around the theater lighting fires while the group performed and pretended not to notice him. This was his maniac thing. It was very original theater, and very satisfying to Edmondo's grandfather. He didn't care if the audience was looking at him or not, because he had his box of matches.

Edmondo and Brigitte moved into our flat. Michael came from a family of diamond merchants in Brussels and stayed in five-star hotels. He felt guilty because he was the only one of us with money, so whenever he came to visit he brought a ton of fancy food and we had a feast. He also backed Maniac Productions.

Another tenant was Piotr, a Polish artist with the most impossibly funny hair: dead straight and cut like a big mushroom. He moved into the living room—only because it was so cold, he slept in a tent in the middle of the room.

On the last Friday of every month, people in nice neighborhoods in Amsterdam would put furniture they no longer wanted out on the sidewalk. And so that was how we furnished our loft. One week, we found a couch and a couple of chairs; another week, a coffee table; still another week, a lamp. And then one amazing Friday, a working refrigerator.

This fridge came to have another use besides the usual one. Piotr had a book of logic—I think it was Wittgenstein translated into Polish—and for reasons best known to himself, he kept it in the freezer. This book was his favorite thing in the world. And every morning he would wake up with this imbecilic smile on his face, take his book out of the freezer, wait patiently until the page he wanted to read unfroze, read to us from it in Polish, then turn the page and put the book back in the freezer for the next day.

The spice loft was our *La Bohème*. It was the first time in my life that I lived in any kind of community, and everybody was so eccentric and different—I loved it. I was always trying to take care of everyone, and everything was constantly falling apart.

For instance, Edmondo (who had been an accomplished Shakespearean actor before he turned to performance art) was madly in love with Brigitte, the fifteen-year-old with the toilet seat around her neck. Brigitte's father had started the pornography industry in Sweden—a very big deal; the porn revolution really began there—and she hated her father; she hated everybody. She was a deeply depressed person: she literally never spoke a word. All of us in the flat ate all our meals together, and she would just sit there, completely silent. Then in the middle of the night one night, Edmondo knocked on our door. I opened it and said, "What's wrong?" "She talks, she talks!" he said. "What did she say?" I asked. "She said, 'Boo,'" he said.

"That's not much," I said.

The next morning, she packed and left. That was all. He'd forced her to say something, and she just left. Edmondo couldn't stop crying. Then his father came from Italy to console him. He was a dentist, and brought with him all his instruments, which he placed neatly over a sheet of newspaper on the table. He then began repairing Edmondo's teeth while also cooking Italian pasta for the rest of us. At the same time, Michael's girlfriend Marinka (a strikingly beautiful Croat) moved in and became the new third member of Maniac Productions.

And Piotr fell madly in love with Marinka. Who was deeply in love with Michael.

It turned out there was another reason, besides comfort, that Michael was living in hotels. It turned out that he had another girlfriend. Ulla was her name. "I'm so happy," he told us one day, about his pair of girlfriends. "The two of them complement each other perfectly." Marinka and Ulla knew (and liked) each other, and knew (but didn't like) the arrangement. Then Ulla got pregnant—not only pregnant, but pregnant with twins. When Michael told Marinka about it, she moved to Australia. And Piotr followed her there, and committed suicide on her birthday. Marinka went on to have a successful career in animation and design and ultimately reestablished a friendly relationship with Michael. Not long after this, Marinka, still young, would die of cancer.

More death. This was a big one: on May 4, 1980, Tito died. He was eighty-seven. Dutch television carried the state funeral, all four hours of it. And my countrywoman Marinka and I prepared a huge funeral feast and lay on the bed watching the entire ceremony, eating and crying, then eating some more and crying some more. Ulay and Piotr looked at us like we were nuts. But we were crying for a reason: we knew that with this one death, everything had changed—that without this strong man to hold Yugoslavia together, everything back home was going to go wrong.

The funeral was gigantic, majestic. Tito died in Slovenia, and the cameras showed the train carrying his body arriving in Belgrade. There was a huge crowd, everyone dressed in black, everyone weeping. Peasant women were ripping their dresses open so that their breasts fell out, beating their chests in sorrow, crying, "Why? Why did you take him? Why didn't you take me? Why didn't you take me?"

Who were they talking about? God? Communism didn't believe in God. But the Yugoslav people kind of believed in God and Tito together as one thing.

I understood. Tito had done great things. In 1948, when Stalin tried to take over the entire Eastern Bloc—Poland, Czechoslovakia, Hungary—Tito kept him from invading Yugoslavia. He had found a way to give the country its own socialist brand of Communism, to stay nonaligned with America or the Soviet Union, to lead his own bloc of nonaligned countries.

And he had done it all with great style. This must be said. He had the spirit of a playboy: he loved Sophia Loren, Gina Lollobrigida, Elizabeth Taylor, and they all came to visit him at his summer estate in the Brijuni Islands, as did Carlo Ponti and Richard Burton, not to mention every important world leader. When Sophia Loren came, Tito threw Hungarian sausages into the sea so she could watch his falcons dive for them. He drank whiskey and watched American movies with Lee Marvin. He hunted big game: he was always posing for photos with his right foot on top of the bear he had just shot. Maybe all of it was decadent (very American), but for the Yugoslav people it was like, "This is Tito—he can do anything."

I felt the same. My father had taken me many times to watch Tito give speeches in Marx and Engels Square—we were in a special viewing area, very close to him. I can hardly describe the experience: his charisma was absolute, overpowering. I felt electricity flowing through my whole body as he spoke; the tears flowed from my eyes. And it didn't matter what he was saying. This was mass hypnosis—a huge number of people, at that particular moment of history, believing every word he said, knowing that it all made sense.

Then Ulay and I did our own experiment with hypnosis.

We wanted to access the unconscious. So over a period of three months we periodically allowed ourselves to be hypnotized, and we tape-recorded the sessions. We instructed the doctor to ask us specific questions about our work while we were under hypnosis. Afterward we listened to these sessions, and collected ideas and images from them that we then translated into performances—four in all, three for video and one for an audience.

The first piece was called *Point of Contact*. In this, the video camera recorded us as we stood face to face, pointing our index fingers at each other, the fingertips just a tiny distance apart, as we looked intently at each other for sixty minutes. The idea was to really feel each other's energy without touching, all through the eyes.

The second performance—this one done for the public at the National Gallery of Ireland in Dublin—was *Rest Energy*. This piece, with a big bow and arrow, was the ultimate portrait of trust. In it

I held the bow and Ulay held the string pulled out with the end of the arrow between his knuckles and the tip pointed at my chest. We were both in a constant state of tension, pulling from either side, with the constant threat that if he slipped, I could be shot in the heart. And meanwhile, we each had a tiny microphone taped to our chests, under our shirts, so the audience could hear the amplified sound of our hearts beating.

And our hearts were beating faster and faster! This piece lasted for four minutes and twenty seconds, which felt like an eternity. The tension was unbearable.

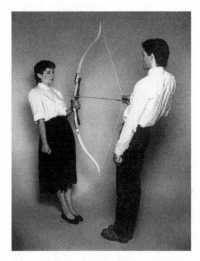

Ulay/Marina Abramović, *Rest Energy* (based on the performance for video, 4 minutes), ROSC '80, Dublin, 1980

The third piece was called *Nature of Mind*—and we actually filmed this one. I was standing by a dock on the Amsterdam harbor; out of sight of the camera, and over my head, Ulay, wearing a red shirt, was hanging on to a crane. In the film I'm just standing there with my hands in the air, for minute after minute, with nothing happening. Then, after what feels like forever, there's a red flash as Ulay plummets by and splashes down into the water below me. All you see is this bright flash, for maybe a quarter of a second. It was like so many things that happen to us in life: a bright instant, never to be recaptured.

And the last performance was *Timeless Point of View*. Unlike the other pieces, which were collaborative, this one was my idea: it came from a vision I had, in one of the hypnosis sessions, of how I wanted to die. We filmed it on a big lake in central Holland called the IJsselmeer: the catalog text for the finished piece described what you were seeing:

> Far in the background, there is a small rowing boat, but it stands out only as a silhouette against the monochrome color. In it, Abramović sits rowing while Ulay is standing at the shore and listening through headphones to the sound of her rowing. The gap between picture and sound is irritating, for the ever-same volume of the sound of the oar dipping into the water cannot be reconciled with the boat becoming smaller and smaller, then disappearing on the horizon.

My work and my life are so connected. And throughout my career, I've produced works whose unconscious meaning only becomes clear to me over time. In *Point of Contact*, we were so close, and yet that final tiny space between us, the gap that ultimately prevented a merging of our souls, was unbridgeable. In *Rest Energy*, Ulay possessed the power to destroy me, and to literally break my heart. In *Nature of Mind*, he was a brief but very important passage in my life, one that blew through like a flash because the emotions were so strong—and then, just like that, vanished definitively.

And *Timeless Point of View* is unavoidably connected with the memory of my father teaching me to swim. It doesn't matter that in real life he was the one rowing out into the Adriatic, threatening to disappear as I struggled through the water toward him. In the work I've corrected the past, making myself the powerful and independent one: Ulay is reduced to being a helpless onlooker as my destiny removes me from him.

I realized that this is a theme I return to constantly—I'm always trying to prove to everyone that I can go it alone, that I can survive, that I don't need anybody. And this is also a curse, in a way, because I'm always doing so much—at times, too much—and because I have so often been left alone (as I wished, in a way) and without love.

Painting in my studio, Belgrade, 1969

An early cloud painting by me, 1965

My early painting *3 Secrets*, 1962

Marina Abramović/Ulay, *Gold Found by the Artists*
(later changed to *Nightsea Crossing*), Gallery of New South Wales, 1981

Marina Abramović/Ulay, beggar turned into a warrior
(production still from *City of Angels*), Bangkok, 1983

Me atop the Great Wall of China, 1988

The Artist Is Present (performance, 3 months), reuniting with Ulay, New York, 2010

Photograph © Marco Anelli

Cleaning the House, slow-motion walk (8 hours), student workshop, Denmark, 1996

Cleaning the House, walking for 10 hours after 4 days without food or talk,
student workshop, Académie des Beaux-Arts, Paris, 1995

Me with gold miners during a research trip, Soledad, 1991

Sleeping Under the Banyan Tree, in collaboration with Tibetan monks,
2001, photograph by Alessia Bulgari

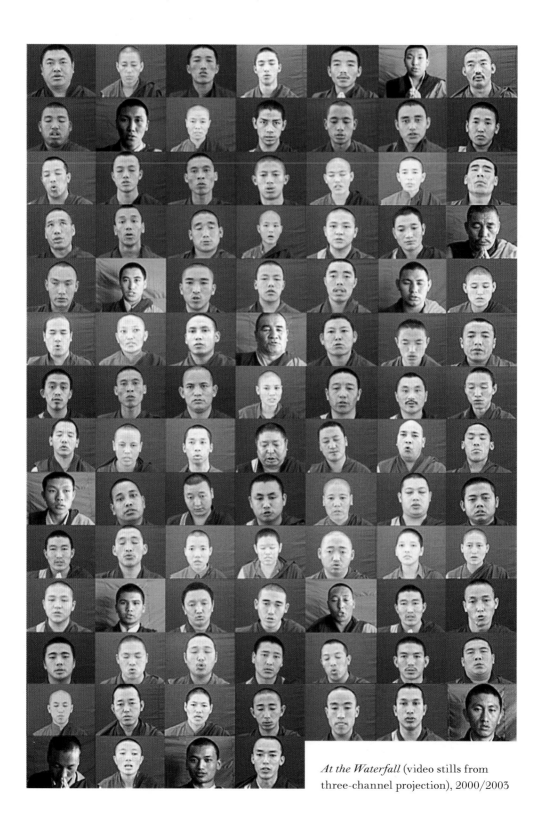

At the Waterfall (video stills from three-channel projection), 2000/2003

Thomas Lips (1975) re-performance from *7 Easy Pieces*,
Solomon R. Guggenheim Museum, New York, 2005

Balkan Baroque (performance, three-channel video installation,
4 days and 6 hours), Venice, 1997

6.

On the night of December 15, 1980, in the outback of central Australia, I have the following dream:

Ulay is going to war, which is starting now.

I am crying on the shoulder of my grandmother, saying "Why, why." I'm desperate, because I know that it is not possible to change anything and that this all had to happen.

They are trying to kill me, by throwing grenades at me.

But not one grenade explodes.

I am taking them from the ground and throwing grenades back at them.

Later on they tell me that I won.

They're showing me the bed in which I am to sleep.

The bed is small, military, with blue bedsheets.

From the mid-1970s to the end of the decade, performance art caught on. There were lots of performances going on, and a lot of them were bad—it seemed everybody was doing it and there were very few good pieces. It got to the point where I was almost ashamed to tell people what I did, because there was so much bad performance art—somebody would spit on the floor and call it a performance.

At the same time, the originators of the medium were no longer young, and this work was very hard on the body. And the market, and dealers especially, were putting increasing pressure on artists to make something to sell, because, after all, performance produced nothing marketable. So as the 1970s clicked over into the '80s, it seemed as though all the bad performance artists were becoming bad painters. Even important artists like Chris Burden and Vito Acconci turned, respectively, to making objects and making architecture.

As all this was going on, Ulay and I were looking for a solution— new ways to make performances. I had no desire to go back to painting, and he had no wish to return to photography. So we said, "Let's go to nature. Why don't we go to the desert?" We always used to joke that Moses, Mohammed, Jesus, and Buddha all went to the desert as nobodies and came back as somebodies, so there must be something in the desert. . . .

In 1979 we were invited to Australia for the European Dialogue Biennale of Sydney. It was a very important event—the first time that Australians would get to see new European artists. Many artists were invited, and we were asked to do an opening performance: a big honor. We accepted, but told the organizers that we would have to arrive early and get a sense of the environment, because we'd never been in that part of the world. We wanted an idea to come spontaneously and organically: we didn't just want to go there with something prepared that wouldn't fit.

I also had an ulterior motive in accepting this invitation.

When I was fourteen, in Belgrade, I discovered this amazing man, a mad, wonderful anthropologist named Tibor Sekelj. He was in his late forties then, and he had been everywhere in the world and done everything. He learned a new language every four years. And every year he would take the most exotic trips—up the Amazon in Brazil or the Sepik River in New Guinea—or into a dozen other wild places. On his journeys he would encounter almost-extinguished tribes, cannibals, or headhunters, and then, at the end of each year, he would come to the university to give talks about his research. I was in the first row every time—at age fourteen, fifteen, sixteen, seventeen. I would devour his every word. My dream was that one day I, too, would go to these places and also have experiences like this.

Once he told a story I'll never forget. Somewhere in Micronesia, there were two circular groups of islands, a smaller circle within a larger one. Sekelj told a story about a ring and a bracelet. He said that the natives on one of the islands in the smaller circle had a ritual: on a particular day of the year, all the villagers would get in canoes and go to the next island bringing a special ring. But when they arrived, everybody there would be shut in their huts, pretending they weren't home. So the ring-bringers would scream and shout and do a dance to make the people come out of their huts, and when they finally emerged, the people who had brought the ring would tell them a story about how difficult it had been to come from their island to this island—there had been a storm; a whale had eaten the ring and they'd had to fight the whale to get it back—a whole saga. Then, finally, they would hand over the ring and return to their own island.

The next year, the natives who had received the ring took it to the next island over, and the same ritual took place—except that this new group of ring-bringers would add their own story to the story of the group who had brought them the ring the year before. So from year to year, the ring would travel around the smaller circle of islands—and the amazing thing was, this same process was going on with a bracelet in the opposite direction in the outer circle! Clockwise with a ring in one circle of islands, counterclockwise with a bracelet in the other. And all the stories adding up. It was like an endless movie for me.

And so when I thought of visiting Australia, what compelled me most of all was the idea of going to the outback, the Great Victoria Desert in the center of the continent, and encountering the Australian Aborigines, much as my idol Sekelj would have. Surely they had amazing stories. Ulay and I started reading everything we could find about the Aborigines, and the more we read, the more we understood what a mind-blowing culture this was.

We learned that every feature in the landscape was sacred to the Anangu, as they called themselves. (As with Native Americans, the term the Aborigines used for themselves simply meant "people," or "human beings.") We learned about the Dreamtime, the Aboriginal concept of the Creation, which exists in the past, present, and future all at once. We read that the creators traveled in paths across the land called songlines. The words of the song in a songline describe the landmarks—those sacred rocks and trees and water holes and mountains—that mark the route. And the creators, we read, existed across space and time: the Aborigines were in touch with them both in dreams and waking life.

I couldn't wait to see this place for myself.

The Biennale's organizers agreed to our plan to come up with a performance after we arrived. And ten days after we landed in Australia, a very simple and beautiful idea came to us. We had, after all, traveled to the other end of the earth, where the seasons were reversed and the light was different, and so we wanted to do something with light and shadow. The result was a piece called *The Brink*. In it, Ulay walked slowly back and forth along a high wall above the Art Gallery of New South Wales's sculpture courtyard; on the other side of the wall was a busy highway. While he paced, in actual danger of falling, I walked the edge of the wall's shadow in the courtyard below, in metaphorical danger. Meanwhile the shadow crept, ever so slowly, across the courtyard—until, precisely four hours and fifteen minutes later, when there was no sunlight left in the space, the performance ended.

Ulay/Marina Abramović, *The Brink* (performance, 4 hours, 15 minutes),
Biennale of Sydney, 1979

After we performed the piece, we had ten days free before we had to fly home. We were consumed with the idea of spending this time in the outback. When we told Nick Waterlow, the director of the Biennale, of our obsession, he said he had a friend named Phillip Toyne who lived in Alice Springs, in the heart of the desert, and knew the territory very well. Toyne was an activist lawyer in Aboriginal land rights, Nick said; he was determined to restore to the tribes the sacred lands that Australian settlers had taken away. Nick gave us a letter of introduction to Phillip. "He's a bit of a crusty character," Nick said, "but if you give him this letter, maybe he'll show you the outback."

It was easier in those days to fly from Sydney to Paris or London than it was to fly to Alice Springs. We got the cheapest tickets possible, showed up at the appointed hour, and set out.

There were only around three streets in Alice Springs then, and not many people walking around. We started asking everybody we saw, "Where is Phillip Toyne?" And finally a guy directed us to this kind of half-destroyed motel out at the end of a dirt road—this was the Aboriginal Land Rights headquarters.

We walked in and found this unshaved, dirty guy screaming at somebody on an army field telephone. Finally he hung up, looked Ulay and me up and down, and said, "And just who the hell might you be?"

"We are friends of Nick Waterlow," we told him. "He gave us this letter to give to you."

He read the letter, and started screaming at us. "You motherfuckers, are you out of your minds?" he yelled. "Get the fuck out of my office! Why is he sending me these idiots? You're just blood-sucking tourists like the rest of them! You want to take pictures of Aborigines, then go back to your nice cozy home and say you saw Aborigines! I want nothing to do with you—get the fuck out of here!" He stood up menacingly; we backed out of his office.

So now we were stuck. We had bought rock-bottom cheap tickets to Alice Springs; there was no going back early. We were stuck for ten days in this town with three streets; you couldn't go anywhere else in the vicinity without permission, and even if you could, we had no idea where we would go or how we would get there.

There were just three places to eat in town, and wherever we went we kept running into Phillip. After a few days he started talking to us. He said, "Okay, what do you want?"

We told him, as best we could, who we were and what we did. We weren't tourists, we said; we were artists. We had been to far-flung places, and had the greatest respect for indigenous populations. We were fascinated with the outback and its tribes; we just wanted to get to know them, and let what we learned find its way into our work.

He shook his head, almost sympathetically. "Sorry, mate," he said. "Not this time. Aboriginal land rights are a very sensitive matter—all kinds of groups are worried about the tribes being exploited, especially by foreigners. But if you actually want to *do* something for them, and you come back with a serious proposal, next time let's see."

So we hung around Alice Springs for ten days, and then we flew home and wrote a proposal to the Australian Visual Arts Council. We wanted to live in the outback among the Aborigines for six months, we said. We wanted to learn who they were and how they lived, and we wanted to let what we learned fill our art with something new. We would then spend the following six months traveling around Australia, performing whatever new pieces our experiences had inspired and giving talks about our time in the desert.

The members of the council had loved *The Brink*. They okayed our proposal and gave us a generous grant for the following year.

In October 1980 we sold the van, took Alba to stay with our friend Christine Koenig in Amsterdam, and flew to Australia.

We bought a used jeep in Sydney and outfitted ourselves with all the gear we thought we'd need for six months in the desert. Then we made the long drive to Alice Springs—it was over a thousand miles; it took us nearly two weeks—and there we were again, and there was Phillip Toyne. He said, "What? You're back already?"

We needed someone to show us around and introduce us to the tribes. He knew the territory and the tribes. We knew he was making a book about Aboriginal land rights to present to the Australian government, so we asked what we could do for him.

"What do you know how to do?" he asked.

Ulay had once been an engineer, so he knew how to make maps; he was also a photographer. I knew how to do graphic design. Phillip needed maps and photographs and graphic design for his book. He agreed to help us.

We spent the next month driving around with Phillip, mapping and photographing the region. Every night, we returned to Alice Springs and ate in one of the three restaurants with Phillip and his friend Dan Vachon, a Canadian anthropologist. We stayed in the broken-down motel that served as Toyne's headquarters. It was quite an unusual place. Snakes would appear in the room frequently, and gigantic spiders. There was no air-conditioning, and my God, it was hot. Autumn in the northern hemisphere is spring below the equator, and central Australia was starting to heat up. Daytime temperatures in the outback can approach 45 degrees Celsius—close to 115 degrees Fahrenheit.

In the Great Victoria Desert, Australia, 1980

Some days we spent the entire day driving along the dingo fence, the 3,500-mile-long barrier that protects the sheep of the country's southeast from the wild dogs of the interior. We couldn't believe that a fence could be so long, or that it could be so effective at keeping out predators—it reminded both Ulay and me of another example, even longer and far more ancient, to the north: the Great Wall of China.

With Phillip's guidance, Ulay mapped all the trees and rocks and water holes and mountains that were sacred to the nearby tribes. We'd read about these things, but here in the desert, in the mind-boggling heat and vast emptiness, everything we heard and saw took on much greater meaning. To the Aborigines, everything on earth and in the sky contains a spirit. It made me think of the presences in the *plakar*, the deep, dark closet in our Belgrade apartment, with whom I used to talk when I was small. Meeting the Aborigines would soon give me proof that I was not alone in thinking this way, that this supposedly invisible world really existed. The Aborigines, I would soon learn, lived in this world all the time. Phillip was finally satisfied that we weren't tourists—he probably thought we were crazy, he probably didn't quite understand what we were doing, but I think he respected it. And so, now that we were finished helping him, Phillip gave us permission to go to the south stations—the territory that was inaccessible to ordinary travelers. He would take us and introduce us to members of the Pitjantjatjara and Pintupi tribes: after that, we would be on our own.

Before we set out, after many months of noncommunication, I wrote a letter to Danica:

Today is our last day in civilization and I will write to you again at the end of the year. In any case I live a very healthy life, much better than in the city. The nature here is incredibly beautiful. We eat rabbits, kangaroos, ducks, ants, worms that live in the hollows of the trees. This is pure protein and is very healthy. On my feet I have canvas boots which are very good protection from snakes and spiders. This year we will celebrate our birthday in the desert around the fire. I will be thirty-four years old and Ulay thirty-seven. I never felt as young in my life as I do now. Traveling makes a person young because he doesn't have time to get old. ... The temperature at the moment is 40–45 Celsius. We are really feeling this temperature. We sleep under the open sky full of stars. We feel like the first people on this planet.

Ulay drinking water after rain, central Australian desert, 1980

It wasn't just the heat that was shocking. Nothing prepares you for the ubiquitous dirt and the overwhelming smell and the swarming, clustering, relentless flies of the outback, and nothing prepares Westerners—even Westerners used to extreme experiences—for meeting Australia's first inhabitants.

Aborigines are not just the oldest race in Australia; they are the oldest race on the planet. They should be treated as living treasures. Yet they are not.

There is (at first) zero communication with them. Tribal Aborigines don't talk to you, because they don't communicate in the way that we are used to. It would take me three months to discover that they actually were speaking to me—in my head, telepathically. That was when everything would start opening up to me. But you have to spend at least three months climbing this wall, which most Australians don't. They would rather go to Paris or London than to the desert.

And then there is the smell.

The Pitjantjatjara and Pintupi don't wash with water—for one thing because there isn't much water in the desert, but for another because they don't want to bother the Rainbow Serpent, the all-powerful creator god who lives around the water holes. Instead they use ashes from their fires to wash themselves, and it doesn't deodorize them. To a Westerner, this scent is unbearable: smelling it is like taking a raw onion and rubbing it on your eyes.

And yet so many things about the Aborigines are fascinating. First, they're a nomadic culture, so ancient and so connected to the energy of the land. The land is filled with stories: they are always traveling through this mythical landscape. An Aborigine will say to you, "This is a snake man just here fight with a water woman"—and all you see are some boulders, maybe a bush that looks like some strange form of fish.

You look at this landscape, and hear this story, and it's not that it happened in the past, it's not something in the future. It's happening now. It is always now. It has never "happened." It *is* happening. This was a revolutionary concept to me—all my ideas about existing in the present came from there.

The ceremony is their way of life. They don't just perform these rituals at a certain time of year: they're constant. You'll see Aborigines all dressed up in feathers and face paint, and walking through the desert—the middle of nowhere, dust flying everywhere and unbearable heat, and you'll ask, "Where are you going?" And they'll say, in this broken English they use, "Oh, we have business"—meaning a ceremony. "But where is the business?" you ask, and they'll show you a rock and a tree in the distance. "There is the office," they'll say.

The thing that fascinated me most was that they have absolutely no possessions. This is connected to the fact that they don't believe in tomorrow; there is only today. For example, it is very rare to find a kangaroo in the desert. When they find one, they have food to eat, which is a big deal for them. But after they kill and cook the kangaroo, they can never finish it: there's always lots of meat left. But since they're always moving from place to place, when they wake up the next morning, they don't take the meat with them. They just leave everything—the next day is the next day.

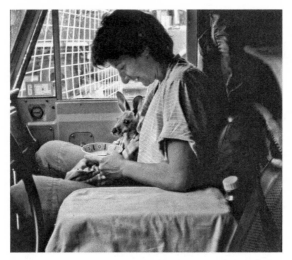

My rescue kangaroo, Frederika, and me,
Great Victoria Desert, Australia, 1981

Ulay and I separated, because among the Aborigines, the men stay with men and the women with women. The two sexes only make love during nights with a full moon, then they separate again. This creates total harmony—they don't get a chance to bother each other! When the women have children, any woman who has milk can be the mother to any child around. The kids just run around playing soccer, then stop for a couple of minutes and suck at a breast, then run out and play some more.

My main job with the women was watching them present their dreams. Every morning we would go to a field somewhere, and in hierarchical order, starting with the oldest women and moving down to the youngest, they would show us, using a stick to make drawings in the dirt, what they'd dreamed the night before. Each woman would then assign the rest of us roles to act out the dream as they interpreted it. They all had dreams; they all had to show them—dreams playing all day long! And sometimes they couldn't finish all the dreams, so the next morning they would have dreams left over from the day before, along with new ones to show. . . . It was so much work.

My strongest memory of the desert is of motionlessness.

The temperature was unbearable. As spring turned to summer, the heat would rise to 50 degrees Celsius or more—130-plus degrees Fahrenheit. It's like a hot wall. If you just stand up and walk a few paces, your heart feels like it's going to hammer through your chest. You can't. There are very few trees; there's very little shade of any kind. So you literally have to be motionless for long periods of time. You function before sunrise and after sunset—that's it.

To stay motionless during the day, you have to slow down everything: your breathing, even your heartbeat. I also want to mention that Aboriginals are the only people I know who don't take drugs of any kind. Even tea is much too strong a stimulant for them. That's why they don't have any kind of resistance to alcohol—it completely wipes out their memory.

In the beginning, there were flies everywhere. I was covered with them—in my nose, in my mouth, all over my body. It was impossible to chase them away, so I began to name them: Jane was the one on the roof of my mouth, George was the one who liked to sit in my ear. Then after three months, I woke up one morning without a single fly on me. It was then that I understood that the flies had been drawn to me because I was something strange and different: as I became one with my surroundings, I lost my attraction.

I don't think it was a coincidence that at the same time, I stopped noticing the Aborigines' smell.

⌒

One night, around the same time that the flies went away, I was sitting around the fire with some tribeswomen when I noticed that they were talking in my head. We were not speaking, but they were telling me something: I was thinking, and they were answering me.

That was when my mind really started opening. I began to notice that we could sit around in total silence and have a full conversation. For example, if I wanted to sit in a certain place next to the fire, one of the Aborigines would tell me in my head that this was a bad spot and I should move. And I would move, and nobody had spoken one word—everything was understood.

Living in this kind of heat, in a tranquil state and with very little food or water, I became a kind of natural antenna. I would receive the most amazing images, as clearly as if they were on a TV screen. I wrote down the images in my diaries, and eerily (as I later found out), many of them seemed to foresee actual events. I dreamed of an earthquake in Italy: forty-eight hours later, there was an earthquake in southern Italy. I had a vision of someone shooting the Pope: forty-eight hours later, someone tried to shoot Pope John Paul II.

This also worked on the simplest and most personal level. For example, back in the spice loft in Amsterdam, my friend Marinka had a bed that was always in a dark corner of her room. And sitting in the middle of the desert in January, I had a vision of her room in front of me, in three dimensions. In this vision, her bed was next to the window instead of in the corner, and she was nowhere to be seen—it was just an empty room, a bed by the window. I made a little note: "Strange image—how great that she put her bed next to the window." That was all. And I wrote the date.

A year and a half passes. I come back to Amsterdam. I go to her room, and I see the bed in the dark corner as always. I said, "Marinka, this is so strange; I had this vision in Australia, in the middle of the desert, that your bed was next to the window. I wrote it in my notebook." She says, "Can I see the date?" She looks at the date. She says, "At that time I went back to Belgrade, and I rented my place to some Swedish couple. And the first thing they did was put the bed next to the window. When I returned, I put it back."

⌒

At the beginning, when I was with the tribeswomen, I had these unbearable migraines because of the heat. Then Ulay brought me a medicine man from his tribe who said he could take care of this migraine. He asked me for a container, any kind of container. So I had an empty sardine can, and I gave it to him. He told me to lie down in the dirt and close my eyes. I could feel him put his lips, very softly, in two different spots on my forehead. Then when I opened my eyes, the sardine can was full of blood. He said to me, "This is the fight, bury it." I buried the can in the ground. Then I looked in the mirror, and at the places on my forehead where he had touched me, I only had two blue spots—the skin was unbroken. And my headache was gone, and I had a remarkable feeling of lightness. As soon as I returned to the city, the migraine came back.

I was pretty much accepted among the women, but the tribesmen more than accepted Ulay. He didn't undergo an initiation, but he did become very close to a Pintupi medicine man named Watuma. And Watuma gave Ulay a tribal name, Tjungarrayi, which meant he was on the path to initiation.

After spending time separately, Ulay and I decided to go out on our own for a little bit. There was a rock formation we wanted to visit—a strange landscape, around a water hole, that looked like the site of a meteorite impact. So we took our jeep, gallons of boiling-hot water, cans of beans, and set out. It was the third week in December, and we wanted to get to this water hole around Christmas.

Visiting a painter of the Pintupi tribe, Great Australian Desert, 1981

We were driving through the outback one night as a huge full moon rose over the desert, when we began to talk about the fact that the only human constructions visible from outer space, according to astronauts, are the pyramids and the Great Wall of China. We both instantly thought of a beautiful line from a second-century Chinese poem, "Confessions of the Great Wall": "The earth is small and blue, and I am a little crack in it." Suddenly we both had chills: this ancient Chinese poet had somehow foreseen the astronauts' vision of the Great Wall from space. It was at that moment that we conceived our next great ambition: we would walk the Wall, starting from opposite ends, and meet in the middle. No one had ever done this before, we were quite sure.

Not only would we meet in the middle, we decided, but we would be married there. It was incredibly romantic.

⁓

We arrived at the rock formation. It was a very strange location indeed—a water hole surrounded by huge boulders and red earth. The sun was just setting; it was Christmas Eve. So I began to make a fire in preparation for cooking dinner, because it was so hot that you

Our floating breakfast, central Australian desert, 1981

could only eat after the sun had gone down. The fire was also important because it created hot ashes that we spread in a circle around our sleeping area, to protect us from poisonous snakes and spiders.

The sun went down and I began cooking. And as I cooked, we suddenly became aware of a huge wedge-tailed eagle circling us in the semidarkness. He circled and circled, then he landed—directly across the fire from us. He just stood there and looked at us: this was a really big bird. I stopped cooking; I couldn't move, the image of this giant bird standing and staring at us was so mesmerizing.

We didn't move. We never ate—we just left our food. As the darkness deepened, the eagle continued to stand there. Finally, exhausted, we fell asleep.

We awoke at first light, and saw the eagle still standing in the same place, stock-still. And then—I'll never forget this—Ulay walked over to the bird and touched it, and it fell over, dead. It had been entirely eaten by ants. Every inch of my body turned to goose bumps. We packed our things and got out of there, fast.

Fast-forward to a couple of months later. We had left the desert and returned to Alice Springs; we were having dinner one night with Phillip Toyne and Dan Vachon, the anthropologist. We were telling them all the stories: about the rituals, the dreams, the healing of my migraine. Then Ulay said, "Oh, and Watuma the medicine man gave me this name, Tjungarrayi." Dan, who had a dictionary of Aboriginal language, said, "Let me look that up." And he looked, and found it. "Oh, that means dying eagle," he said.

Somewhere west of Lake Disappointment, Australia, 1980

What did we learn from the desert and the people who lived there? Not to move, not to eat, not to speak. And so when we came back to Sydney to begin the next six months of our project, the performance part, we decided to do a piece that was exactly that: not moving, not eating, not speaking. We called it *Gold Found by the Artists*.

The title was both literal and metaphorical. Literally speaking, we *had* found gold in the outback, 250 grams of it, with an Army-surplus metal detector we'd bought. Metaphorically, our experiences with the Aborigines had been pure gold. We had discovered stillness and silence. In the desert we had sat and stared and thought, or not thought. We both felt we had communicated telepathically with the Aborigines. How would it be to sit and stare at each other for as long as humanly possible, and then much longer still? Would we attain a new state of consciousness? Would we read each other's thoughts?

The new piece would go as follows: for eight hours, we would sit across a table from each other, in chairs that were neither too comfortable nor too uncomfortable, and look into each other's eyes without getting up, without moving at all. On the table we placed a gold-covered boomerang, the gold nuggets we'd found in the desert, and, once again, a live snake: a three-foot diamond python named Zen. The snake symbolized life, and the Aborigine creation myth; the objects stood for our time in the outback.

Sitting unmoving all day sounds simple. It was anything but simple. At our first performance, we found out how hard it would be.

The first day, at the Art Gallery of New South Wales, in Sydney, everything was fine for the first three hours. But then the big muscles in our legs, thighs, and calves began to cramp, and our shoulders and necks began to throb with pain. Yet our commitment to remaining still meant that any kind of movement to relieve the pain was impossible.

The experience is indescribable. The pain is a huge obstacle. It comes like a storm. Your brain tells you, *Well, I can move if I really have to*. But if you don't move, if you have the willpower to make no compromise or concession, the pain becomes so intense that you think you'll lose consciousness. And it's at that moment—and only at that moment—that the pain disappears.

We performed *Gold Found by the Artists* for sixteen straight days in Sydney. We fasted for the entire period, only consuming juice and water in the evenings, and never spoke to each other throughout.

We began on July 4, 1981. And after I had stared at Ulay for two hours, trying not to blink, I began to see an aura around him—"a clear shiny yellow luminous color," I wrote in my diary. The familiar bodily pain returned: in order to remain completely still, I imagined that someone in the audience was pointing a pistol at me and would pull the trigger if I moved.

I made diary entries after each day's performance. "Today I felt I would lose consciousness," I wrote on the fourth day, July 7.

A strange heat came into my body. I succeeded in stopping the pains in my head, neck, and spine. I know by now that no position is more comfortable than another. Even the most comfortable position after a period of time would become intolerable. I know by now that I must simply accept the intolerable: confront the pain and accept it.

It happened at once: everything motionless—without pain—only heartbeats—everything became light. This state was so precious to me. Out of this was pain and change. Ulay continued to change. In fractions of seconds he transformed into hundreds of faces and bodies. This lasted until he became an empty blue space surrounded by light. I feel something very important is happening. This empty space is real. All other faces and bodies are only different forms of projection. I am this space, too. This helps me not to move.

I had discovered a new version of myself, one in which pain didn't matter. It's not that my shift of mind had made the pain disappear. It had just gone somewhere else. It was there but not there. And as I sat and looked at Ulay on that fourth day, he disappeared in front of my eyes. Only his outline was present. Inside the outline was pure blue light, the bluest blue imaginable, like the sky in the middle of a cloudless day in the Greek islands—that kind of blue. It was shocking. I had been trying not to blink; now, because I couldn't believe that I wasn't hallucinating, I blinked and I blinked—and nothing changed. It wasn't Ulay across the table from me any longer. It was just blue light.

Years later, a comparison occurred to me between this state of mind and something that happens in Dostoevsky's *The Idiot*. In that novel, Prince Myshkin describes with acute precision the sensations that overcome him before an epileptic attack: he experiences the most powerful feeling of harmony with everything around him, and a tangible sense of lightness and luminosity in nature. As Dostoevsky describes it, those sensations are so profound that the nervous system can't take it, and the epileptic seizure comes on as a result.

These sensations sound very similar to those I've experienced while performing long-duration pieces. These pieces are very repetitive, very constant: there are no surprises for the body, and so the brain kind of checks out. That's when you get into a state of harmony with everything around you: that's the moment when what I call "liquid knowledge" comes to you.

I believe that universal knowledge is everywhere around us. It's only a question of how we can achieve that kind of understanding. Many people have experienced moments when something in their brain says, "Oh my God, now I understand." And those moments feel so rare, but the knowledge is always out there for the taking. You only have to tune out all the noise around you. In order to do this, you have to exhaust your own system of thinking, and your own energy. That's extremely important. You must really be exhausted, to the point where there's nothing left: where you're so tired that you can't take it anymore. When your brain is so tired of working that it can no longer think—that's the moment when liquid knowledge can enter.

That knowledge has been very hard for me to win, but I have won it. And the only way to win it is by never, under any circumstances, giving up.

⌒

"Today the time was long," I wrote on July 8. "In the end I had an intense sense of myself, particularly smell." That night, I wrote, "I dreamed of an operation on my brain. I had a tumor. I had only a few days to live. The name of the doctor is strange."

The next day, I once more had the feeling that I could smell everybody and everything in the room, like a dog. Then, I wrote in my diary,

> a feeling of loving everything and everyone. There was warm air coming from inside and outside at the same time. Today I didn't move. I passed five hours and overcame the physical pain and the wish to move. In the remaining three hours there was no pain. I only felt light and silence. With pain I established the contact. I could control it if I breathed properly and stopped the flow of my thoughts. Today something scared the snake. It contracted violently, first transmitted to Ulay and then to me. I felt pure clear physical pain in my right temple. By now I am able to notice the most subtle changes in Ulay's aura. I take time differently, I surrender to it. Nothing is important to me. I feel from time to time a strong flow coming out of my body. When eight hours pass I get up from the chair and I see everything as if for the first time—little dizziness—not tiredness, but pain in the body. Tiredness and pain are no longer the same thing. I love *malog* ["little"] Ulay.

At the table on July 10, the pain in my shoulders was so strong that I was forced to let my hands drop to my knees. "I became angry with myself because of that movement," I wrote.

> After this everything went easily. Today the time was the shortest. Two hours before the end the real devil came in the form of some Yugoslav. He came to me and said, "How are you, Marina?" That disturbed me so much in my condition that my heart started beating out of control.
>
> It took me a long time to get quiet again. After this the same man disturbed me in many different ways, trying to make me pay attention to him. He tapped his foot. He coughed and at last he said good-bye. I couldn't believe that I could be so disturbed by

that. I needed an enormous force to get quiet again. Tomorrow I will ask chief curator Bernice Murphy for a guard.

This man who disturbed me was just some gallery visitor who spoke to me in Serbo-Croat, trying to get a reaction. I showed nothing, though inside I felt totally panicked.

And the next day, the man came back:

JULY 11

Only pain in my spine. Legs start trembling out of control. But after all this the time passes quickly. The same Yugoslav came again and asked me twice, "How are you, Marina?" This time I was less disturbed. Again a feeling of peace. At home an undescribable pleasure of drinking orange juice—happiness—

The next two days were very tough.

JULY 12

Crisis. No concentration. The public is ordinary. Too much noise and smell. Time doesn't move. I'm nervous. Ulay has a pain in the lower section of his abdomen. We have seven days left. I'm hoping that we will succeed in finishing them. At one moment a sensation of losing my body, but quickly I return. The public served [helped] me not to move my body. Who will serve me to stop thinking?

JULY 13

Difficult day—I wish to cry. I have pain everywhere. I'm not able to concentrate. How to make it till the end?

And then on the 14th, a real crisis:

JULY 14

After noon, Ulay stood up all at once and left. A little later someone came to me and put a small note in my hand from him. He wrote that I must decide for myself if I continue. His pain in his lower abdomen is so acute that he can't. I continue to sit. Light on his chair stays. Two circles and in the center a bright point. After seven hours, at home.

After I left the gallery that night, I wrote him a letter:

Dear Ulay,

Our rational minds want us to stop. Your mind never before had this treatment. Concentration drops down, temperature drops down, this is all possible.

Ulay, we are not having a good or bad experience. We are having an experience in a period of 16 days. Whatever comes—good or bad—we are in it. I also think that a bad experience has the same importance as a good one. It is all in you. It is all in me. I don't agree with you that [if we continue] it would fulfill a quantitative promise and not a qualitative one. I see 16 days as a condition, fasting as a condition, not talking as a condition. When the Tibetan lama said 21 days in silence and fasting: do you think it is not very difficult? But he said 21 days. We said 16 days. We also could have said ten or seven, but we said 16 days. We want to break the physical body. We want to experience a different mental state. . . . I have my good days. I have my bad days. I want to stop. I don't want to stop. You will have good experiences again. It goes up and down and up. I see this work and the 16 days as a discipline.

The next morning, we went to the hospital. Ulay's spleen was dangerously swollen, and he had lost twenty-six pounds. I had lost twenty-two. The doctor warned us that our bodies might fail if we continued. We looked at each other and decided to continue.

SNAKE COUPLE GO ON, read the headline in the *Sydney Morning Herald*.

JULY 15

I feel good. Today the snake fell four times together with the boomerang on the floor. After this it became tranquil again. I'm worried about Ulay. Are we able to continue? It has occupied my mind so much that I have forgotten my own pain. I am not able to stop the flow of my thoughts.

The next day, the excruciating pain and sudden cramps continued, but with them came a new phenomenon: 360-degree vision. I actually had the sense, like a blind person, that I could see what was happening behind me. But, I wrote in my diary, "I have less and less wish to write about all this."

And then Ulay had to leave the table once more. Once again I remained.

"I can deal with the pain more easily," I wrote that night. "Ulay again has the problem to continue. For me it is incomprehensible. We said to ourselves sixteen days. There's nothing to think about. We must continue. I hope for the best."

He returned, and we finished out the sixteen days. In one sense, the difference between us was merely gender-related, simply anatomical: I had more flesh on my rear end, and I did not have testicles. Ulay's butt was so thin that his bones were almost in direct contact with the chair through his skin.

But we also had different expectations about *Gold Found by the Artists*. He thought that when he stood up in the middle of the performance, I would stand, too—and I didn't. My thinking was simply that he had reached his limit, but I hadn't reached mine. To me, the work was holy, and the work came before everything else.

Maybe another difference between us was my partisan heritage, the walk-through-walls toughness my parents had passed along to me. There was also an echo of *Expansion in Space*, when Ulay walked away and I kept pushing the column.

Whatever it was, it got under his skin and festered. We continued performing *Gold Found by the Artists*, but things between us became subtly different. And then not so subtly.

When we'd done pieces like *Relation in Space* or *Light/Dark*, running into each other or slapping each other, or *AAA-AAA*, in which we screamed at each other till my voice or Ulay's gave out, we were getting our aggressions out, letting off steam. Discharging energy. But the moment we were quiet and meditative together in a performance, building up energy, something else began to happen, and it wasn't good.

⌒

We returned to Amsterdam recharged. We had decided to perform *Gold Found by the Artists* ninety times over the next five years, in museums and galleries all around the world. Except that we'd come up with a new name for the piece: *Nightsea Crossing*.

The title was not to be taken literally: the performance was not about crossing the sea by night. It was about crossing the unconscious— *nightsea* meant something unknown, the thing we'd discovered when we went deepest with the Aborigines, farthest into the desert. It was about invisible presence.

From March to September 1982, we performed *Nightsea Crossing* over forty-nine days, in Amsterdam, Chicago, New York, Toronto, a number of times in Germany (in Marl, Düsseldorf, Berlin, Cologne, *documenta* in Kassel) in Ghent, Belgium, and finishing in Lyon, France.

Here there was an explosion.

Once again because of excruciating pain in his butt and abdomen (I suspect his spleen was enlarged again), Ulay had to get up and leave in the middle of the eight hours. And once again I stayed seated.

Before the next performance, we argued. It was the same fight as before: he felt I should have risen and left the gallery in solidarity; I felt, strongly, that the integrity of the piece took precedence over any personal considerations. It was the same fight, only this time it escalated into screaming, and then all at once Ulay slapped me, hard, in the face.

This was not a performance piece, this was real life. It was the last thing I was expecting. The slap stung; tears came to my eyes. It was the first and last time he ever hit me in anger; he later apologized. But a boundary had been breached.

⌒

On our birthday in 1982, Ulay got a phone call from Germany: his mother was dying. He packed a small bag and went to her side at once. I stayed in Amsterdam, not because I wanted to, but because Ulay did not want me to come along with him.

He stayed with her in the hospital for her last days; after she died, he called me and I came to attend her funeral. That night, he told me he wanted to conceive a child with me. I refused, for the same reason as before: I was and would always be an artist, absolutely. Having a child would just get in the way. And now not having a child was one more thing in the way of my relationship with Ulay.

We were exhausted, and so we took a break. At the end of the year we traveled to northeast India, to visit Bodh Gaya, the place where Buddha received his enlightenment.

Siddhartha Gautama was a prince who lived in a palace with the king. Everything was done for him, and he never knew how it looked outside the walls, in the real world of India. And one day his manservant, who was also his friend, said, "Let's go outside of the walls, just to look around." So for the first time they opened the door of the castle, and went out.

Siddhartha was shocked at what he saw: poverty, hunger, leprosy, people dying in the streets. He said, "If the world looks like this, I don't want to be a prince in a palace." So he renounced his princehood. He adopted the clothing of an untouchable, just dirty patches and rags, and with his manservant, began looking for the truth. He wanted to find a way free from suffering. He wanted to know what life was all about: why people were poor and sick and dying, why people got old, what death itself was. He wanted to experience enlightenment. He spent years searching.

But at one point he had all but given up. He had spoken to holy men, he had practiced yoga and the highest degrees of meditation. And then he said, "This is all nonsense." He was in Bodh Gaya, where a big Bodhi tree whose leaves looked like a flame stood alongside a little river. Siddhartha decided to sit under the tree without eating or drinking anything until he had achieved enlightenment.

He sat beneath the tree for many days, meditating. A cobra passed by and saw him: the sun was so fierce that the snake rose up to make a shadow to cool him. Siddhartha sat for many days more, turning to skin and bones. Soon he was on the verge of death.

It happened that in the neighborhood, a young girl from a rich family was tending her family's ninety-nine cows. When she saw this young man, so thin, meditating, she said, "Oh my God, he's going to die, he's starving." So she took a huge pot and milked all ninety-nine cows, and then she cooked the milk down to its creamy essence, and then she cooked rice in that concentrated milk, and then she put the mixture in a golden bowl. And she went to Siddhartha and gave it to him. He felt guilty at breaking his meditation, but he realized that if he starved to death, the meditation would be over. So he ate this delicious rice dish, and the food gave him back his energy. He handed the golden bowl back to her, but she refused to accept it. The girl turned her back and left.

Now Siddhartha felt doubly guilty. He had interrupted his meditation, and he had taken this girl's golden bowl. So he went to the river and said to himself, "I am going to throw this bowl in the river. If it goes downstream, I will never receive enlightenment. If it goes upstream, maybe I have a chance." He threw the golden bowl in the water, and it floated upstream. But by now he was so exhausted that he went back to the Bodhi tree and fell into a deep sleep—and woke up enlightened.

This is how I read the story: that to achieve a goal, you have to give *everything* until you have nothing left. And it will happen by itself. That's really important. This is my motto for every performance. I give every single gram of energy, and then things either happen or they don't. This is why I don't care about criticism. I only care about criticism when I know I didn't give 100 percent. But if I give everything—and then 10 percent more than everything—it doesn't matter what they say.

Bodh Gaya is a kind of mecca of every temple you can imagine—Burmese, Vietnamese, Thai, Japanese, Chinese, Sufi, Christian. Every kind of religion has a little headquarters there, and people come to sit in Samadhi meditation for a long period of time. It's a huge pilgrimage place, and the best time to go there is around the time of the full moon, when the energies are strongest.

The Sufi temple there is well-known. We had corresponded for a long time with a Sufi philosopher and master, and we made an appointment to meet him at Bodh Gaya. At the time, I wasn't particularly interested in Tibet, but Sufism was very important to me. I was reading the poetry of Rumi, and I was fascinated by the dervish dances and everything else.

So we arrived in Bodh Gaya, and we were looking for a place to stay. There were no hotels there, just a few guest rooms. But the Chinese temple was huge, and it had these very Spartan dormitories—basically just areas with wooden benches where you could unroll your sleeping bag and stay for hardly any money, about a half dollar a night. It was already dark, and we went there, and we found a couple of available benches.

We ate something and then we went to sleep. In the middle of the night, I had to go to pee. You had to go outside, because there was no bathroom, just an outhouse some meters off. It was very dark, and I didn't have a flashlight—I was just feeling my way. And I tripped over a step and fell, badly twisting my ankle. When I woke up the next morning my ankle was grotesquely swollen, blue, and hurting like hell. I couldn't walk at all on that foot.

Yet at the same time, we had an appointment with the Sufi master at three o'clock that afternoon. This felt like a matter of life and death—we *had* to see him. Ulay was very doubtful about my ankle. I said, "At least let's go to the temple; maybe we can do it somehow."

We got in a pedicab and went to the temple. And there it was—at the top of a big hill, three hundred steps up. I said, "Oh my God." And then I said to Ulay, "You know what I'm going to do? I'm going to crawl up the steps. I am going to be there at three o'clock, but I am going to take my time." We bought a couple of umbrellas, because the sun was blazing. It was ten in the morning, and I started to crawl up the steps.

Ulay walked straight up and I went up on my butt—slowly, slowly. I had a little food, some water, and my umbrella. The sun was terrible, the pain was terrible. But by three o'clock, I had made it.

At exactly three P.M., they brought us to a special chamber in the temple. I sat down with my foot up on a chair, with a towel wrapped around it—the ankle looked like hell, and it hurt worse than ever. Then the Sufi master arrived and sat in front of us. The first thing he did was look at my ankle. "What happened?" he asked. I told him the story. He said, "But how did you make it up the steps?" I told him I'd started at ten in the morning, and crawled up. He seemed impressed.

Then we had a conversation. It was very interesting—we discussed the passage between life and death, how the soul can leave the body through the center of the fontanel of the head. These were all questions I'd been interested in for a long time.

At the end, a couple of disciples served us tea. And at the end of the tea, the master said, "Please take it easy and finish your tea—I have another meeting. It was very pleasant to meet you." He left, and we sat there finishing our tea. I was postponing the inevitable: I knew that I would soon have to stand up and go back down the three hundred steps. Then I stood up—and I had no pain. Zero. It was very strange, because the ankle was still swollen. I had heard that these people had the power to remove pain, but this was the first time I experienced it myself. I simply walked down the steps. The ankle was swollen for another three weeks, but the pain never returned.

We'd been there a few days already, and there were rumors that the teacher of the Dalai Lama was coming. This was Ling Rinpoche, the most important teacher of all. It was said he was going to come to the Tibetan temple. I'd never been to a Tibetan temple.

Someone said to me that if I wanted to see him and get his blessing, I should go and buy this special white shawl. When I stood in front of him, I was to give him the shawl. He would then bless the shawl and put it around my neck.

We went and bought our shawls, then joined a big line in front of the temple. Ling Rinpoche was inside. We waited for a long time, then I finally got to the front. He was an old man, at least eighty, and he was sitting in the lotus position. He had a big belly under his red robe. I gave him the shawl. And he gave the shawl back, but he did something that I hadn't seen him do for other people. He gave me a tiny finger-flick on the center of my forehead—very gentle—and smiled.

Ulay came after me, but I didn't see his interaction with Ling Rinpoche. I just went to the rear of the temple and sat down. And about five minutes later, my body felt like it was on fire. I turned strawberry-red, and I began weeping uncontrollably—great gulping sobs, bursting from my chest. I couldn't stop. I was so embarrassed that I had to leave the temple, and I still kept crying for the next three hours. My whole face was deformed.

I kept wondering: "Why am I weeping like this? What's going on?" Then it began to dawn on me: there was something about this man who had flicked my forehead so gently, something unbelievably humble and innocent and pure. I think that innocence opened my heart. If that man had told me to open the window and jump, for whatever reason, I would have done it. It was something I'd never experienced—complete surrender. Pure love. It came so unexpectedly, like a wave.

Then His Holiness the Dalai Lama arrived, and we attended his spiritual talks. He was so easy to meet in those days; he talked to everybody. I learned one very important thing at that meeting. He said that you can tell the most terrible truths if you first open the human heart with humor. Otherwise, the heart closes and nothing comes in. It was such a beautiful experience just to be in his presence. But this was only our first encounter with him; there would be many more.

Afterward, we did a twenty-one-day retreat in Vipassana meditation. Vipassana is about mindfulness: of breathing, thoughts, feelings, actions. We fasted, and we did everything—sitting, standing, lying down, walking, even eating—in slow motion, in order to better understand what we were actually doing. Vipassana would later become one of the cornerstones of my Abramović Method.

⌒

We were back in Amsterdam, staying at Christine Koenig's house. After the heat of Bodh Gaya, it was a very rough winter—it was so cold, even indoors, that the toilets were frozen. There's a picture of me from that time, peeing in Christine's sink: I wasn't doing it to show off, but because it was the only place to go.

One day Christine returned from town and told me she'd run into a friend who said, "I saw Ulay's son, and he's looking more and more like him."

"Which son?" I asked. The only son I knew about was in Germany. When I asked Ulay if it was true, if he had another son in Amsterdam, he denied it, saying people were gossiping and trying to break us up.

⌒

Early in 1983, our Belgian friend Michael Laub brought us to Thailand to help with a video work he'd been commissioned to do; instead, we wound up conceiving our own video idea, which Michael produced for Belgian TV: it was called *City of Angels*.

Michael Laub and me, Bombay, 1999

The piece took place north of Bangkok in Ayutthaya, the ruined former capital destroyed by the Burmese army in a war against the Siamese in the eighteenth century. We wanted to give a rich sense of this strange and wonderful place, with its many ravaged temples, and we had very strict rules. First, only local people—a beggar from the streets, a rickshaw driver, fruit sellers in the market, young guys who drove boats on the canals, a little girl—would appear in the video; Ulay and I would not be on camera at all. There would be no narration: the only language heard would be Thai, so the music of people's speech rather than the sense of what they said would be in the foreground. And to lend the piece visual beauty, we shot only in the very early morning, just after sunrise, and in the late afternoon, around sunset.

This was a brand-new thing for us, the first time a piece of ours was all about people other than ourselves. We wanted to capture, in sight and sound, the strangeness of the life among these ruins, and the past deaths they signified. In an especially mesmerizing sequence, a beggar stood with a mirror in one hand and a sword in the other: as the mirror reflected the rays of the setting sun, the beggar slowly lowered the sword toward his head, transforming before our eyes into a mythic hero. In another scene, the camera seemed to float over a long line of adults and children lying on the ground, hand in hand, until it stopped on a shot of a turtle—which poked its head out of its shell and walked quickly away.

It felt important to bring the rich cultures we were experiencing into our work. Later that year we conceived of a way to expand on *Nightsea Crossing* that would do exactly that.

The idea was to have a circular table this time, with four people seated around it, two pairs facing each other: Ulay and I, and, representing two of the places that had been so important to us, an Australian Aborigine and a Tibetan monk. We would call the piece *Nightsea Crossing Conjunction*.

Now that I think of it, besides being an expansion, perhaps this new piece was also a way of diffusing the intense pressure that had built up between Ulay and me every time we performed *Nightsea Crossing*.

The Dutch government and the Museum Fodor of Amsterdam agreed to sponsor *Conjunction*. The museum's curators tried to bring a monk from Tibet—only to discover that most Tibetan monks did not have passports! Instead, they somehow managed to locate a monk in a Tibetan monastery in Switzerland. Meanwhile Ulay returned to the Australian outback and reconnected with the Pintupi. When he asked his old friend Watuma the medicine man if he would like to come to Europe to perform with us, Watuma laughed and said he wouldn't just like to; he would love to.

We performed *Nightsea Crossing Conjunction* over four days in April, in a Lutheran church in Amsterdam. This time, in deference to our guests, we did the piece for four hours at a time rather than eight: not a terrible ordeal, but not exactly a walk in the park, either. On the first day we began at dawn; on the second, at noon; on the third, at sunset; and on the fourth, at midnight. The round table at which the four of us sat—Ulay and I, in chairs with arms, at the circle's east and west points; Watuma and the monk, Ngawang Soepa Lueyar, on cushions at north and south—was about eight feet in diameter and covered in beautiful gold leaf. Ngawang sat serenely in the lotus position; Watuma, on the other hand, sat with his legs twisted tensely beneath him, like the watchful hunter he was—if a rabbit had run by, I swear he would have jumped and caught it.

This was a truly pioneering piece. These two cultures, the Aboriginal and the Tibetan, had never met before. I think we helped open the rest of the world to the other worlds. Today, multiculturalism is commonplace. Then it was brand-new, so new that there was grumbling in Holland about public funds having been spent on this strange and immaterial work. Frank Lubbers, one of the Museum Fodor curators, had a wonderful response. "With the same amount of money that would buy you a middle-class car, you got a Rolls-Royce," he said.

Years later, an amazing thing happened. In the mid-1980s, while the late Bruce Chatwin was in the outback researching *The Songlines*, his great book about the Australian Aborigines, he interviewed a tribesman whom he called Joshua. As Chatwin described him, Joshua was an exuberant middle-aged man, "all leg and less body, very dark-skinned in a black cowboy hat." The Aborigine described (and sang) for the writer a number of "Dreamings," or songlines: one described the perentie, a huge, carnivorous lizard native to the outback; others told of fire, wind, grass, the spider, the porcupine. And then there was a songline that Joshua called "Big Fly One."

"Aboriginals, when tracing a Songline in the sand, will draw a series of lines with circles in between," Chatwin wrote.

The line represents a stage in the Ancestor's journey (usually a day's march). Each circle is a "stop," "waterhole," or one of the Ancestor's campsites. But the story of the Big Fly One was beyond me.

It began with a few straight sweeps; then it wound into a rectangular maze, and finally ended in a series of wiggles. As he traced each section, Joshua kept calling a refrain, in English, "Ho! Ho! They got the money over there."

I must have been very dim-witted that morning: it took me ages to realize that this was a Qantas Dreaming. Joshua had once flown into London. The "maze" was London Airport: the Arrival gate, Health, Immigration, Customs, and then the ride into the city on the Underground. The "wiggles" were the twists and turns of the taxi, from the tube station to the hotel.

In London, Joshua had seen all the usual sights—the Tower of London, Changing of the Guard and so on—but his real destination had been Amsterdam.

The ideogram for Amsterdam was even more perplexing. There was a circle. There were four smaller circles around it. . . . Eventually, it dawned on me that this was some kind of round-table conference at which he, Joshua, had been one of four participants. The others, in a clockwise direction, had been "a white one, a Father one," "a thin one, a red one," "a black one, a fat one."

It turned out that Chatwin had changed the tribesmen's names for his book. In reality, "Joshua" was none other than Watuma, and the very strange scene he was describing was *Nightsea Crossing Conjunction*. The "white one, Father one" was Ulay, the "black one, fat one" was Ngawang, and the "thin one, red one" was me.

What made it all even stranger was that we had actually become part of Aboriginal culture—and Dream Time.

We immediately followed the sublimely successful *Nightsea Crossing Conjunction* with one of the worst pieces I have ever done.

Positive Zero was our first theater piece, and it was an ambitious one: this time, there would be not one Tibetan lama but four (we managed to find monks with passports), two Aborigines (but not Watuma, who had gone back to Australia), and Ulay and I. The Holland Festival and de Appel sponsored the piece; Dutch Public Television was to film it; and the Goethe-Institut, the Austria Council, and the India Arts Council funded it. A big production.

The performance was to be a series of tableaux vivants based on tarot cards, depicting conflicts between youth and age, male and female—very serious. The lamas would chant, the tribesmen would play their didgeridoos, and as we rehearsed these staged tableaux with people who had never been on stage before, I began to realize this was not a good piece.

Maybe it would jell as we got further along, I thought. It didn't.

And then came the night of the premiere, at the Royal Theatre Carré in Amsterdam: the public was there, and there was no turning back. In addition to this I had come down with a virus and had a fever of 104 degrees. The whole evening felt like sheer, nightmarish delirium. In one scene, I cradled Ulay on my lap in a *Pietà*: in a screen-grab from the taped performance, you can see my eyes are red—not from mourning but from my high temperature. It was the only real moment in the entire piece. The rest was kitschy and shitty and descriptive and naive—incredibly naive. It was just bad.

The four lamas of *Positive Zero* stayed in our home during rehearsals for the piece and for a couple of days afterward. Every morning they would wake up at four A.M. to meditate, and then they would make this tea, Tibetan tea. Tibetan soup was more like it—it was thick and rich, full of butter and salt and milk. I remember one morning at around five thirty I was awakened by laughter, and not just a little bit: loud, hearty laughter that went on and on, coming from the kitchen. I went in to see what was going on, and I found that it was the lamas who were the source of all the hilarity. I asked the translator, "What is happening with these monks?" He said, "The bubbling of the milk has made them so happy." I was astonished.

Positive Zero might have been terrible, but at least the performers were paid well. The lamas received 10,000 gulden—so much money for them that an entire monastery of seven hundred monks could live for four years on it! After the performance, on their last night in Holland, they went shopping. The stores in Amsterdam were open late on Thursday night.

So the monks took their 10,000 gulden and went downtown with their translator, beautifully dressed in their red robes—they all looked like the Dalai Lama. And they were gone for hours: seven o'clock, eight o'clock, nine o'clock, ten o'clock passed. We were saying, "Oh my God, the monastery money—it's gone. They've spent it all." Finally they returned at ten fifteen, after the shops had closed, and they were super-happy, extremely excited. I said, "What did you buy?" They grinned with delight and showed me: two umbrellas.

⌒

Failures are very important—they mean a great deal to me. After a big failure, I go into a deep depression and a very dark part of my body, but soon afterward I come back to life again, alive to something else. I always question artists who are successful in whatever they do—I think what that means is that they're repeating themselves and not taking enough risks.

If you experiment, you have to fail. By definition, experimenting means going to territory where you've never been, where failure is very possible. How can you know you're going to succeed? Having the courage to face the unknown is so important. I love to live in the spaces in between, the places where you leave the comforts of your home and your habits behind and make yourself completely open to chance.

This is why I love the story of Christopher Columbus—Columbus, who was sent by the queen of Spain to discover a different way to go to India, who was given a crew of convicts, because everybody was convinced the earth was flat and you would fall off the edge if you sailed across the Atlantic. And then, on their way out into the unknown, they made one last stop on El Héro, in the Canary Islands, and had dinner—I always imagine this dinner, the night before setting out to God knows where, before taking this unfathomable risk. I imagine Columbus sitting at the table with the convicts, all of them feeling this might be their last supper together.

That must have taken even more courage than going to the moon, in my point of view. You think you might fall off the edge of the earth, and then you discover a new continent.

Then again, there's always the chance that you really might fall off the edge of the earth.

7.

Two stories that turn into one story.

I had a friend in Belgrade, a very intelligent guy who went to the film academy with my brother. His name was Lazar Stojanovic. And for his thesis work, Lazar made an amazing avant-garde film called Plastic Jesus. *The plot is indescribable, but basically it was an allegory about Tito. Tito was the Plastic Jesus, and he was played by the filmmaker (and later performance artist) Tomislav Gotovac.*

The movie was hilarious, and deeply satirical about Tito and the decline of the Yugoslav political system. There was one long scene in which the leader debated with his commanders about whether it is better to go into battle shaved or unshaven. Finally they decided it was best to be unshaven during the battles but that after winning, they should be clean-shaven.

The head of Lazar's thesis committee gave the film the highest possible grade. But then, in a government crackdown, the committee head was questioned by the secret police and fired by the academy, and Stojanovic was sentenced to four years in prison for his anti-Tito film.

Now we go to deepest Bosnia, where among poverty-stricken villages on the edge of deep forest there was a game warden who everyone hated. This warden was very strict—if villagers shot a few rabbits out of season, he would write down all their names and turn them in to the police.

So the peasants decided to get revenge. They happened to know that almost every day, the game warden went to a forest clearing, whistled a signal that brought a young female bear out from the trees, then fucked the young bear.

The villagers told the police what was going on, and the police and the villagers hid in the bushes and watched while the game warden walked into the clearing and whistled. Very soon, the bear came into the meadow, and the game warden did it again. The police then arrested the warden. Why? Not on moral grounds, but because bears were protected wildlife under national laws. The game warden went to prison.

Now back to my friend Stojanovic. After four years in prison, he finally got out and we threw him a big party. Lots of food, lots of drinking and laughter. Four years for making a movie? We still couldn't believe it. Somebody asked Lazar, "What was the worst part about prison?" And he said, "As an intellectual, the worst thing in the prison for me was having to share a cell with the game warden who fucked the bear."

Before the lamas returned to Tibet, they told us they wanted to make *puja*, a big ceremony for removing obstacles and ensuring a long life. The ceremony was to start at five in the morning, with prayers and bells and chanting, and offerings of food and fruit and flowers, and the monks wanted all the organizers of the Holland Festival to be present, along with Ulay and me. The *puja* was to take place in our house, so we had to wake up anyway, but then it turned out that the other five people, for different reasons, didn't come. One couldn't wake up, one was feeling sick, another one forgot—various things. So with just Ulay and me, the monks made this entire *puja*, ensuring long life, and redeeming the negative energy of *Positive Zero*. Then they went home.

Positive Zero had taken so much out of us, and turned out so terribly, that we were exhausted: we decided to go on holiday.

Do you remember Edmondo, the performance artist from our spice loft, who had been madly in love with the depressed Swedish teenager who never spoke? After he forced her to talk, she moved back to Sweden, and he was distraught—but then she wrote him a letter and said that the whole problem had been Amsterdam. She just hated living in the city. If he lived in the country, she said, she would come back to him.

It turned out that Edmondo's grandfather, the pyromaniac, owned a farmhouse in Tuscany. So Edmondo told his grandfather, "I don't want to wait until you die—can you give me this little house, and the farm, so I can bring my girl there and we can live together happily?" So his grandfather gave him the house. The Swedish girl came back, and they went to Tuscany to live happily ever after—except that after three months, she fell in love with the shepherd next door and got pregnant by him and left Edmondo, who was now distraught once more and desperate for company. Could we—Ulay and I, Michael Laub, Marinka, and a new friend, an artists' agent we had just started working with, Michael Klein—come and visit him?

A free vacation in Tuscany sounded perfect. So we drove down there, only to find that Edmondo's farmhouse was an utter ruin, with only half a roof and rats running around everywhere. There was no way we could sleep there, we realized. So we went to the village nearby to buy a tent so we could sleep on Edmondo's property.

The Tuscan landscape was beautiful, but Edmondo's farm was totally out of whack. There was a rat embryo in the olive oil. He had chickens with epilepsy—every time you fed them, they would fall over. He had a pig called Rodolfina who had a hernia, and a donkey who had fallen in love with the pig: the donkey kind of didn't know he was a donkey, and he slept with Rodolfina. The only successful part about this farm was Edmondo's marijuana crop, which he watered regularly—he was always walking around with a joint in his mouth.

So we pitched our tent and stayed there, and it was a lovely holiday. We had been there about a week when Ulay went to the village one morning to phone de Appel in Amsterdam, to find out whether any performance offers had landed in our shoebox. When he came back, his face was drained of all color—he could hardly talk. I said, "What happened?"

It turned out that all five people who had been instrumental in the Holland Festival—all five people who'd missed the *puja* ceremony that morning—had died in a plane crash in Switzerland. Wies Smals had been one of them, along with her six-month-old son. They had gone to Geneva to see an installation by Daniel Buren, the French conceptual artist, and were on their way back to Amsterdam. It was a small jet: the pilot didn't have much experience flying it, and they hit a sudden downdraft over the Alps and went into a mountain.

It was unthinkable, really—an absolute nightmare. We packed everything and drove straight back to Amsterdam, a ten-hour drive.

When we arrived, it turned out the bodies were still in Switzerland. I remember walking into the gallery, and everything was just as it had been: our shoebox, Wies's glasses, three apples sitting on the table. . . . Little tiny things, but the kind of things that mean so much. I remember thinking how very much these small things mattered.

While everyone was standing around in confusion, I went into the kitchen and filled a bucket with hot water. Then I got a couple of rags, and I started washing the gallery floor. At this moment I needed to do something real—something very simple.

Then the most incredible thing happened. The bodies were brought back, a funeral had to be organized. And during this time, a letter arrived from the monks who had appeared in *Positive Zero*. The envelope was postmarked the day before the plane crash. And the letter said, "We are so sorry for your loss."

Wies Smals at the Royal Palace, Amsterdam, 1979

I had believed that happiness could protect you. I had thought it was like an invisible shield that guarded you from all misfortune. Wies had been so joyous about having her baby—she was in love. Surely nothing could ever harm them. Their deaths brought an end to that belief.

⌒

From one crack in the earth to another.

At first, like almost everybody else, we'd thought that the Chinese had built the Great Wall to protect themselves from Genghis Khan and the Mongol tribes. But as we did more reading, we found that this wasn't true. What we discovered was that the Wall had been designed in the form of a gigantic dragon, as a mirror image of the Milky Way. The ancient Chinese had started the Wall by sinking twenty-five ships at the edge of the Yellow Sea in order to create the foundation for the dragon's head. Then, after the dragon rose from the sea, its body twisted across the landscape and through the mountains, corresponding exactly to the shape of the Milky Way, until it reached the Gobi Desert, where the tail was buried.

Now we made a formal proposal, once again to the Museum Fodor curators who'd helped us get the government funding for *Nightsea Crossing Conjunction.*

We wrote:

That edifice which best expresses the notion of the Earth as a living being is the Great Wall of China. In the case of the Great Wall it is a mythical dragon who lives under this long fortress like structure. . . . The dragon's color is green, and the dragon represents the unification of two natural elements, earth and air. Though it lives underground, it symbolizes the vital energy on the surface of the earth. The Great Wall marks the dragon's movement through the earth, and so embodies the same "vital energy." In modern scientific terms the Wall lies on what are called geodetic force lines, or ley lines. It is a direct link to the forces of the earth.

Our plan was for me to start the walk at the Wall's eastern, female end, the Gulf of Bohai on the Yellow Sea, and for Ulay to start at the Wall's western, male end, the Jiayu Pass in the Gobi Desert. After walking a total of 2,500 kilometers each, we would meet in the middle.

About our original plan, to marry when we met there, we now spoke less and less.

The truth is that my relationship with Ulay was falling apart. Since the death of his mother—specifically since I had refused, on the night of the funeral, to conceive a child—we had been furious at each other, but saying little to nothing about it.

Actually, our transition from frequent and ardent lovers to a couple living in mere physical parallel had begun with *Nightsea Crossing*. The performance required abstinence and distance during our off hours. And Ulay wanted so badly to do the piece all the way through, but he kept having to stop, which was killing him—and which distanced us still further. And we were still performing the piece here and there, trying to reach our goal of doing it ninety times.

He was taking his humiliation out on me. He would flirt with waitresses, airline stewardesses, gallery assistants—anybody—right in front of me. I feel certain, in retrospect, that he was having affairs.

That summer we went to Sicily to make another video piece, one inspired in a way by *City of Angels*. In the new piece, as in *City of Angels*, we would not appear. We had spent time there before, and the division between the sexes fascinated us: the women were always indoors, dressed in black and sitting in clusters as they talked together; the men were always outside, talking in their own groups. We wanted to base our film on these phenomena.

We were in Trapani, which is in the middle of nowhere. When we first got there, we wrote a newspaper advertisement saying that we were looking for women from age seventy to a hundred to appear in our film, and also any virgins from eighty to ninety years old. We would pay them for their time, we said. The ad went in the paper. And then we sat in our hotel for three days, and no one came. Absolutely nobody. Then, on the fourth day, a very proper older lady arrived, dressed like an elegant widow. She had a friend with her, similarly dressed, but the first lady did all the talking. She said, "What do you want? Tell us the story."

So we told them, in all our enthusiasm, about the film we had in mind. We were drinking coffee together, in small Italian cups. The woman looked at me. Then she said, "We're going to help you; we're going to talk to our brother." And on the next day, the entire town mobilized to help us. We were given an old mansion to film in, as well as full permission to film anywhere outdoors. Young men materialized to help carry the equipment, and even more important, our equipment was safe. There in Sicily, where everything was controlled by the Mafia, I felt like your belongings could vanish in three seconds if you didn't watch them like a hawk. Now we could leave our cameras in our unlocked car and nothing would be touched— the Mafia protected us. I think they just liked us, because we were so insanely strange: they were entertained by us. We even found two virgins, eighty-six-year-old twin sisters. They blushed very sweetly when their moment on camera came.

We called the film *Terra degli Dea Madre*—roughly translated, "Land of the Matriarchs." In it, the camera's point of view floats eerily from a dining room full of old ladies chatting together (the soundtrack is me speaking in tongues) out to a cemetery, where a group of men in black suits and white shirts stand talking in their rough voices. To create this floating effect, we used a Steadicam. Ulay, the camera enthusiast, was fascinated by this device and wanted to try it out. It was a big, heavy apparatus—you had to strap yourself into it, and almost as soon as he was wearing it, he felt something in his back crack. No pain, but a definite crack.

That night, after we had dinner at a local restaurant, we went for ice cream in the village square. The waiter put the bill on the table, and just as Ulay reached for it, a sudden gust of wind blew the paper up in the air. He playfully grabbed for it—then fell to the ground in agony. His back had turned into a mass of muscle spasms.

He looked so scared: he was in overwhelming pain. And the local hospital was no help at all—if you went to the bathroom, another patient would come and take your bed from you: families were literally sitting on patients' beds to hold them. After a couple of bad nights there, we flew back to Holland and checked Ulay into a decent hospital. He was diagnosed with a herniated disc, and the doctor wanted to operate immediately. Ulay refused to have the operation.

He was afraid to have his back operated on, but I believe he was afraid of many things at that point—afraid and angry and confused. We found an Ayurvedic doctor, Thomas, who began giving him alternative treatments, a combination of acupressure and the application of medicinal oils, and his condition improved. But our relationship continued to decline, even more rapidly than before.

Since his back was in a delicate state, our sex life stopped altogether. For almost a year, I was reduced to being his nurse, and nothing I did for him was ever good enough. If I brought him food, it was always too cold or too salty, or too something else. If I offered him sympathy, he was distant and rejecting. I was hurt and angry, but there was more: I was now in my late thirties, and feeling fat and frumpy and bad about myself in general.

The following spring, we got an invitation to teach a two-month summer course at the San Francisco Art Institute. It was a very well-paid position, and by now Ulay was feeling much better, but he didn't want to go. He said, "I think we need time off; you go and I'll stay." So I went, and he stayed.

⌒

The first thing I did when I got to San Francisco was to announce a five-day fast for the students in my performance-art workshop, an exercise for improving willpower and concentration. As always, I participated.

The second thing I did was to have a mad affair.

This was the first time I'd ever been unfaithful to Ulay. And this had been building up in me for a long time. He hadn't exactly been making me feel wanted or desirable. And there was a simple biological fact: I might've been getting close to forty, but I was still a young woman. While Ulay recuperated, he claimed to have become interested in certain tantric practices that would unleash his kundalini life force. Abstinence, he said, was part of the program.

This was not my program.

Robin Winters, a painter I'd met years before in Amsterdam, was also teaching a summer course at the Institute. And one night after a lecture we found ourselves alone together, and we started kissing, and that was that. For the next week we did little else but have sex. It was great, but then I started to feel terribly guilty, and I just stopped. Then it was time for me to go home.

I'd been gone for two months, the longest Ulay and I had ever been apart. In those days there was no e-mail, of course, and overseas phone calls were ridiculously expensive. We'd corresponded, but only a tiny bit. In his letters he didn't say much more than that he was doing fine. And my guilt kept boring its way into me.

Ulay was waiting for me at the airport in Amsterdam. He looked thinner than ever, and I could tell just by looking at him that he was still in some physical pain. This only increased my guilt. On the drive home, we chatted about this and that, but the pressure was building up inside me, and then it just blew: I burst into tears and told him everything. It had only been one week, I said; it meant nothing. I was really, really sorry.

His response amazed me. He was calm; he was sympathetic. "I understand," he said. "Don't worry; everything is fine." *Wow. Maybe the tantric discipline really has worked wonders for him*, I thought.

This is the greatest man I've ever known. How inconceivable, how beautiful, that he really understands.

I'd landed in the morning. It had been a very long flight from San Francisco to Holland, and I fell asleep as soon as I got home. I finally woke up at about six P.M., and Ulay wasn't around, so I went to the square with a couple of friends to have coffee. I told them about everything that had happened—the affair, my confession, Ulay's amazing reaction. They looked at each other. Then they told me: three days after I'd left for San Francisco, Ulay had taken up with a girl from Surinam, and he'd lived with her in our home literally until the morning I returned.

I went back home, and when Ulay returned, I asked him if it was true. He said he had gone to some opening where he met this Surinam girl, and then they went to eat something, and they both got some kind of food poisoning from the fish they ate. So they went to the hospital to get their stomachs pumped, and then he invited her home and she stayed.

He was actually trying to enlist my sympathy!

Instead I went totally nuts. I smashed everything in the house, and when I ran out of things to smash, I re-smashed what I'd already smashed. It would've been one thing if he'd confessed to me when I confessed to him. But to leave it all on me and pretend he was above it all . . . the arrogance (or cowardice) of it was breathtaking. After smashing a final dish, I walked out and went to stay with friends. After a day, I came home to pack, and then I moved out for good. And then I went to India.

He came to India after me, and we started again. All my friends told me it was a terrible idea. I should have listened.

⌒

The Museum Fodor curators agreed to help us with our Great Wall walk. Together with them we created a foundation, called Amphis, to move the project forward. We contacted the Chinese embassy in The

Hague to ask their advice. An official there told us, off the record, that the Chinese government would be more receptive to a film about walking the Wall than a performance piece celebrating the first people ever to do it. And one more thing: They didn't want us to be the first people to do it. One man at the embassy quoted Confucius: "It is impossible to walk a road that has never been walked before."

A long dance began.

The embassy put us in touch with an important group in Beijing, the China Association for the Advancement of International Friendship—the CAAIF. In reality, of course, they were just an arm of the Chinese government. We wrote to them about our project— this time mentioning that we wanted to make a film—and they wrote back very politely, but agreeing to nothing. They also added that though our proposed film sounded interesting, the idea of foreigners walking the Wall before a Chinese ever accomplished the feat seemed to demand further consideration.

Over the next couple of years we continued to write to the Chinese, and we continued to receive vague and polite replies about international friendship. After a while, we went to consult with a friend who was doing some business in China. We said, "Excuse me, what are we doing wrong? We can't move forward with this project." We showed him some of the letters. He looked at me and started laughing. "What's so funny?" we asked.

"You know," he said, "in the Chinese language there are seventeen ways to say no, and in this correspondence they've used all seventeen ways."

"What should we do?"

"You have to go through the Dutch minister of culture," he said. The government had a huge cultural foundation, he reminded me. Why hadn't we thought of this in the first place? So we sent the foundation our proposal and got an immediate response. A very interesting project, the government said. They wanted to talk to us. We were very excited.

The background of all this was that just at this moment, the Dutch government and the electronics company Philips were building a big factory in China—but at the same time, the Dutch government had signed a contract to build a submarine in Taiwan. Because of that contract, the Chinese ambassador had left the country in protest, and China had cut all ties with the Netherlands.

Strangely enough, the Dutch government saw our project as a way to restore relations with China. They canceled the submarine contract with Taiwan, and they proposed to China this wonderful friendship walk on the Great Wall. And the Chinese got interested, too, because they wanted the Philips factory. A long series of negotiations began.

Finally the Chinese said they would sign on to our project, but they wanted one million Dutch guilder—about $300,000—for security, accommodations, food, and guides. And this turned out to be just fine with the Dutch government: the price of restoring good relations with China. We were in the middle of the whole thing.

Then we were told we had to postpone our project for another year. We had no idea why.

And then, miraculously, a Chinese man walked the Wall.

In 1984, a remarkably short time after the Chinese government agreed to our proposal, a railway clerk from western China named Liu Yutian set out on a solo walk across the Great Wall. The official Chinese news release said that in 1982, Liu had "read an article in a newspaper that some foreign explorers were planning to explore the whole length of the Great Wall. . . . He was not happy after hearing that news. In his mind, the Great Wall belongs to the Chinese nation, and if someone was going to explore it, it should be a Chinese."

An interesting story. And fascinating timing.

A year later, we were invited to China for the first time—not to begin our project, but to meet the heroic Liu Yutian, the first man ever to walk the Great Wall, and to discuss our walk further. There was a big ceremony to celebrate our meeting with Liu; many photographs were taken. All the publicity made clear the fact that the Chinese man had gone first and Ulay and I would be second.

Beijing scared me. We felt under constant surveillance. There

Ulay with the first Chinese man to walk the Wall, 1988

were hardly any cars, just thousands of bicycles—only government officials had cars. We were housed in a concrete apartment block with a toilet: the rest had to go to the public toilet at the end of the street. But we had indoor plumbing—and we understood that this was luxury. It was all too reminiscent of the Eastern Bloc drabness of Belgrade, but so much worse: this was Communism combined with fanaticism. We sat through meeting after meeting, and I never had any idea what was really going on or if any progress was being made. And in this chilling atmosphere, Ulay and I were growing more and more distant from each other.

⌐

Because of his long association with Polaroid, Ulay had access to the company's giant, room-size camera in Boston. This camera took tremendous, literally life-size (80 by 88-inch) pictures. We made several series of these big Polaroids. One group, from *Modus Vivendi*, showed Ulay and me each posed as a hunched, weary figure carrying a box. His box was empty, mine was full. The images had a grave, timeless quality.

Our friend the artist's agent Michael Klein began to sell these giant pictures—to museums, banks, corporations—and for the first

Marina Abramović/Ulay, *Modus Vivendi*, Polaroids, 1985

time in our relationship, we weren't dirt poor. As always, I paid no attention to the money: Ulay took care of all that.

In the spring of 1986 we had a show of some of the giant Polaroids, also called "Modus Vivendi," at the Burnett Miller Gallery in Los Angeles. On the night of the opening there was a big crowd. Ulay hung around for a little bit, but then he said to me, "Oh, you know how to deal with people; I'm just going to have a walk." And he left.

He was gone for a couple of hours. It occurred to me once or twice during the opening that he was on quite a long walk. . . . Did I know, on some level, what was actually going on? Did I suspect? There I was, smiling and making small talk with people I had no interest in talking to, doing our business, while he was off somewhere screwing the gallery secretary, a pretty young Asian woman. Friends told me about it later. I wish they'd never told me.

This is when the failure of my working relationship with Ulay began.

For the last three years we were together, I was hiding, even from our closest friends, the fact that our relationship had fallen apart. I was hiding it from everybody, because I could not stand the idea of this failure. (And I was terrified—I kept thinking, *This is the moment you get cancer, when the emotions you're hiding make you sick.*) I had given up working on my own for an ideal that I thought was higher: making art together and creating this third element we called *that self*—an energy not poisoned by ego, a melding of male and female that to me was the highest work of art. I could not stand the idea that it actually didn't work.

And that we failed for the stupidest, pettiest reason—the failure of our domestic life—was the saddest thing of all. For me private life was part of the work, too. For me our collaboration was always about sacrificing everything for the bigger cause, the bigger idea. But in the end we failed because of smallness. . . .

⌒

We did the final performance of *Nightsea Crossing*, day ninety, in October 1986 at the Musée des Beaux-Arts in Lyon. Ulay wore black, I wore white. To commemorate the completion, the museum also held an exhibition of artifacts documenting our previous five years of work: there were photographs of the robes of various colors we'd worn for each of the performances; there were segments of the big round table we'd used for *Nightsea Crossing Conjunction*. The museum acquired for its collection the entire installation of *Nightsea Crossing*, as well as the Citroën van in which we lived for so long while crisscrossing Europe to perform our work.

Not long afterward, for the Kunstmuseum Bern, we did a piece called *Die Mond, Der Sonne* ("The Moon, The Sun") that consisted simply of two enormous black vases we'd made, exactly the size of our bodies: one had a slick and shiny surface; the other was matte, completely light-absorbing. The vases represented us and our inability to perform together anymore. And this piece was a clear end to our personal relationship.

Marina Abramović/Ulay, *Die Mond, Der Sonne* ("The Moon, The Sun"), twin lacquered vases, Kunstmuseum Bern, Switzerland, 1987

Maybe I should've seen something that happened on my fortieth birthday as an omen. Our friend Tony Korner, the owner of *Artforum*, threw Ulay and me a party on November 30, complete with a huge cake shaped like the Great Wall—it stretched all the way across a long dinner table, with a little figure of Ulay on one side and one of me on the other side. There were eighty-three candles in all, since he was forty-three and I was forty. And once all these candles were lit, they flared up and created a blaze that melted the cake and almost set the house on fire. How funny: a collapsing cake, to celebrate a collapsing relationship.

In early 1987 Ulay made another trip to China to continue the negotiations for our Wall walk. The Chinese were constantly changing the terms; it was infuriating. But then there was a breakthrough and we were finally given a definite date: the walk would take place that summer. I was to meet him in Thailand to make final plans for the piece.

I have to tell you my state of mind at this point: I felt like a failure. Ulay had cheated on me again and again, both behind my back and in plain sight. And so when I arrived in Bangkok, I was desperate. I was insane with jealousy, dying to know who he was having an affair with now, and determined to play a role: the happy woman who doesn't care. I was having a mad affair with a French writer, I told him; the sex was fantastic. It was a complete fabrication.

And it served the desired purpose—he instantly told me what he was up to. She was a rich, Waspy American, whose husband, a musician, was in prison in Thailand on a drug charge.

"Great!" I said, still in my role as the happy, liberated woman. "Why don't we have a ménage à trois?"

This was how low I had sunk. And sexual excitement had nothing to do with my idea.

But Ulay, naturally, was turned on—and surprised and delighted that I had morphed into a different woman. No more mad jealousy, no more scenes with smashing things. He smiled. "I'll ask her," he said.

And the next day, smiling again, he brought back her answer: it was fine with her, he said.

That night we went to the house where he was staying with her, a woman straight out of the world of rock and roll, and the two of them got really drunk and did a lot of cocaine. I didn't touch a thing, but soon, all three of us were naked. I couldn't have been less turned on. It's hard to explain the terrible state of mind I was in: *I had to see.*

I'll never forget that night for the rest of my life. First Ulay and I had sex, very briefly, and then the two of them fucked in front of me. And it was as if I didn't exist—even I somehow forgot that I existed.

Later, it was around five in the morning, and I was lying on the bed next to them, wide awake, while they slept, exhausted. I just lay there as the slow luminosity of the new day crept in, and the roosters began to crow outside. . . . And then I heard an old Thai woman in the kitchen, washing the dishes while preparing breakfast. I remember everything: the smell, the stillness, the two of them beside me in this bed. . . .

I had put myself in so much pain that I no longer felt any pain. It was like one of my performances, except that it wasn't—this was real life. But I didn't want it to be real. I felt nothing. People always say, when they're hit by a bus and lose a leg, that they feel no pain: that the nerves simply can't transport so much pain to the brain. It's a total overload. Yet I had done it on purpose. I had to do this. I had to put myself in this situation, to give myself this much emotional pain, in order to get rid of it, to exorcise him. And I did it. But the cost was very high.

I felt complete stillness, absolutely nothing. Numb. Then I got up, took a shower, and left. That was the moment I stopped liking his smell. And the moment I stopped liking his smell, it was over.

Later that day, I took a flight back to Amsterdam.

The Chinese had received their fee, and the date was set. Then suddenly they wanted more money. It was like something out of the Mafia. The Chinese government sent us a telegram demanding an additional 250,000 guilder, some $80,000, for "security and soft drinks." At this point the Dutch government had already paid them a huge amount; there was nothing left in the budget. But there was no alternative—too much time and money had already been invested. The additional funds had to be raised. And our summer start date was postponed.

The thought of spending another winter in Amsterdam with Ulay was unacceptable. I wanted to get as far away as possible, geographically and spiritually, so I decided to go to the Tushita monastery, in the foothills of the Himalayas, to do the Green Tara retreat. I had first learned about Green Tara, the Tibetan goddess who removes obstacles in your life, when I visited Bodh Gaya.

Now I had lots of obstacles. There were the problems with the Chinese; there were all the issues with Ulay. I was feeling miserable. This long retreat, I felt, could help cleanse me for walking the Wall.

The retreat was very strict. In complete isolation, seeing no one, talking to no one, you would repeat a certain mantra, one million, one hundred and eleven thousand, one hundred and eleven times—all while imagining you *were* Green Tara. The whole process took about three months. I was eager to begin.

I flew from Amsterdam to Delhi, and took a very long train ride north to Dharamsala, the home of the Dalai Lama, a beautiful little hillside village with a magnificent view of the snowy Himalayas. The Tushita monastery was in the hills above town. I arrived at about three o'clock in the afternoon and went to the information center, where a man told me, "You should stay here tonight and go to the monastery tomorrow morning—a rickshaw can take you then." I said, "No, no, no, please—I am not interested in staying overnight; I want to go to the monastery immediately. I can walk." I was single-minded about this. The guy said, "But it gets dark at around five thirty." And I said, "I was told that it's only a two-and-a-half-mile walk, maybe forty-five minutes. I'll be there by four or four thirty." The guy said, "There are lots of monkeys in the forest; you really shouldn't walk alone." I said, "Just tell me which road to take."

He showed me on a map, and the path looked very simple—just three turns. So with my rucksack on my back, I set out.

There really were monkeys in the forest, little nasty beasts, and they kept jumping at me as I walked: I kept having to shout at them and chase them away. I walked and walked, for over an hour. I was sure I'd taken every turn I was supposed to take—except now it was getting dark, and there was no sign of the monastery; there was no sign of anything. I was in the middle of nowhere, totally lost, with no idea what to do.

Then I saw a little light, far off among the trees.

I walked toward the light, and soon I saw it was coming from a small house in the forest. An old monk was standing in front of the house, washing his rice bowls. I said, "Tushita monastery, Tushita monastery"—and he laughed and laughed. "Come in, come in," he said. "Tea, tea." Hospitality is very important there, and there is always tea.

"No, no," I said. "Time, time, dark. Walk to monastery."

"No, no, no," he said. "Come in." He said nothing about the monastery. I realized I had no choice. It was his house, after all.

I went inside and followed the monk to the living room. And there in the middle of the living room sat the mummified body of Ling Rinpoche, the teacher of the Dalai Lama, the man who had gently flicked my forehead and made me weep uncontrollably in Bodh Gaya five years before. The body had been preserved in salt: it looked eerily alive.

The monk brought my tea, put it down on the table, and left, quietly closing the door behind him.

I had heard he'd died, three years after I met him. I thought that I would never see him again. Now here he was, and I had had to lose myself in the forest to find him.

The same feelings of overwhelming tenderness and love washed over me, once more, like a wave. I prostrated myself in front of him, weeping and weeping. After a while I sat up and drank my tea, just looking at Ling Rinpoche and shaking my head.

I think I stayed for about an hour. Then I went out and the old monk was just sitting there. "Tushita monastery?" I said.

"Tushita monastery is next door," he said.

And he took me by the hand and led me through the trees to the monastery, which was about a hundred meters away.

The Tushita monks greeted me, and I began. Scattered around the monastery, deep in the forest, were little retreat cells: tiny huts on raised platforms with room for just one sleeping bag and an altar. I was given my own hut, and my instructions.

I was to say the Tara prayer one million, one hundred and eleven thousand, one hundred and eleven times. Using prayer beads, I was to count each prayer I completed, and there was no relaxing—I was to pray and count for three hours, sleep for three hours, then wake up and pray and count for another three hours, over and over and over and over, all the while trying to imagine that I was Green Tara. I soon found, however, that this was very difficult to do. I couldn't stop thinking how unhealthy I would look if I were green.

Every morning, there would be a soft knock on the door of the hut, meaning one of the monks had left my food for me. There was no talking with the monks, no communication of any kind—the food would just be left, the monk would leave, and I would open the door and eat. There was just one vegetarian meal a day. Very bland—salt and spices were thought to excite the emotions. And a bottle of water. You were supposed to eat before noon.

I had some bad moments during the three months, some deep depressions. But repeating the mantra again and again and again has a stabilizing effect on the mind and body: your sleeping and awake states become one; dreams flow into reality. And the moment you step into this other state of mind, you are tapping into a limitless energy, a place where you can do anything you want. You're no longer little you with all your limitations—"poor Marina," the person who cries like a baby when she cuts herself slicing an onion. When this kind of freedom comes, it's as if you're connected with a cosmic consciousness. It's the same thing, I would soon find, that seems to happen in every good performance: you're on a larger scale; there are no more limits.

It was a very important lesson to learn.

After three months of counting prayers, I put a message outside my door saying that I had finished. Then the monks came and took me to the monastery, where I was supposed to burn all my possessions, making me newborn. The monks were very practical—you weren't supposed to burn your money or passport, or else they'd never be able to get rid of you. But you did have to give up anything that was important to you, and what was important to me was my sleeping bag. It was very expensive, very warm; it was like part of my body. I loved it. I burned it. And then I was free.

⌒

When the retreat was done I went down to Dharamsala. It was a little village, just three streets, but after I had been there for fifteen minutes I felt like I was in the middle of Times Square and got a huge migraine. I had to flee back to the monastery for ten days to rebalance myself.

Then I decided to take some time off. I took a train to Dal Lake in Kashmir, where you can stay in these wonderful houseboats. It was very pleasant but a little boring. After a few days of floating and smiling, I decided to go to Ladakh to see the dancing lamas.

Every year in Ladakh there are several festivals in which these Buddhist monks, wearing ornate costumes and masks of the gods' faces, dance and chant all day long for days at a time, to the accompaniment of tremendous, unending drumming. This incessant dancing and chanting requires almost supernatural physical force: the masks and costumes are very heavy. I was fascinated from a performance point of view to know how the lamas prepared for this festival.

Visiting the lama dance festival in Ladakh, India, 1987

The bus trip from Kashmir to Ladakh, through the Himalayas just after the snow melted, was more or less suicidal. The roads were narrow, the cliffs tremendous. Rounding curves, you could see your wheels practically going over the edge. A year earlier, I learned, one convoy of buses had been hit by an avalanche. Five buses dropped straight into the nothingness: everybody died. It turned out that the brother of our driver had been driving one of those buses. When we got to the spot where it happened, our driver stopped, got out, and climbed down the cliff to find his brother's body—the snow was melting, so it was his chance to see him at last. He just left us in the bus: we had to sleep there that night. The next day another bus came to pick us up, and we finally arrived in Ladakh.

Ladakh is 4,000 meters high—you take three steps and you get dizzy. It takes days just to get used to the altitude. Finally I got acclimated, and hired a guide to take me to the monastery. I arrived, and they had a room for me. I was standing in front of the monastery— the sun was just going down, very early as always in the mountains— when I saw this crazy-looking blond woman in Tibetan clothes, with flowers in her hair and a rucksack on her back, coming down the hill, singing. This seemed pretty interesting! I went over and talked to her.

She was a landscape architect from Chicago who spoke three Tibetan dialects, and she had been appointed by the Dalai Lama to reconstruct the garden of the Buddha in Bodh Gaya at the time of his enlightenment. She said to me, "Oh, don't sleep in the monastery; sleep with me in the tent—it's much better." I was a little worried: once the sun goes down it's freezing, and I had burned my wonderful, expensive sleeping bag, which kept me warm in any weather, and bought a cheap new one. But I felt I had to say yes, because this woman was kind of amazing.

Night fell; I went to her tent, which she had pitched right in front of the monastery. She was inside, naked, with only a little blanket to cover her. "How can you sleep like that?" I asked. She told me she had learned Tummo meditation from the Tibetans, a very special exercise that took four years to master. By visualizing a fireplace above your solar plexus, it's possible to raise your body temperature to a point where you feel hot in the middle of the snow. To practice, Tibetan monks sit in the snow, naked, in the lotus position while students put wet towels on their shoulders. Whoever can dry his towels first wins. This woman from Chicago knew that technique. I was impressed.

The monastery had twelve monks, men of all ages, shapes, and sizes. Two were very young and very tall; one was middle-aged, and quite short and fat—really almost square. I spent ten days hanging out with them, eating meals with them, watching them prepare for the festival in the courtyard where the lama dance was to take place.

I liked these lamas very much. We laughed a lot. But I was seriously underwhelmed by their exercises. A little bit of drumming—tap tap tap—and a little dancing, but nothing at all impressive. I began to think I was in the wrong place with the wrong people.

The big day came. Four thousand people arrived, from all over the Himalayas. They seated themselves all around this big courtyard, just before dawn. The drummers were ready to drum, the lamas were ready to dance. Everything starts at the moment the sun comes up. There was total silence. The little fat monk stood in the center of the courtyard in heavy red robes, a big gold mask of a goat on his face. Waiting, waiting for the sun. Silence, mesmerizing. Then the first sliver of sun appeared over the horizon, and the drumming began.

The drums were deafening. The same rhythm, over and over and over, and so loud that your body vibrated. And the little square monk, short and fat and burdened with his heavy mask and costume, jumped straight into the air and did three *salto mortales*—CHUK-CHUK-CHUK—just like that, landing effortlessly on his feet. He wasn't even breathing hard. He repeated the same routine every day for ten days.

Later on I asked him how this was possible. I had seen the rehearsals: nothing had prepared me for the real thing.

"But it's not us doing the jumping," he said. "The moment you put on the face and dress of the Divine Entity, you are not you anymore. You are Her, and your energy is limitless."

8.

The most famous incident in the history of Yugoslavia's fight against the Nazis during World War II is the Igman March. In January 1942, in the hills north of Sarajevo, the Germans had encircled the 1st Proletarian Brigade and were about to close in and kill all of them. The only route to safety for the partisans was to cross Mount Igman. This was clearly impossible. It was the dead of winter, the snow was deep, a wide and only partially frozen river was in the way, and the temperatures on the mountain were minus 25 degrees Celsius. But the partisans crossed the mountain anyway. Many froze to death. My father was one of the few people who survived and crossed this mountain.

When I called my father and told him that I was going to walk the Great Wall, he said, "Why are you doing this?"

"Well, you survived the Igman March," I said. "I can walk the Great Wall."

"How long will this Chinese Wall walk take?" he asked.

"Three months," I said. "Ten hours a day of walking."

He said, "Do you know how long the Igman March was?"

I had no idea. To me, it had always seemed like an eternity.

"One night," he told me.

We had conceived our grand romantic idea of walking the Great Wall of China eight years earlier, under a full moon in the Australian outback. The notion had loomed so powerfully in our shared imaginings. We had thought—back then—that the Wall was still an intact, continuous structure that we would simply hike along; that each of us would walk alone; that we would camp out on the Wall each night. That after starting at opposite ends (the head in the east, the tail in the west) and meeting in the middle, we would marry. Our working title for the piece, for years, had been *The Lovers*.

Now we were no longer lovers. And, as always seems to be the fate of romantics, nothing was as we had imagined. But we still didn't want to give up the walk.

Instead of walking alone, each of us would have an entourage consisting of a small company of guards and a translator/guide. The guards were supposedly there to protect us, but the Chinese were also paranoid about our going to the wrong places and seeing the wrong things. There were whole sections of the Wall that were in restricted military areas: instead of walking through these areas, we would each have to detour around them, in a jeep with a driver. And camping on the Wall was out of the question, because in China nobody who had been through the Cultural Revolution wanted to be uncomfortable on purpose, especially the soldiers assigned to accompany us. Instead we stayed in inns or villages along the way.

As for the Wall itself, this colossal dragon-shaped structure, visible from outer space, was largely in ruins, especially in the west, where vast sections of it had simply vanished under the desert sands; in the east, where it ran across the spine of a mountain range, winters and time itself had done their destructive work: in places, the Wall was simply treacherous piles of rock.

And as for our initial motivation, it was gone. *We* were gone. I told the *Village Voice* performance critic Cynthia Carr, who cashed in her life savings to travel to China and cover our walk,

Before, [there] was this strong emotional link, so walking towards each other had this impact . . . [it was an] almost epic story of two lovers getting together after suffering. Then that fact went away. I

Walking on a destroyed section of the Great Wall of China, 1988

was confronted with just bare Wall and me. I had to rearrange my motivation. Then I always remember this sentence of John Cage saying, "when I throw I Ching, the answers I like the less are the answers [from which] I learn the most."

I'm very glad we didn't cancel the piece, because we needed a certain form of ending. Really this huge distance we walk toward each other where actually we do not meet happily, but we will just end—it's very human in a way. It's more dramatic than actually just having this romantic story of lovers. Because in the end you are really alone, whatever you do.

My guide's name was Dahai Han. He was twenty-seven years old (and, by the way, a virgin, he later told me). He spoke perfect English, and he hated me.

I would later find out why. His English was so good that he had translated for all the big Chinese officials and traveled all over the world with them. He had led a very privileged existence up to the previous year, when he went to America with a government delegation, and, while he was there, saw break dancing for the first time. He loved it; he became obsessed with it. He took many photographs of break dancers, and when he returned to China, he Xerox-published a little underground booklet on break dancing in America.

The government found out about it. He was removed from his government translating post and sent to be my guide and translator while I walked the Great Wall. I was his punishment.

He arrived in a gray Chinese suit and black dress shoes. After three days of walking, he was sick with a temperature and his shoes were in pieces. I had to give him my spare shoes. He had such small feet that he had to put newspaper in them. I even gave him half my clothes to wear—it didn't matter; he still hated me. I remember he talked about how good it was that China had invaded Tibet, because after all, Tibet was Chinese. I said, *"What?"* He really knew how to get to me—I hated him back.

I learned afterward that Ulay also couldn't stand the changes the Chinese had forced on us: the crowds of soldiers and officials that constantly accompanied each of us, the dirty inns we had to stay in instead of camping, the restricted areas we had to avoid. For him, the purity of our initial concept had been spoiled.

I was always one to take things as they came, though that didn't mean—at all—that I was happy with every part of my walk. There were many, many difficulties. And I had expected no less.

This was pre-Tiananmen Square China, a China that very few Westerners had seen. I had to pass through twelve provinces that were forbidden for foreigners. There were areas that were polluted by radioactivity. I saw people tied to trees, left out to die, as a form of punishment. I saw wolves eating corpses. This was a China that nobody *wanted* to see.

The terrain in the east was extremely steep and rocky, and the rocks could be very slippery. Once I fell and injured my knee and had to stop and rest for a few days. In the mountains, the sheer drops on either side of the Wall were terrifying; sometimes the winds at high altitude were so strong that we all had to lie down to avoid being blown off.

It drove me crazy to be constantly accompanied by seven Red

Army soldiers—and it made me even crazier when they tried to walk in front of me. I didn't want to look at their backs! I'm sure it was my headstrong nature, as the daughter of tough partisans, but *I* wanted to walk in front. Even though it was so hard. Every evening, my knees hurt like hell. I was in pain, but I didn't give a damn—I was going to lead the way.

There were always seven guards with me, but my detachment would change as I moved from province to province. In one area there was a Red Army major who was so fascinated by me, this woman walking the Great Wall, that he brought a few of his soldiers to accompany me. One day we came to a super-steep hill, almost straight up, and as I started to climb it—still leading the way—these soldiers all started yelling.

"What are they saying?" I asked Dahai Han.

"They say we have to go around this hill; we can't climb it," he said.

"Why?" I asked.

"This is called Never Standing Hill," the translator said. "Nobody has ever stood on top. You can't climb it."

"But who said that?" I asked.

He looked at me as though I was the stupidest person in the world. "That's just how it is," he said. "It's always been like this. We have to walk around it."

Now the major and his soldiers had sat down and started to eat lunch. I looked at Dahai Han, said, "Okay," and I started walking up the hill. Straight up, it didn't matter—up and up I went as they all sat there eating. Finally I got to the top and looked back down. And then the major started screaming at the soldiers, and then they all walked up the hill. That evening, in the village where we stopped, the major gave a big speech about me. *You can't take obstacles for granted*, he said. *You have to face them and then see if it's possible to overcome them. This foreign woman has taught them all the lesson of courage*, he said. I was so proud.

One day, after weeks of walking, I noticed that my translator was always walking at the very rear, behind me and the soldiers. I asked him, "Why do you always walk way back there?"

He looked at me and said, "You know, there's a Chinese saying: 'Weak birds fly first.' "

I began to let my guard walk in front sometimes.

⌒

I was so fascinated by the relationship of the Wall to the ley lines, the energy lines in the earth. But I was also becoming aware of the changes in my own energy as I walked over different kinds of terrain. Sometimes there was clay under my feet, sometimes iron ore, sometimes quartz or copper. I wanted to try to understand the connections between human energy and the earth itself. In every village I stopped in, I would always ask to meet the oldest people there. Some of them were 105, 110 years old. And when I asked them to tell me stories about the Wall, they would always talk about dragons, a black dragon fighting a green dragon. I realized that these epic stories were literally about the configuration of the ground: the black dragon was iron, the green dragon was copper. It was like the Dreamtime tales of the Australian desert—every inch of land was full of stories, and the stories all related to the human mind and body. The land and the people were intimately connected.

I understood why the soldiers didn't want to camp, but I hated having to leave the Wall each night and walk two hours to the nearest village, and then, every morning, walk two hours back and climb up the Wall again, by which time I was exhausted before even beginning the day's journey. One morning I was so out of it when I started that I turned left instead of right and walked four hours in the wrong direction! I only realized it when I came to a point in the countryside I had photographed the day before. I had to turn our whole detachment around and head back. The soldiers didn't care—it was all just a job for them.

Even the bigger inns were depressing—undecorated concrete blocks without indoor toilet facilities. The lighting was terrible; where the walls were painted, they were painted that hospital green I remembered all too well. It was like Belgrade squared. And the villages were a nightmare. They all had these very Communist dormitories, consisting of three rooms. The middle chamber was the kitchen. On one side were the men's sleeping quarters, on the other side the women's. Heating pipes ran left and right from the kitchen stove, under the sleeping platforms in the men's and women's areas.

Females of all ages, including old ladies and little kids, slept all clumped together in the women's quarters—I would wedge in between them. They all had pissing pots next to their heads, because it was too cold to go out and pee in the middle of the night. The smell was unbearable.

I would try to get up early so I could go to the latrine alone, but it was impossible. The second I was up, they were up. There were always ten women running alongside me, all trying to hold my hand at once because I was such a novelty—for them, a woman with no man, with no children, a foreigner walking the Great Wall, was unthinkable. They were always trying to grab my nose—when I asked my interpreter why, he said they thought it was a fertility aid, because it was so big that it looked like a phallus to them.

The latrines were unspeakable—just barracks where you shit on the floor. Piles of shit, millions of flies. We would all have to squat together, holding hands and singing friendship songs: this was the Chinese way. In the beginning, it made me so constipated. I just couldn't do it. After a while, I got to a point where I didn't care anymore—I was squatting and singing friendship songs with the rest of them.

When Cynthia Carr showed up to walk with me for a while, I was so happy. The evening she arrived, when it was time to leave the Wall and go down to the next village, I asked her if she had to pee. She said she did. I said, "Can I hold your hand?"

She thought I'd lost it. "No!" she said.

"Okay," I said, "I was just trying to prepare you."

The next morning, there she was, holding hands with ten women while she squatted. "Now I know what you meant," she said.

In the villages in the morning, they would give you a big pot of boiling pig's blood to put on your tofu—milk was supposed to be bad for you. Boiled pig's blood was supposed to clean the system. That was a difficult breakfast to face.

One morning in a village somewhere, I woke up early to try to get to the latrine unmolested, and an old man came out of a house and started running after me screaming like he wanted to kill me. I had no idea why this guy was screaming, and of course I was in better shape than he was, so I ran around and around the square, trying to tire him out, all the while screaming to my guide to wake up. The old guy couldn't catch me, but he kept running like a maniac—it was terrifying. Finally my guide woke up and ran over to him and said something, and the guy just walked away.

"Excuse me, what was this about?" I asked my guide.

"He was saying, 'Bloody Japanese, out of here—I kill you!' " my guide said. This old man had never seen a foreigner before, and he thought I was a Japanese invading his village.

I realized that I was also a kind of invader to Dahai Han. And slowly, slowly, he and I became less hateful toward each other. Sometimes, over our shared meals, we would talk; the story of how he came to be demoted from government translator to my guide finally came out. He glowed with enthusiasm when he talked about his break-dancing photographs.

And so I decided to photograph him. I made a piece called *Le Guide Chinois* ("The Chinese Guide"). I styled his hair with sugar and water and posed him on the Wall, shirtless, making Tantric mudra hand gestures. The pictures were very beautiful.

Dahai Han and I became friends. After I finished my walk, because his punishment was over, he went back to the government. And the first time he returned to America, he defected. He wound up in

Kissimmee, Florida, next to Disney World, selling hamburgers and married to an American woman. This was a complete disaster. He divorced.

When China became more open, he went back. Now he is a very distinguished diplomat-writer in Washington, a correspondent for the Xinhua News Agency. This was his destiny.

Dahai Han, my guide, 1988

One day, halfway through the walk, a messenger brought me a note from Ulay, still far away in western China. "Walking the Wall is the easiest thing in the world," it read. That was all it said.

I could have killed him. Of course the walk was easy for him—he was traveling through the desert, where the path was flat. And all I was doing was climbing up and down mountains. On the other hand, this asymmetry wasn't his fault. Since fire is the masculine principle and water symbolizes the feminine, the plan had always been for Ulay to begin his walk from the desert and for me to begin at the edge of the sea.

And I will also confess that despite everything, at this point I still had hopes of salvaging our relationship.

⌒⟩

We finally met, on June 27, 1988, three months after we'd started, at Erlang Shen, Shennu, in Shaanxi Province. Only our meeting wasn't the one we had planned, not at all. Instead of encountering Ulay walking toward me from the opposite direction, I found him waiting for me in a scenic spot between two temples, one Confucian and one Taoist. He had been there three days.

And why had he stopped? Because this scenic spot was the perfect photo opportunity for our meeting. I didn't care about photo opportunities. He had broken our concept, for aesthetic reasons.

The handshake that marked the end of our personal
and professional relationship, 1988

A small crowd of onlookers was there to watch our meeting. I wept as he embraced me. It was the embrace of a comrade, not a lover: the warmth had drained out of him. I would soon learn that he had impregnated his translator, Ding Xiao Song. They would marry in Beijing in December.

My heart was broken. But my tears weren't just about the end of our relationship. We had accomplished a monumental work—separately. My own part in it felt epic, a long ordeal that was over at last. I felt almost as much relief as sadness. I flew back to Beijing immediately, and spent one night there, in the only Western hotel in the city at the time. Then I flew back to Amsterdam. Alone.

Ulay and I had been together, as collaborators and lovers, for twelve years. I would suffer from him, I told my friends, for at least half that long.

⌒

Ulay had always been in charge of our money; I had no idea what went on. When we split, he gave me 10,000 guilder, about $6,000 at that point, telling me it was exactly half of all the money we had. I didn't question it.

We had long since given up our warehouse loft on Zoutkeets-gracht; I was staying at my friends Pat Steir and Joost Elffers's place. One day, as I went to the square to have coffee, I passed a wreck of a house with a piece of wood nailed across the front door. Scrawled on the plank were the words FOR SALE and a phone number.

I wrote down the number; I wasn't sure why at first. But after I had coffee, I called, and a guy said this house was a bankruptcy case: the bank owned it. I asked if I could look at the place that afternoon. "Sure," he said.

I went to see the house. Actually it was two houses: the one in back was seventeenth century; the one in front, eighteenth century. Both had six floors and the two buildings were connected by a courtyard; the interior space was 1,150 square meters.

The place was a squat—thirty-five heroin addicts were living there. The chaos was palpable. It smelled like dog shit, cat shit, piss. A bunch of totally stoned guys were throwing knives at the seventeenth-century carved-wood door. One floor was literally burned—it was nothing but charred floorboards with a toilet sitting in the middle. This place looked terrible. But underneath it all, it was beautiful, with elegant stucco work and marble fireplaces. I had a vision.

"How much?" I asked.

Forty thousand guilder, they told me. They clearly just wanted to dump this house. But if you bought it, you were also getting the heroin addicts who were squatting in it, and under Dutch law, it was all but impossible to get them out. For any normal human being to buy this place would be like throwing money out the window. So I said, "Okay, I'm interested."

I talked about it with my friends. "You're nuts," they said. "It's not money you have—what the hell are you going to do?"

Next day I went to the bank. They told me they needed at least a 10 percent deposit, and I would have three months to find a mortgage. If you couldn't find one after a month and a half, you could tell the bank you weren't interested anymore and you'd get your deposit back. But if you decided to keep trying after that point, and you wound up not able to get a mortgage, you would lose your deposit.

The house that changed my life, Amsterdam, 1991

I gave them 4,000 guilder—almost half of all I had in the world. Really, it was insane. Then I started visiting banks.

I still had a Yugoslav passport, but no visa to stay in Holland. I had been illegal there forever. Whenever I came and went, the Culture Ministry had always given me letters of passage; I'd never had a problem. I'd never had a bank account before: I opened my first account with the money Ulay gave me. And every bank I approached for a mortgage, the moment they walked in the door, before they even got to the end of the corridor, said, "We're not interested." The house was worth something, but you'd never get a mortgage as long as these squatters were in it, and you'd never get them out. This is why the price was so low.

One-and-a-half months passed; the bank called. "Do you have a mortgage?" they asked.

"No," I said.

"Are you quitting the contract?" they asked.

"No," I said. I just couldn't let it go, even if I lost my whole deposit. I was obsessed by this point—kind of out of my mind. I started smoking then.

I put the telephone down and said to myself, *Okay, Marina, now you have to take a new approach. You have to get some information about this house.*

So I went to the neighbors on both sides of the house, knocked on both doors. The neighbors were pretty nice: they told me the story of the house. The first owner anyone could remember was an opera singer. Then an old Jewish family moved in. And then, after another owner or two, a drug dealer bought the place. But he didn't pay the mortgage. And he didn't pay and he didn't pay, and finally he was in such financial trouble that he decided to burn the place down for the insurance. Except that the fire was stopped in time and only the one floor was damaged. And then the insurance investigator found that the drug dealer had done it intentionally, and the bank took the house away from him. And this was how it turned into a squat for heroin addicts.

"But where is this guy?" I asked.

"He's still living in the house," the neighbor told me.

This house had two entrances. One went to the first floor and the other to the second. The door with the board across it was the entrance to the first floor, where I'd already been; the drug dealer was living on the second floor. So I went around and knocked on the door, and he answered. "I want to talk to you," I said.

He let me in. There was a table in the middle of the floor, covered with Ecstasy, cocaine, hashish, all ready to go into bags. There was a pistol on the table. This guy was bloated—he looked like hell. And he looked at me, and suddenly I poured my heart out to him.

I told him everything—about Ulay, the walk across the Great Wall, the pregnant Chinese translator, the money he gave me; everything. I said that this house was what I wanted—all I wanted—the only home I could afford with the little money I had. I was weeping. This guy was standing there with his mouth open; he must've thought I'd landed from another planet.

He stood there looking at me. Then he said, "Okay. I am going to help you. But I have a condition."

He told me that for two years he'd been squatting in this house that used to belong to him, living there for free because the bank couldn't sell it. He rented sleeping space to heroin addicts for five guilder a night. This was his life.

"I hate these bank bastards, I hate the government," he said. "But you are different. This is my deal. I'll get everybody out; you'll get your mortgage. But the moment you sign the contract and get the house, you're going to sign a contract that I can stay on this floor for the rest of my life for the lowest rent possible. That's the deal. If you cross me . . ." He showed me the pistol.

"Give me two weeks to get everybody out," he said.

At this point I had maybe a month left to sign the contract. I came back two weeks later and all the addicts were out of the house. The dealer was all by himself in his apartment. But the house still looked like hell.

I got a Dumpster, and I got all my friends in Amsterdam to come, and we threw out everything in the place. Everything. We could've made a drug supermarket with all the shit we found. We threw it all out. We threw out all the carpets that were wet from piss. And then I sprayed the whole place with copious amounts of lavender spray, installed industrial lights to erase all the dark corners, and stood back and took a look at what my friends and I had done.

What I now saw was a house with amazing potential. It was in a good neighborhood, where a comparable place would sell for forty to fifty times the price. And it was empty—not a heroin addict in sight. So I contacted three banks. The first bank looked at the house and said they were interested; they would let me know. The second bank looked, too, and also said they'd let me know. And the third bank said yes at once. I got a mortgage in less than a week.

But now, since my bank knew the house was empty, Dutch law gave them the right to buy the house for themselves. So I went back to the drug dealer and said, "Can we get some addicts back into the place? Because it's too good now."

"How many you want?" he asked.

"About twelve," I said.

"No problem," he said. He got twelve addicts back. I took curtains I found in a Dumpster and put them on the windows. Then I scattered some more debris around the place.

Now all I had to do was wait. My contract signing was two weeks away—it was the longest two weeks in my life. Finally the day came. I put on the most formal dress I had, took an expensive Mont Blanc fountain pen my father—not my mother—had bought me for my birthday, and walked into the bank.

The atmosphere was very serious. One of the bankers looked at me and said, "I heard that the unwanted tenants have left the house."

My stomach was rumbling. I just looked at him very coolly and said, "Yeah, some left; there are plenty of them still there."

He cleared his throat and said, "Sign here." I signed. "Congratulations," the banker said. "You're the owner of the house."

So I looked at him and said, "You know what? Actually everybody left the house."

And he looked back at me and said, "My dear girl, if this is true, you have just made the best real-estate deal I've heard of in my twenty-five-year career."

⌒

The house was mine. I immediately went to a lawyer to get a contract drawn up for the drug dealer's apartment. That was in the morning. That afternoon, I took the contract and a bottle of champagne and knocked on his door. I didn't want to mess around. The dealer opened his door. "Here's your contract, here's a bottle of champagne," I said. "Ready?"

"Wow—I see you keep your promises," he said. And he signed.

As soon as we popped open the champagne, he started crying. He told me his wife was in a hospital somewhere, dying from heroin overuse; he had two kids, twelve and fourteen, who were delinquents, in some kind of special-care facility. "I want so much for my kids to be with me," he sobbed. "Everybody's gone from my life—it's terrible." I sat listening to him; now our situations were more or less reversed. His place still looked like hell.

I began living in the house. In Amsterdam it is always raining, and in this house it was raining indoors. I put pots everywhere to collect the water. I had a very large cupboard, as big as a closet (another *plakar*): this was where I slept. It was the only place it didn't rain. The one burned floor was still burned. Everything was wrong, and I had no money to fix it. Plus, every five minutes some heroin addict was ringing the bell asking if he could crash or use the toilet. (Only one toilet was working, by the way.) People were shooting heroin on my doorstep: the steps were spotted with blood every morning. All my friends were saying, "You are crazy to have to go through all this for this shitty house."

Ulay had also returned to Amsterdam, and was living in a house just a couple of blocks away. One day I was sitting in my big house—it was raining, and the rain was pouring through the holes in my roof and drip-drip-dripping into all the pots—and I was looking out my window at the canal in the rain, and there, standing on a bridge, was Ulay, kissing his pregnant Chinese wife.

Time to get out of town, I told myself.

⌒

When I split with Ulay, I felt fat, ugly, and unwanted. It would have been very easy to lie in my bed with the covers pulled up and eat whole boxes of chocolates. But I was always one to make things happen, so I made things happen. Besides buying the house, I soon made two other big changes in my life, one very bad and one very good.

The bad change was a young Spaniard—though of course he didn't seem bad at first. He worked for Michael Klein's agency; he was thirty to my forty-two, and very good-looking. Also very narcissistic. He spent hours in the gym every day. But he gravitated to me at a moment when I badly needed someone, and I didn't ask questions. I should have.

Early on he took me for a ride on the back of his bicycle, and we crashed: I fell off and really hurt myself. *If my grandmother could see me now,* I said to myself, *She would say, "Stop right there, because this is going to end badly."*

In China I had felt so strongly the relationship between the minerals beneath my feet and the human body. The ancient people I spoke to in the villages reinforced this idea, with their stories of battles between dragons of various colors. And I had brought back some of the beautiful minerals I found there: rose quartz, clear quartz, amethyst, and obsidian. In the gray city of Amsterdam, in the depths of my despair, I had an inspiration. I would construct objects that would express the relationship between minerals and the body—objects that would transmit the energy of these minerals to those that came in contact with them. It was also important to introduce the public to the Great Wall walk, as this was the first performance of ours for which they had been absent.

I constructed a series of these pieces—I called them transitory objects—that spring. They resembled Spartan beds: long, oxidized copper–covered planks with mineral pillows of rose quartz or obsidian. Each was to be fixed to a wall, horizontally or vertically, for public use in three basic body positions: sitting, standing, and lying. I called them *Green Dragon*, *Red Dragon*, and *White Dragon*, and they neatly reversed my usual relationship to my audience: this time the public was on the wall and I was free in the gallery space, looking at them. That summer the Pompidou Center in Paris acquired all three, and set a show for me in the fall.

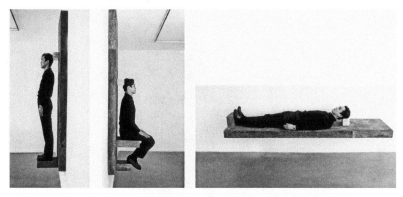

White Dragon, Red Dragon, Green Dragon, from the series
Transitory Objects for Human Use, oxidized copper, black obsidian,
rose quartz, 1989 installation, Victoria Miro Gallery, London, 1991

At the same time, the Pompidou gave me a grant to produce more work, and I signed a three-year contract to teach performance at École nationale supérieure des Beaux-Arts. So I decided to rent an apartment in Paris—and the Spanish guy moved in with me. Now I could afford to improve my new house, but I didn't want to live there for the time being. For the present I'd had it with Amsterdam.

It was the first time in my life I had real money, and one of the Span-iard's first goals was to help me spend it. He used to say to me, "I will make a baby for you if you buy me a car and a boat." He always smiled when he said it, and we both laughed, but he was only half joking.

When he wasn't thinking about himself, he seemed to be think-ing about me. Thinking about me, that is, in the most superficial way possible. "I will help you feel better about yourself," he would tell me. This meant mirroring his narcissism: going to the gym and the hair-dresser, and buying couture clothes. I wasn't immune to this physical self-improvement, not at all. And beautiful clothes became a whole new phase in my life. I went to the Yamamoto shop and I bought

My first fashion photo shoot, dressed in
Yohji Yamamoto, Paris, 1989

an amazing suit: black trousers, an asymmetrical jacket, and a white shirt with just one collar point protruding. I still own this suit, and can wear it anytime—it's classic.

This suit was a revelation. It was so comfortable and elegant; it just felt right. I couldn't believe how it changed the way I felt about just walking down the street. I no longer felt self-conscious. I felt beautiful.

In advance of the Pompidou show, I did a lot of interviews. I had done many interviews before, but the French were very different. The big interview was for a fashion magazine, and they wanted a list of the designers I wore! At first I was like, "What?" Then I said, "Yamamoto."

They sent a whole rack of clothes for me to try on; they sent makeup artists. I spent three hours being styled and photographed, and then the interview took twenty minutes. But when the magazine piece came out, I have to say I looked pretty good. Paris was suddenly a whole new world for me—I felt I had to dress up just to go get a baguette for breakfast.

The new clothes made me feel better about myself, but my Spanish boyfriend didn't.

Before the Pompidou show I had a show in Brussels. I'd turned parts of the Great Wall film into a video installation, and also created new wall pieces made from minerals: vertical triptychs against which the public could press their head, heart, and sex to exchange energy. At the time, I wrote the following about these pieces:

> All the transitory objects have one thing in common: they do not exist on their own; the public must interact with them. Some objects are there to empty the viewer, some to give energy, and some to make a mental departure possible.
>
> The individual should never cause an interruption in the circuit of nature; he should never use energy without restoring it again.
>
> When transformation takes place, the object receives the power to function.

The Spanish guy helped manufacture some objects and install the show—and while he was there, began an affair with a young gallerist. I heard about it very quickly.

My best friend at the time, the German artist Rebecca Horn (she was three years older, and everything that was happening to me had already happened to her: I called her Dr. Horn), said, "Marina, this is your moment—you're so lucky that he's having this affair! Get rid of him now."

So I called him. "I know you're involved with so-and-so, and I totally understand," I said. "She's younger, she's prettier, she's much better than me." I was very convincing. And he left.

〜〜

Danica had heard I was living in Paris, and she called, very excited. For her, Paris represented art at its highest, and everything that was refined and elegant. It brought back wonderful memories of her years as a UNESCO delegate. I told her very proudly that I was having a show at the Pompidou, and it would be great if she could come to the opening.

"Are you naked in it?" she asked.

I told her that I was not, that I was showing my transitory objects. When I explained what they were, she actually sounded intrigued. "I'm coming," she said.

You will recall my mother's obsession with hygiene. She was staying at the George V, but she wanted to see my apartment. And so I cleaned the place to the point of surgical sterility—I mean, everything was sparkling. Danica arrived, and squinted at the premises. She gave a little nod, not making an immediate judgment. And then she gave the apartment a thorough inspection, running her hand over every surface. Finally she nodded again. "Relatively clean," she said.

On the day of the opening, I didn't want to arrive exactly on the dot, so I got to the Pompidou a half hour late. And as I arrived, I

With my mother at my opening at Galerie Charles Cartwright, Paris, 1990

looked in the window and saw my mother standing in the gallery, in her trademark blue suit with the brooch, surrounded by a small crowd. People were taking pictures of her. I went inside. Danica was holding forth (in perfect French, *naturellement*) to a group of critics, discussing my work. She had taken over—my presence wasn't necessary at all.

I took a second mortgage on the Amsterdam house, and had a new roof put on—no more pots of rainwater—but I made no improvements at all to my living quarters. Instead, I had the drug dealer's apartment renovated.

Once again everybody told me, "You don't know what you're doing; you've lost your mind." And once again, I was following my intuition.

The workers came and made the dealer's apartment beautiful. He was still stuck in his old ways, still doing drugs—but also still obsessed with getting his children back. And now he had a nice home for them to come back to. So he went to the facility where they were living and told them this. The social worker, an English girl, said she had to see his place first.

She went and looked, and his apartment was perfect-perfect. The facility decided to give him back his children—with the condition that the social worker come every week to make sure everything was all right.

With his children there, he started to clean up his act. He took fewer drugs; he made good food for the three of them to eat. When the heroin addicts knocked on the door, he turned them away. Little by little, he changed. And little by little, the social worker, who was from a very nice aristocratic British family, fell in love with him.

⌐

In 1991 the Parisian gallerist Enrico Navarra became fascinated with my transitory objects. He gave me a big advance to produce new works, money that allowed me to travel to Brazil to find crystals and minerals. In order to go to the mines, I would need permission from the owners—permission I didn't have when I left Paris. Fortunately, though, when I arrived in São Paulo, friends introduced me to Kim Esteve, a lover and collector of art who invited me to stay with his family in Chácara Flora. And there Kim introduced me to several mine owners, and I got the authorization I needed.

One of the first places I went was Serra Pelada.

Serra Pelada was an enormous open pit of a gold mine near the mouth of the Amazon. The great Brazilian photographer Sebastião Salgado had made it infamous with his unforgettable pictures of tens of thousands of men clustered together, half-naked and filthy with mud, desperately clawing at this hillside for flakes of gold.

Serra Pelada was called the place where the gods say good-bye. This was hell on earth. It was completely lawless and incredibly dangerous—there were dozens of murders every month, all unsolved, because there was no one to investigate them. The only women there were prostitutes. Any other woman would be crazy to go: you would be raped and killed.

The only way to get to Serra Pelada was by boat or plane—there were no roads. I went on a plane with no seats, with a donkey in the middle of the plane tied to a rope. Next to the donkey were a bottle of sleeping pills and a shotgun. He had been tranquilized with the sleeping pills. We were told that if he woke up, we would have to shoot him, because he would freak out and bring down the plane.

I went alone, with just a rucksack and three crates of Coca-Cola. No camera. I had heard that just a few weeks earlier, Steven Spielberg had tried to film a sequence there for one of his Indiana Jones movies; some people got upset at his cameraman for taking pictures and shot him to death. I didn't want to upset anybody. The Coca-Cola was for making friends.

I stayed in a place called the Dog Hotel, which deserved its name. Even Alba would have hated it there. (By now, Alba was almost fifteen, ancient in dog years. Her muzzle was gray; her dark eyes had a bluish cast—cataracts. She could barely climb the stairs in my Amsterdam house. I took her to Majorca, to the beautiful home of my friend Toni, and Toni and I built her a small doghouse under a tree, in sight of the ocean. She died peacefully there one morning, and we buried her under the tree.) The Dog Hotel was filthy, and the only other occupants were old prostitutes. The streets were just mud. And the miners were walking around in clothes that were in shreds, covered in red mud; their teeth were replaced with gold. I saw one man, missing a finger, with a gold prosthesis.

Everything was paid for with gold, even tomatoes and bananas. And to get this gold, these hordes of half-naked men climbed down into the pit, which was clay and unstable. There were frequent collapses, many deaths daily.

Why did I go there? It wasn't for gold. Instead I had an even more insane idea: to create a video piece called *How to Die*. (Eventually, I thought, I would figure out a way to bring a camera in without bodily harm.)

The idea was this: when you see real death on television, footage of some terrible disaster or other, you might stare for a moment, but then you can't take it anymore; you just change the channel. When you watch an opera, theater, or film, and you see the heroine die, you identify with this kind of organized, aesthetic death. You look, you're moved emotionally, and you cry.

So my idea was to juxtapose in a video a few minutes of opera death (in my mind it was always Maria Callas—I had become obsessed with Callas, with whom I identified tremendously) and a few minutes of real death: to put them together in a scene. The most real death I could think of was in Serra Pelada. So I went to Serra Pelada to see these deaths.

On paper, my idea was intriguing. I had proposed it to France's Minister of Culture and received an encouraging response. And when I got to Serra Pelada, nothing was as I had imagined.

I wanted to talk to these gold miners in the most open, honest way, with no camera, no agenda. The Coca-Cola I'd brought was a great conversation-starter. I would sit down with them, hand them a couple of Cokes, and start talking about opera: *La Traviata, Othello.* One guy I talked to, black as night, had all gold teeth—the sun was shining and he was smiling, and the teeth were reflecting the sun. I said to myself, *This is Othello right here.* Another one, Italian, knew *Traviata*: he was singing it for me. The guys I met liked me; they seemed to want to protect me. And not only did they want to protect me, a couple of them who had their own cameras even started taking photographs for me—they gave me the pictures, some amazing images: I put them in my book *Public Body.*

I spent three days there, absolutely convinced, the more I thought about it, that *How to Die* would be a powerful piece. The idea evolved in my mind. I would commission seven different fashion designers to create the clothes for the opera segments. I would ask (for example)

Azzedine Alaïa to design the dress in *Carmen* with fifty yards of red silk. José would stab Carmen, and then the camera would show a real death in Serra Pelada. Then Karl Lagerfeld would design another costume for *La Traviata*, then I would direct this death, too. It could all be edited together and presented as a video installation.

And in the end it was too expensive. I never made the piece. But the idea stayed with me: I never really gave up on realizing it someday.

A year later I returned to Brazil, this time with twenty-six other artists, on a trip up the Amazon sponsored by the Goethe-Institut and the Museum of Modern Art of Rio de Janeiro. Our only assignment was to create a work with indigenous materials that would promote ecology—it was a scenic trip, relaxed and fun. One of the artists was an old friend of mine, the Portuguese painter Julião Sarmento, so I had somebody to laugh with. One night, in Belém, there was a beauty contest, the Miss Boom Boom competition, to pick the most magnificent ass in Brazil! Julião and I were actually asked to be judges.

A film crew from a television arts network in Germany, ZDF, accompanied us on this trip, and the director, Michael Stefanowski, became fascinated with me. This was very nice for my ego, especially in the wake of my self-destructive fling with the Spanish guy. Michael was the opposite of the Spaniard in almost every way: he was short and smart, his face was wrinkled, and he didn't give a damn about his body. His solution to the stresses of the TV business was to chain-smoke and drink a lot of vodka.

We started a relationship. He had just separated from his wife. He was such a sweet man, so loving—I felt completely comfortable with him. I never needed to pretend anything. When I felt insecure, he encouraged me. When I was anxious, he told me not to worry, and I listened. For the next few years, whenever we were both in Europe, we found ways to get together. We also traveled together: to Thailand, to the Maldives. While we were in the islands, he took a snapshot of me, one of my favorite pictures of myself, smiling in an old-fashioned swimsuit and holding a beach ball. I look happy. I was happy. I wasn't really in love with Stefanowski, but I was so fond of him that at one point I thought I wanted to marry him. He said, "Why marry?" I didn't really have a good answer.

In 1992 I got a big grant from a German organization, DAAD, to come to Berlin and work there for a year. They gave me a beautiful studio, a generous stipend, and a very nice apartment in the Charlottenburg district. I got to see a lot of my friend Rebecca, who also had a studio in Berlin. And I made friends with Klaus Biesenbach, a young curator who had started the new art institute there, Kunst-Werke. Klaus was intriguing: very smart, very interested in my work, kind of cool and warm at the same time. For an intense period we were more than friends—we were more like soulmates with a shared intuition and intimacy that made us challenge each other. But over the years we both saw that a working relationship was the best kind of relationship to have.

Klaus Biesenbach and me, 1995

With Charles Atlas during rehearsals of *Biography*
at the Kunsthalle, Vienna, 1992

This new studio was very important for me—the first studio of my own I'd had since Belgrade—and I immediately began working on a very ambitious extended performance, a massive theater piece called *Biography*. My collaborator was Charles Atlas, an American video artist I'd met in London a couple of years earlier. The subject was to be nothing less than my life and work, staged as a theater piece.

In a way *Biography* was my definitive declaration of independence from Ulay. It even had a farewell sequence—I called it the bye-bye scene. To the sound of Callas singing Bellini's heartbreaking aria "Casta Diva," I recited:

BYE-BYE
EXTREMES

BYE-BYE
PURITY

BYE-BYE
TOGETHERNESS

BYE-BYE
INTENSITY

BYE-BYE
JEALOUSY

BYE-BYE
STRUCTURE

BYE-BYE
TIBETANS

BYE-BYE
DANGER

BYE-BYE
SOLITUDE

BYE-BYE
UNHAPPINESS

BYE-BYE
TEARS

BYE-BYE
ULAY

After the Wall walk, the show about our project had toured museums in Amsterdam, Stockholm, and Copenhagen, but since my former partner and I were no longer speaking, there needed to be two press conferences and two dinners for each opening. I know this was difficult for me; I suspect it was even harder for the curators.

Around that time, a cultural TV program in Munich wanted to make a documentary about us. They planned to call the film *An*

Arrow in the Heart, after our piece *Rest Energy*, but also making reference to the pain of our separation. The only problem was that we wouldn't be interviewed together. The Germans agreed to film us separately, with the condition that they ask us the same questions.

They came to my house in Amsterdam, which was beautiful by now, and I dressed up for the camera in elegant clothes and high heels, presenting myself as the happy survivor. The interview went very well, I thought. A couple of months later, when the documentary was aired, I went to Berlin to watch it with Rebecca Horn, who translated for me. My sections were fine, but when I saw Ulay's, I nearly had a heart attack. Instead of being interviewed in his house, he'd chosen to be filmed in an abandoned schoolroom with the floor ripped up, presenting himself as a poor, homeless artist. A little fire burned in a wastebasket in the middle of the room. They asked, "Why wasn't the arrow pointed at you?" He said, "Because her heart was my heart." Then he called, "Luna, Luna," and at that moment, a beautiful little half-Chinese girl ran into his arms. It was the first time I had ever seen her—after this I went to bed for three days with a migraine.

That year I performed *Biography* across Europe: first in Madrid, and then, refining and developing it as I went along, in Vienna, Frankfurt, and Berlin. It was a demanding piece: there were re-performances of old solo works like *Rhythm 10* and *Thomas Lips*, complete with real blades and my actual blood. There were split-screen projections of pieces I'd done with Ulay—the split screens a dramatic physical symbol of our actual separation. There was a recorded chronological narration:

    1948: Refuse to walk . . .

    1958: Father buying television . . .

    1963: My mother writes "My dear little girl, your painting has a
           nice frame" . . .

    1964: Drinking vodka, sleeping in the snow. First kiss . . .

    1969: I don't remember . . .

1973: Listening to Maria Callas. Realizing that the kitchen of my grandmother is the center of my world . . .

And there was humor. Onstage, I recited a list of words that applied to me: "Harmony, symmetry, baroque, neoclassic, pure, bright, shiny, high heel shoes, erotic, turning around, big nose, large ass, *et voilà*: Abramović!"

9.

Once more, I was in Thailand, but this time alone. One afternoon I went looking through some ruins, and it was stiflingly hot, and nearby was a little road full of trucks passing, dusty. I suddenly realized I was hungry. All around me were little stands where you could buy things to eat, and I was trying to decide which one to go to. Finally I chose one run by an old woman. She had a big wok and six or seven rickety little tables, and that was her whole restaurant. Everything she cooked was with chicken. Chicken wings, chicken liver, chicken breasts, chicken whatever. And all around her were dozens of baskets of chicken in various stages. One big basket was full of live chickens. Another one just had chicken livers. Another, just chicken legs and feet. Still another basket was filled with dead chickens with the feathers still on. And another was stuffed with plucked chicken cadavers ready to be cooked.

I sat at one of the little tables, and the old woman brought me spicy chicken wings. They were so delicious. While I ate them, she kept cooking more for me. Then, as I was eating, I looked under the table and saw something I will never forget.

Just as I looked down, a ray of sunshine came out of the clouds and lit this little scene under the table—chicken life: a mother hen and her chicks. A bunch of tiny little chicks, yellow and fluffy, were hovering around their mother in this ray of sun, peeping loudly, so happy. Their mother looked very proud.

This, for me, was like a spiritual revelation. That moment of happiness under that ray of sun, in the midst of cadavers, baskets of every kind of chicken part.... This mother hen was going to be the next one in the pot. And I thought, This is it. This is us. Even if we have a tiny moment of happiness, soon we, too, are going to be in the pot.

I left Michael Klein's agency soon after I left Ulay. Michael still represented Ulay; he also still employed the Spanish guy. I needed to move on. I also needed to make a living. I always wanted to live for my work, the thing I knew best, and to live *by* my work.

But strangely, for one who was so bold in performance, I felt unsure about showing my other work. Besides my performances, I was producing transitory objects, video installations, and photographic works. But would galleries really be interested in me? I had met the great Ileana Sonnabend a few times in Rome, yet I was shy about approaching her. I felt the same about Nicholas Logsdail, of London's excellent Lisson Gallery.

Then my friend Julião Sarmento came to the rescue. He was represented in New York by a Brit named Sean Kelly, and Julião loved him. He told me, "I think Sean is the one person who can really understand your work and figure out how you can actually sell some stuff."

I could have asked Julião to introduce me, but I also felt insecure about this. I didn't want there to be any kind of personal pressure on Julião or on Sean Kelly. In my mind the only clean way for me to come to Kelly's attention was a spontaneous meeting.

Clearly a spontaneous meeting would have to be arranged.

Julião was going to New York to meet with Sean, and so I decided to go along with him.

We worked out a plan. Julião and Sean were going to have lunch on such-and-such a day at Jerry's, a little restaurant on Spring Street in Soho. Julião said to me, "Just pass the window a few times. When you see we've finished the meal and we're going to have coffee, just come in and say, 'Oh, Julião, so nice to see you,' and I will say, 'Please sit down and have coffee with us.' " It seemed like a good plan.

The day came. I kept walking by Jerry's, like five times, because in those days there were no mobile phones to make planning easy. Whenever I looked in the window, they still hadn't finished this stupid lunch. *Patience*, I kept telling myself. Finally I saw that the lunch dishes had been cleared and coffee was on the way. I walked in and went over to their table. "Hey, hello!" I said.

"Marina, wonderful to see you," Julião said. "Please, sit. This is Sean."

We started talking, and finally I worked up the courage to say to Sean, "I'd really love to work with you."

And Sean said to me, "You know what? You've picked the worst day of my life to say that. I've just been thrown out of my job." He had been the director of the L.A. Louver Gallery in Soho, which had a Californian owner. And that day, this Californian owner had told Sean he wanted to show some Californian artists, and when Sean saw the work, he absolutely hated it. "It's kitschy, it's horrible," he said. And the owner said, "I'm paying you; this is my gallery. I want to show these artists." Sean said, "I can't do it." So he just resigned.

With Sean Kelly making power objects, Alicante, 1998

Sean had a mortgage on an apartment. He had two kids, one four years old and one six. He was in New York without a job, and still without an American passport. He said, "You want to work with me? I just lost my gallery. I've got nothing."

"Perfect," I said. "I don't want a gallerist with a gallery. I want a gallerist without a gallery. You'll be able to give me much more time."

This was just how it worked out. Sean started working from his home in Soho, where he lived with his wife, Mary, and their two children, Thomas and Lauren, and he began to succeed on his own. Mary was so important in this process—without her, I don't see how Sean would have managed at all. Aside from the household, she had to take care of their active social life, with a constant round of dinners and parties, and frequent visits by collectors coming to look at work. For many years to come, I would spend the best Christmases with the Kellys—I grew especially fond of Mary's British bread sauce, of which I always had extra servings and which I ate with a big spoon.

Sean came to Amsterdam and looked through the photographs of my early solo performances, beginning with *Rhythm 10*. There were a lot of photographs. He went through them all, putting aside one or two from each piece. *Thomas Lips* provided especially strong (and bloody) images: me whipping myself, the star I cut into my stomach. "Okay," he finally said, "let's make a small edition of these. You'll write some text about each one, and we'll put them out there and see what happens."

And this is how we began.

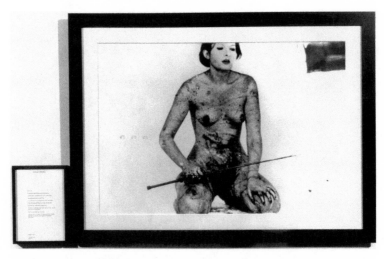

Thomas Lips, black-and-white photograph with letterpress text panel,
Krinzinger Gallery, Innsbruck, 1975

⟳

Tito had held Yugoslavia together by sheer force of personality—plus the huge sums he borrowed (brilliantly playing all sides against each other) from Russia, China, the United States. The moment he died, everything flew apart. Russia, China, and the United States all wanted their money back. And the country's six republics, formerly united by the leader's iron hand, now became separate entities. Whereas once they'd been interdependent—copper mines in the south, for example, sending copper ore to factories in the north to be processed—now they were all at odds.

Tito had stipulated in his will that after his death, each republic should be governed by a president who would serve a one-year term. This was a total disaster. Each president would rule with no thought about what would happen after he left—and grab as much money as he could, for himself and his republic, while he was in office.

Yugoslavia was no more.

It all came to an end in early 1992, with the outbreak of the Bosnian war. The ethnic groups that had been coexisting easily, the Serbs and the Croats and the Bosnian Muslims, all suddenly remembered they hated each other's guts. It was a vicious, disastrous conflict, as stupid a war as any that was waged in the twentieth century.

Though most of the fighting—and the massacres—were taking place in Bosnia and Herzegovina, leaving Belgrade untouched, I worried about my parents. They were in their seventies now, and trapped in this country in flames.

My father in particular was suffering. Though he never wrote to me, not even a postcard, we talked on the phone now and then, and suddenly he sounded old and sad. He had married his beautiful blond girlfriend, so sexy in her short skirt and high heels; she became a judge, the youngest judge in the country. Fine. She had divorced her handsome husband, who was the same age, to marry my father, also very handsome and a revolutionary, but thirty-five years older. And now the age difference was really starting to show.

Now Vojin was stuck in Belgrade, and poor, and suffering. All commercial flights in and out of the city had been suspended: the city was racked by shortages of everything. My mother never complained, but I knew she was suffering, too. I decided to go and do what I could to help. I also decided to take Charles Atlas with me and do video interviews with Danica and Vojin. I had a new piece in mind that would include them—the Theater am Turm in Frankfurt had given me production money for it—but I also wanted to document my parents while I still had the chance.

The wartime shortages were absurd. I saw a newspaper story that said citizens of Belgrade could now buy entire slaughtered pigs on easy credit terms—people were buying these pigs on installment plans and bringing them home to cut up for sausage. People's bathrooms were filled with hanging pork. Whenever a truckload of anything—toilet paper, cans of tomatoes—would arrive, mobs would descend to buy the goods at inflated prices and take them home to store. Entire apartments were stacked with toilet paper.

I asked both my parents what they needed. Their answers were true to form. My mother wanted Chanel lipstick, perfume, and moisturizing cream; my father wanted penicillin, lightbulbs, and batteries. Charles and I flew to Budapest, where I bought all the goods we could carry, and we took a bus into Serbia.

After a long, nerve-racking ride—we were stopped by soldiers at several checkpoints along the way—we arrived late at night in Belgrade. Vojo was there to meet us, and I was shocked at how much older he looked. I also saw immediately that he had tears on his cheeks. I had never seen my father cry before. With a grim look, he showed us that he was carrying a pistol. "This is what it has come to," he told me. A few days before, some young guy had spat at him on the street. "You Communist," the guy said. "You and Tito got us into this fucking mess."

When we got to his place—he walked with a slight limp; he was having trouble with his hip—he showed us the old photographs of himself with Tito that he had cut in half. Now his tears were running freely. "This is not what I fought for," he said. "My life is completely wasted." He really seemed like a broken man.

⌒

When I was in my late twenties and still living in my mother's large Belgrade apartment, I had an idea. "Why don't we split this big place into three parts?" I asked her. She could have one apartment, I suggested; I could have one, and my brother could have the third. "Everybody could be independent," I said. "It would be a good solution."

This was not even a possibility for her—she had to control everything. So I just escaped home at twenty-nine. Then, after I had been gone for a year and she finally understood that I wasn't coming back, she did exactly what I'd suggested and changed the place into three apartments. The place she gave herself was quite modest, my brother's apartment was huge, and the space she saved for me was smallish, like hers. After three years, my brother sold his place and spent the money. Then Danica called me and said, "What shall we do with your place? How would you like to paint the kitchen? I have some good ideas for organizing everything. . . ."

I told her I didn't give a shit and that she could do whatever she wanted with the place.

Then my grandmother started living there to keep it for me, until she died—she died in this apartment. When I finally got the place back, I sold it. I didn't want any part of it—I even sold all the furniture. Eventually my mother moved into one of these new socialist apartment buildings. And this is where I found her when I came to Belgrade at the beginning of the war.

I asked if I could bring the video crew to her apartment to interview her. "With dirty shoes and electrical cables?" she said. "People I don't know? No way."

So I rented a theater for her. She arrived like Callas. Black dress, strings of pearls, perfect chignon. I put a chair right in the center of the stage, and arranged the lighting so it would flatter her. And the moment the camera went on, it was as though she had performed forever. She was so comfortable, so perfectly talkative.

I was behind the camera, in the dark. I just wanted her to talk about her life, though sometimes I had specific questions for her. "Why did you never kiss me?" I asked, out of the darkness.

A look of astonishment came over her face. "Why, I didn't want to spoil you, of course," she said. "My mother never kissed me, either."

That was very interesting to me, since my grandmother had kissed me often. But then, as I've said, my grandmother's relationship with my mother was not a good one. Worse than not good. There really was more hate than love because after the Second World War, my mother, the good Communist, had had all my grandmother's possessions taken away by the Party.

Yet my mother, the good Communist, had many surprisingly romantic memories. As a girl, she recalled, she had loved wandering the palace of her uncle, the Orthodox Patriarch. She spoke about sneaking into a movie theater at fourteen to see Greta Garbo in *Camille*. But her favorite film of all, she sighed, was *Gone with the Wind*; she had first seen it when she was seventeen. She was in love with Rhett Butler! Or maybe it was Clark Gable whom she really had a crush on.

Then there were some not-so-romantic memories of fighting as a partisan. Once, she said, one of her comrades had caught an Italian grenade, which exploded before he could throw it back. She assisted with the amputation of the man's hand: he was given one sip of grappa before being knocked out with the butt of a pistol—this was the anesthesia. Her face turned hard. "As for pain, I can stand pain," she said. "It is a rare case, especially in a woman giving birth, that the whole hospital doesn't hear her screaming. I never let out a single sound. When they were taking me to the hospital, they said, 'We shall wait until you start screaming.' I said, 'Nobody has, and nobody ever will hear me scream.'"

I asked, from the darkness, if she feared death.

Danica smiled. "I'm not afraid of death," she said. "Our presence in this world is only temporary. I think that it's beautiful to die on your feet, out of bed, without being ill."

Unfortunately her wish would not be fulfilled; she was to die such a terrible death.

I later interviewed my father in his apartment. He spoke almost exclusively of his wartime experiences, and the horrors he witnessed: men picking maggots out of each other's wounds with sticks; people infected with typhus eating horse guts. People taking refuge inside cow carcasses in the dead of winter. Starving people being torn apart by wolves. He had survived by being tough, he said, taking out his pistol and showing it to the camera.

Video stills of my parents in *Balkan Baroque* (performance, 4 days, 6 hours), XLVII Biennale Venice, 1997

While I was in Belgrade, I also did a third interview, with a man who had caught rats for the city over a span of thirty-five years. The rat-catcher's tales were very much on my mind when I put together *Delusional*, the five-act theater piece Charles Atlas and I staged in Frankfurt in the spring of 1994 at the invitation of Tom Stromberg, the artistic director of Theater am Turm, one of the most avant-garde theaters in Europe. It was a big, complicated piece—too complicated, really, yet it contained the seeds for works I would complete more successfully later on.

Delusional took place on a Plexiglas stage covered with canvas. In the middle of the stage I lay on a bed of ice, wearing a black cocktail dress. Scattered around the floor were 150 dead-looking black plastic rats lying on their sides. Meanwhile the video interview I'd done with my mother ran on a screen in the background. After a while I got up and danced energetically to a fast Hungarian folk tune. When I became exhausted, I lay back down on the ice bed.

While I reclined there, still breathing hard, a new video was projected, showing me in a white lab coat, giving a lecture about rats. In New York City, I said, there were six to eight rats per person; in Belgrade, there were twenty-five. I continued speaking about the amazing reproductive abilities of rats—and then, while the video changed to the interview with Vojin, I changed my costume.

This costume, the Rat Queen costume, had been created for me by the London performance artist and cult figure Leigh Bowery. Bowery was a huge man, very tall and fat—he was a kind of nude muse to the painter Lucian Freud—and an extreme character, who performed in extreme costumes that exposed his flesh in strange and distorted ways. Watching him, you couldn't help feeling ashamed for him, and this was exactly what he wanted. Shame is a very strong emotion, and *Delusional* was really about all the things I was ashamed of: the unhappiness of my mother and father's relationship, my feelings of being unloved, my mother beating me, my parents beating each other.

The Rat Queen costume was transparent plastic. I wore nothing underneath. It clung tightly to my whole body, including my face—to the audience it looked like I was suffocating, and this was the point: I was suffocating, from shame.

As Vojo waved his pistol on the screen behind me, I pulled the canvas off the Plexiglas stage to reveal four hundred live rats running around underneath. My initial idea had been to have an iron stage with four hundred rats wearing magnetic shoes, doing their best to run around on it. I found somebody in Belgium who told me he could make these shoes. But after three months, he said that the rats' feet were so many different sizes that the process of fitting them all would be endlessly long and too expensive.

I'd spent lots of time studying rat behavior. I learned they had the quickest reproductive cycle of any animal on the planet. Fifteen minutes after giving birth to a litter, a female rat could become pregnant again. For this theater production, we initially bought twelve rats and took them to a laboratory: in less than two months, we had four hundred.

Standing on the Plexiglas stage, I took off the Rat Queen costume and, naked, opened a trapdoor and crawled down to join the rats—at least that's what it looked like, though I was protected by a mirrored enclosure. At the piece's climax, I returned to the stage and, still naked, ate a whole raw onion (including the skin) while crying. Then I lay down on the stage, my head tilted back and facing the audience, and told the story of my "Image of Happiness": I am pregnant, sitting on a rocking chair and doing needlework by the fireplace, when my husband, a coal miner covered with coal dust and sweat, walks in the door. I go to the fridge, take out a milk bottle, and pour him a glass of cold milk. With his right hand he takes the milk; with his left hand he touches my belly: gently, gently. Was this the destiny my parents would have wished for me?

Delusional was so soaked with my shame that Rebecca Horn found it deeply upsetting. After the performance, she came to my dressing room and said, "You have to sue Charles Atlas—I can get you the best lawyer."

I told her the piece had expressed exactly what I wanted to say.

Delusional (theatrical performance), Theater am Turm, Frankfurt, 1994

By now I had moved from Berlin back to Amsterdam. The art market was terrible in the early 1990s, but Sean still managed to sell some of my photographs here and there. To make up the rest of the money I needed, I taught.

My teaching, and the workshops on which my teaching was based, were an extremely important part of my career, not to mention the main source of my income, for more than twenty-five years. I taught in so many places: Paris, Hamburg, Berlin, Kitakyushu in southern Japan, Copenhagen, Milan, Rome, Bern, and (longest of all—eight years) Braunschweig in northern Germany.

In each place I taught, I always started with a workshop for the students. The workshops taught endurance, concentration, perception, self-control, willpower, and confrontation with mental and physical limits. This was the core of my teaching.

For each workshop I would take between twelve and twenty-five students outdoors, always to a place that was either too cold or too hot, never comfortable, and, while we fasted for three to five days, drinking only water and herbal teas, and refraining from speaking, we would do various exercises. Some examples:

BREATHING. Lie on the ground, press your body against the ground as forcefully as possible without breathing, keep this position as long as you can, then breathe deeply and relax.

BLINDFOLD. Leave home and go to the forest, where you are blindfolded, then try to find your way back home. Like a blind person, an artist needs to learn to see with his or her whole body.

LOOKING AT COLOR. Sitting in a chair, look at a sheet of paper printed with one of the primary colors for one hour. Repeat for the other two colors.

LONG WALK IN LANDSCAPE. Start walking from a given point, proceeding in a straight line through the landscape for four hours. Rest, then return along the same route.

WALKING BACKWARD. Walk backward for four hours, while holding a mirror in your hand. Observe reality as a reflection.

FEELING ENERGY. With your eyes closed, extend your hands in front of you toward another participant. Never touching the other person, move your hands around different areas of their body for one hour, feeling their energy.

STOPPING ANGER. If you get angry, stop breathing and hold your breath until you can't hold it anymore, then inhale fresh air.

REMEMBERING. Try to remember the very moment between being awake and falling asleep.

COMPLAINING TO A TREE. Hold a tree and complain to it, for a minimum of fifteen minutes.

SLOW-MOTION EXERCISE. For the entire day, do everything very slowly: walking, drinking water, showering. Peeing in slow motion is very difficult, but try.

OPENING THE DOOR. For three hours, very slowly open a door, neither entering nor exiting. After three hours the door is not a door anymore.

Students have asked me what I expect them to get out of these workshops, and what I get out of them. I tell them that after the workshops, participants get a burst of positive energy and a flow of new ideas; their work becomes clear. The general feeling is that the hardship was worth it. And a strong sense of unity is created between the participants and me. Then we go to the academy and work.

For the first three months, I place each student at a table with a thousand pieces of white paper and a trash can underneath. Every day they have to sit at the table for several hours and write ideas. They put the ideas they like on the right side of the table; the ones they don't like, they put in the trash. But we don't throw out the trash.

After three months, I only take the ideas from the trash can. I don't even look at the ideas they liked. Because the trash can is a treasure trove of things they're afraid to do.

Then, for the rest of the year, they have to create four or five performances. And I coach them through. I constantly repeat to them something Brancusi said: What you're doing is not important. What is really important is the state of mind from which you do it. Performance is all about state of mind. So in order to get to the right state of mind, you have to be mentally and physically prepared.

I remember that in Braunschweig, the students were very easygoing. They seemed very lethargic, unmotivated. So I went to the Kunsthalle, the art museum in Hannover, and asked the director if, after closing a show, he waited for a certain period before opening the next show. He said yes, usually three or four days. I said, "Can you give me those three or four days for a student performance?"

"I'll give you twenty-four hours," he said.

I took it. But I also negotiated to use the entire infrastructure of the museum—phones, secretaries, everything—during that time. The kids got motivated fast. In fact, they went absolutely crazy, creating a twenty-four-hour series of performances. We called the series *Finally*. We provided sleeping bags, sandwiches, and water to the members of the public who came to the event.

As a result of this experience, we formed a body called the Independent Performance Group (IPG). As invitations started pouring in, we created events in every museum in Europe that would give us space. We went once to *documenta*, twice to the Venice Biennale.

Some strong performance artists later emerged from this group. I taught them everything I knew: What is performance? What is the process from beginning to end? How is it documented? How does one write proposals? Once a month, I did an open class. Many students would come from all over—Korea, China, England, Europe—to show their work. At the time I was the only professor in Europe specializing in teaching performance.

At first my field of action was restricted to art academies. But soon I would discover how to teach my methods to everybody.

⌐⌐

Holland was really too small for me to earn a living in—Ulay and I had already shown our work at most of the country's major museums. So I traveled around Europe a lot during these years, not just teaching but also performing and installing shows. I called my house at Binnenkant 21 "temporary forever." Every time I got some money, I put it into the house. And little by little, piece by piece, the place that had been so horrible became transformed into my dream place.

I had so much space in those six floors. I thought of the house as an extension of my body. I had a thinking room, a room just for drinking water. I had a room with just one chair facing a fireplace, for sitting and staring into the fire. All the living spaces were clean and spare, with perfect wood floors. In the basement there was a gym with a sauna. On the ground floor, a modern kitchen and dining room. A big studio and guest bedrooms above, which my friend Michael Laub rented from me. A roof garden. And right below it, on the top floor, my bedroom.

"The bedroom is very important," I told a French magazine that did an article about the house.

> It's a kind of concentration of sleep, dreams and eroticism. If you are not passionate in life, you can't be passionate in art. If you have this sexual or erotic energy in a very strong and condensed way, you project this energy in your work. . . . Making love is an important part of my life—eroticism, sexual desires, passion—the bedroom has to be a space where these things happen.

And the really beautiful part about the house was that it had all grown from the core I'd established by renovating the drug dealer's place first.

Now the drug dealer was no longer a drug dealer. While I was in Paris, he'd phoned me to say he and the beautiful English social worker were going to get married, and they wanted me to be their best man. So I flew from Paris to attend the ceremony. It was a study in opposites—these were two families you could never imagine connecting in real life. His relatives were from the lowest class: tattooed, impossible-looking drinkers. Her relatives were sophisticated and aristocratic. But these two people had fallen in love and created a new family. And they were living in the heart of my house.

I met the English curator Chrissie Iles in Amsterdam in the mid-1980s, and we became instant friends—in no small part because she, too, was born on November 30 (though even today, I still don't know her age—she's always made a big point of not telling me), but even more important, because she understood my work deeply, helping me to see things in it that I hadn't even seen myself. In 1990 she invited me to perform at the Museum of Modern Art at Oxford, where I did a piece, *Dragon Heads*, in which four big pythons and a boa constrictor crawled around my head and shoulders.

Now Chrissie was about to curate a retrospective of my work, again at Oxford. When we split, Ulay had taken all the documentation of the pieces we had done together, so the show could only include my early performances and new work. To strengthen the exhibition I created a trilogy of video performances called *Cleaning the Mirror*.

It was the year before I was to turn fifty, and mortality was on my mind. I had also read a book about the Tibetan *rolang* ritual, in which a monk is made to get used to the idea of death by sleeping in a cemetery with corpses in various stages of decay.

In one of the *Cleaning the Mirror* pieces, I lay naked with a (very realistic) skeleton model on top of me for ninety minutes, breathing easily, the skeleton rising and falling gently with every breath I took. In another piece I sat with the skeleton on my lap and, using a hard scrub brush and a pail full of soapy water, spent three hours furiously scouring its every nook and cranny.

Cleaning the Mirror III involved several ancient and amazing objects from Oxford's Pitt Rivers anthropological museum: a mummified ibis bird from ancient Egypt. A magic medicine box from Nigeria. Kadachi shoes made of emu feathers from Australian Aborigines. A mercury-filled bottle from Sussex, England, said to contain a medieval witch. As I sat at a table in a darkened room of the museum, a curator of the collection would very carefully bring each object on a

Left: *Cleaning the Mirror II* (performance for video, 90 minutes), Oxford University, 1995; *right*: *Cleaning the Mirror III* (performance for video, 5 hours), Pitt Rivers Museum, Oxford, 1995

tray, using white gloves, and place it on the tabletop in front of me; I would hold my open hands over the object, never touching it, just feeling its energy.

If energy could transcend time, I wondered, why couldn't the human body?

And why couldn't the human spirit transcend anger? That year I had a big Christmas lunch at Binnenkant 21, and on the advice of my wonderful Stefanowski, I invited Ulay and his wife, Song, along with their little daughter, Luna.

The three of them came, and many of the smiles around the big table were genuine. The six years I'd predicted it would take me to get over Ulay had passed. At the same time, he still controlled the records of the work we'd done together, a fact that upset me every time I thought about it. On the other hand, half a reconciliation seemed better than none at all.

⌒

Soon afterward, during a three-month residency at the University of Texas, I did a video piece called *The Onion*. This was a strange three months: I was feeling my age acutely, also feeling acutely alone. The university housed me in a motel, miles from campus. And since I still didn't drive at that point, I had to call a taxi whenever I wanted to go anywhere.

I constructed *The Onion* very carefully. I was shot against a bright-blue-sky background, wearing bright-red lipstick and nail polish, while I ate an entire onion (just as in *Delusional*) and complained about my life. As I complained, I gazed heavenward, like the Madonna suffering. And since I was eating a raw onion, with the skin, the tears streamed down my face.

I really did suffer for that piece. I actually had to eat three onions. For the first one, the sound wasn't right. For the second, something was wrong with the light. By the time I finished the third onion, my entire mouth and throat felt burned. But we got the video! My lament while I chewed the onion:

> I am tired of changing planes so often. Waiting in the waiting rooms, bus stations, train stations, airports. I am tired of waiting for endless passport controls. Fast shopping in shopping malls. I am tired of more career decisions, museum and gallery openings, endless receptions, standing around with a glass of plain water, pretending that I am interested in conversation. I am tired of my migraine attacks, lonely hotel rooms, room service, long-distance telephone calls, bad TV movies. I am tired of always falling in love with the wrong man. I am tired of being ashamed of my nose being too big, of my ass being too large, ashamed of the war in Yugoslavia. I want to go away, somewhere so far that I am unreachable by fax or telephone. I want to get old, really old so that nothing matters any more. I want to understand and see clearly what is behind all this. I want to not want anymore.

This video is still very important to me. Videos are the most immediate document of a performance, retaining the piece's energy far better than still photography ever could. And this video is kind of a time capsule—both of the 1990s and of my life at that time. It's at once self-centered (notice how I give third billing to shame about the war in Yugoslavia, after shame about my big nose and ass) and universal. It speaks of the superficiality of the art scene, and of all the fears I was feeling about being alone in my fiftieth year.

Late that summer, the National Museum of Montenegro invited me to give a lecture. While I was there, I went to see the village where my father was born, near Cetinje. His old house was in ruins, just a pile of stones. But in the middle of this ruin, growing right up through the stones, was a huge oak tree. And as I sat there in what had probably once been my father's living room, thinking about the vitality of that tree, and the extremes of my life, two horses came up, a black one and a white one, and began to make love, right in front of me! It was like a Tarkovsky movie. *If I ever told anybody about this*, I thought, *they would never believe me.*

But that wasn't all.

Near the ruins of my father's old house was a little house where people were still living. Goats all around it. While I was sitting watching the two horses, an old shepherd with a big Balkan nose came staggering out of the little house, drunk—it was eleven in the morning—and said, "You are Abramović? My name is Abramović, too."

I shook his hand. I could smell the liquor on his breath. I asked about my father's family, and he told me a couple of stories about the village when he was a boy. He pointed out the old landmarks. And then he said, "Abramović—can you lend me four thousand dinars? I just lost a lot of money playing cards."

⌒

For my fiftieth birthday I wanted to do something really big. My exhibition was opening at the same time at S.M.A.K., the museum of contemporary art in Ghent, so I invited 150 people, all my friends from around the world, to come celebrate with me at a big dinner.

And once again, in the spirit of reconciliation, I invited Ulay, with his wife and daughter. After all, it was his birthday, too—at the time it seemed the right thing to do.

A theme for the occasion came to me, almost as if in a dream: I decided to call the party *The Urgent Dance*. What could be more urgent, I thought, than dancing in the face of age? And what dance could be more urgent and sexy than one I had been fascinated with my whole life—the Argentinean tango? I'd always wanted to learn the tango, and so I took lessons. I got pretty good at it.

We began the party with tango dancing. My partner was my tango instructor. It was an evening to remember—great food, great music, and some great surprises. Earlier when I'd asked Jan Hoet, the director of the museum, if he could have a special birthday cake for me, he seemed outraged. "We spent money on an orchestra, we spent money on your exhibition, we spent money on everything!" he said. "Are you out of your mind? We can't afford anything more. And a cake—it is so bourgeois."

But secretly he'd taken the naked photo of me from *Thomas Lips* to the best *patisserie* in Belgium, and they made a life-size marzipan cake of me, replete with chocolate stripes on my stomach like the cuts I made in the piece. At a quarter to midnight, a door opened, and out came five guys carrying this amazing cake. Everyone burst into applause as the guys put the cake on the table, and everybody wanted a piece of me, cutting my marzipan breasts, feet, head.

Then, just before midnight, the same door opened and the same five guys carried in another huge platter—with Jan Hoet lying on it, naked except for a bow tie.

Imagine any other museum director in the world doing that.

To make my big birthday complete, another museum director, Petar Cukovic of the National Museum of Montenegro, gave me a very special present: an invitation to represent Serbia and Montenegro at the next summer's Venice Biennale.

But the evening still had one more climax: Ulay and I performed together again.

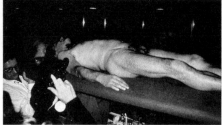

Left: Urgent Dance, 1995; *top right:* My fiftieth birthday cake, made of marzipan with chocolate scars; *bottom right*: Jan Hoet, the director of S.M.A.K, offers his body as a birthday gift, Stedelijk Museum voor Actuele Kunst, Ghent, 1996

We repeated a piece we'd done in Australia fifteen years earlier, *A Similar Illusion.* In it we stood locked together for three hours in a dancers' embrace, his hand holding mine up. To the tune of "The Jealousy Tango" playing on and on, our clasped hands dropped with infinite slowness. In Melbourne in 1986, the piece had lasted three hours. On this night of my fiftieth birthday, it lasted for only twenty minutes, but for everyone there, the experience was still powerfully emotional. For me, however, the electricity I'd once felt when my body touched his was gone forever.

I thought and thought about Cuković's invitation, and what I might do for the Biennale. And the more I thought, the more certain I became that I had to react somehow to the disaster of the war in the Balkans. A number of international artists—Jenny Holzer, for one—had done pieces about it. But for me, the war felt too close: I was deeply ashamed of Serbia's part in it.

What's more, Sean Kelly kept telling me that I shouldn't accept the invitation, that representing Serbia and Montenegro at the Bi-

Left: Marina Abramović/Ulay, *A Similar Illusion* (performance, 96 minutes),
Sculpture Triennial, National Gallery of Victoria, Melbourne, 1981; *right:*
Ulay and I reunite to re-perform the work at my fiftieth birthday party

ennale would be aligning myself with that bastard Milosevic. But I pushed back. All the sides in the war bore blame, I felt. I wanted to grieve for war everywhere, not produce a piece of propaganda related to this particular conflict.

So I wrote a proposal and sent it to the Montenegrin Ministry of Culture. The piece I had in mind was a strange and upsetting one, I said, but nothing was more upsetting than war. The performance I proposed would partake equally of the rat motif and videos of my parents from *Delusional* and the scrubbing of cow bones from an earlier piece called *Cleaning the House.* I would require three high-resolution projectors and 2,500 bones from freshly slaughtered cows, plus refrigeration facilities to keep the bones fresh until the performance began. The total cost, I said, would be about 120,000 euro. A lot of money. But in fact the equipment was less expensive to buy outright than to rent for the whole Biennale (after my performance was complete, the installation and the videos would stay up for the remaining four months of the event). And I was also proposing to donate the piece, equipment and all, to the National Museum of Montenegro, as they didn't have any work by me in their collection yet.

Nevertheless, Montenegro's minister of culture, Goran Rakocevic, chose to misunderstand my proposal completely. Though he had approved Cuković's invitation, he now fired Cuković and turned on me. Not only was the vast cost of this monstrosity being taken out of the pensions of elderly Montenegrins, he said, but the piece I was talking about wasn't really art at all, just an ugly and smelly pile of bones. In an article in the Montenegrin newspaper *Podgorica* titled "Montenegro Is Not a Cultural Colony," he wrote:

> This outstanding opportunity ought to be used to represent authentic art from Montenegro, free of any complex of inferiority for which there is no reason in our exquisite tradition and spirituality. . . . Montenegro is not a cultural margin and it should not be just a homeland colony for megalomaniac performances. In my opinion, we should be represented in the world by painters marked by Montenegro and its poetics, since we have the luck and honor to have brilliant artists of universal dimensions living among us.

In other words, socialist realist or abstract hack painters. Rakocevic was saying not only that I wasn't a real artist, but I wasn't a real Yugoslav.

I saw red.

Two days later I sent a statement to newspapers in Serbia and Montenegro, saying I was ending "any further communication with the Ministry of Culture of Montenegro and all other Yugoslavian Institutions responsible for the exhibition in the Yugoslav Pavilion." Rakocevic, I wrote, had "incompetently . . . tried to misuse my artwork and reputation in some strange purpose, most probably of a political nature." His "evil intention," I said, "is not tolerable."

Hearing of the controversy, the Italian art historian and critic Germano Celant, who was curating the Biennale, invited me to participate in the international section. However, he said, "There's only one place left, because you are so late—I'm so sorry, it's the worst of all." The space was the basement of the Italian pavilion in Giardini: dark, damp, and low-ceilinged.

"The worst is the best," I told Germano.

With Germano and Argento Celant, Paris, 2000

A month before the Biennale, a gallerist in Rome, Stefania Miscetti, invited me there to give a lecture about the Great Wall walk. After the talk, which was on a Saturday morning, Stefania introduced me to a friend and artist of hers, Paolo Canevari. Black, slicked-back hair; dark emotional eyes: movie-star good looks. As he held my hands in his, he told me that my lecture had moved him to tears—that he couldn't believe that a lecture could be so incredible, and that he wanted to get to know me better.

Was I skeptical about his smooth Roman charm? Not very. He really did seem moved. And he didn't let go of my hands. And—there's no other way to put it, because it really happened—time stopped as we stared into each other's eyes. Suddenly Stefania broke the spell. "We have to go to lunch," she said curtly.

"Can I come?" Paolo asked.

"No, you can't—Marina and I have something to discuss," Stefania said.

This surprised me, since as far as I knew, she and I were just going out for a friendly lunch. I was also disappointed. But at lunch, Stefania told me what was up: her best friend, Maura, was Paolo's girlfriend. And the instant chemistry between Paolo and me had been all too clear to Stefania, who wanted to be loyal to her friend. Who, at forty-one, was seven years older than Paolo.

A few days later, I attended an opening for an installation of mine in a palazzo outside of Rome. Paolo showed up, alone. On a motorcycle.

It was a rainy day. After the reception, he asked me if I wanted to go to a street fair in a little town nearby. Sure, I said. So off we went, me on the back of his motorcycle, in the rain. We stopped at the fair and walked and walked. There were food booths under tents, and the cooking smells in the cool, wet air were dizzying—especially at one booth that sold *porchetta*, a very thin-sliced, slow-cooked pork. "Oh my God," I said. "Let's get some."

Paolo looked uncertain. "I'm a vegetarian," he said.

"Oh," I said. "That's okay—we'll get something else."

He shook his head. "No, I'll eat with you."

And so we ate, and walked some more, and talked and talked. Then he had to go back to Rome, so he dropped me off at my hotel— where, the moment I closed the door of my room, I dropped onto the bed and, imagining his hands on my body, brought myself to a mind-blowing orgasm.

We hadn't exchanged numbers. But over the next few days in Rome, I kept looking for him everywhere I went, like a teenage girl in love—hoping I'd see him when I walked down the street, but never seeing him.

Then I did a TV interview at Stefania's gallery, and afterward she hosted a dinner at a nearby restaurant, and there he was, at the other end of this long table. With his girlfriend. Throughout the dinner, I kept looking at him, but he never met my eyes. At the end of the meal, Paolo and Maura stood to leave, and as they passed me, he gave me a quick, cold hello.

And that, I thought, was that.

⌒

The title of my piece, *Balkan Baroque*, didn't refer to the baroque art movement, but rather the baroqueness of the Balkan mind. Really you can only understand the Balkan mentality if you're from there, or spend a lot of time there. To comprehend it intellectually is impossible—these turbulent emotions are volcanic, insane. There is always war somewhere on this planet, and I wanted to create a universal image that could stand for war anywhere.

In *Balkan Baroque*, I sat on the floor of the basement of the Italian pavilion, on an enormous pile of cow bones: five hundred clean bones underneath; two thousand bloody, meaty, gristly bones on top. For four days, seven hours a day, I sat scrubbing the bloody bones while still, silent images from my interviews with my mother and father— Danica folding her hands over her heart then putting her hands over her eyes, Vojin waving his pistol—flashed on two screens behind me. In the un-air-conditioned basement, in the humid summer air of Venice, the bloody, meaty, gristly bones rotted and filled with maggots as I scrubbed them: the stench was unholy, like the stench of bodies on the battlefield. The public filed in and stared, repulsed by the odor but transfixed by the spectacle. As I scrubbed the bones, I wept and sang Yugoslav folk songs from my childhood.

And on the third screen was a video of me in glasses, a lab coat, and heavy leather shoes, very scientific-looking in a Slavic way, telling the story of the Wolf Rat.

The story had come from the rat-catcher I interviewed in Belgrade. Rats, he told me, never kill anybody from their own family. They are very protective, but at the same time, extremely intelligent—Einstein said that if rats were bigger, they could rule the world.

It's very difficult to kill rats. If you try to give them poisoned food, they will first send out sick rats to try it, and if the sick rats die, the healthy rats won't touch the bait. The only way to kill rats (the rat-catcher told me) is to create a Wolf Rat.

The rats live in nests, with many holes, one hole per family. And

Video stills from *Balkan Baroque* (performance, 4 days, 6 hours), Venice, 1997

the rat-catcher would fill all the holes but one with water, so that the rats from one of the rat families would have to flee through the single exit. When they fled, the rat-catcher would trap them and put thirty to forty of them, only male, in a cage. With no food, just water to drink.

Rats have an unusual anatomy: their teeth grow constantly. If they're not always chewing on something, grinding something, their teeth grow so long that they can suffocate. So now what the rat-catcher has is a cage full of male rats from the same family, just drinking water, without food. They won't kill family members, but their teeth are growing. Finally they're forced to kill the weakest one, and then the next weakest one, then the next weakest one. The rat-catcher waits until only one rat is left.

The timing is very important. The rat-catcher waits until the last rat's teeth have grown almost to the point of suffocating it, then he opens the cage, gouges the rat's eyes out with a knife, and lets him go. This blind and desperate rat then runs into its family's hole, killing every rat in its way, family or not—until a bigger and stronger rat kills him. The rat-catcher then repeats the process.

And this is how he creates the Wolf Rat.

I told this whole story in the video playing behind me while I scrubbed the rotting and maggoty bones. Then, in the video, I looked at the camera seductively and took off my scientific-looking glasses and lab coat and dress, stripping down to a black negligee, and did a sexy, manic dance with a red silk handkerchief to the sound of a fast Serbian folk tune—the kind of dance you see in Yugoslav bistros, where heavily whiskered men guzzle rakia, smash their glasses on the floor, and put their money in the bras of the singers.

Here you have the essence of *Balkan Baroque*: horrifying carnage and an intensely disturbing story, followed by a sexy dance—then a return to more bloody awfulness.

Four days, seven hours a day. Every morning, I had to come back and embrace this pile of maggoty bones. The heat in that basement was overpowering. The smell was unbearable. But that was the work. For me, it was the essence of *Balkan Baroque*–ness.

Each day at the end of the performance, I would go back to the apartment I was renting and take a long, long shower, trying to wash away the smell of rotten meat that had permeated my pores. By the end of the third day it felt impossible to get clean.

That was when Sean Kelly knocked on the door, smiling broadly and telling me that I had won the Golden Lion for best artist in the Biennale. I broke down in tears.

And there was still one more day of performance to go, seven more hours of this overwhelming stench.

It was an indescribably gratifying award: I had put my whole soul into this piece. In my acceptance speech, I said, "I'm only interested in an art which can change the ideology of society. . . . Art which is only committed to aesthetic values is incomplete."

During the ceremony, the Montenegro minister of culture was sitting two rows behind me and never got up to congratulate me.

Afterward, the new curator from the Yugoslav pavilion (where

Me after receiving the Golden Lion for best artist at the 1997 Venice
Biennale for my performance *Balkan Baroque*

they'd replaced me with a landscape painter) came up to me and invited me to their reception. "You have a very big heart and you will forgive," he said.

"My heart is big but I am Montenegrin," I told him. "And you don't hurt Montenegrin pride."

Later that day I walked across San Marco Square with Sean Kelly and his wife, Mary. The square, as usual, was packed with tourists—but it seemed every one of them had seen *Balkan Baroque*. I couldn't go five paces without someone stopping me and saying how moved they'd been by the piece, and how grateful they were to me for it. Ulay and I had been able to connect with a larger public together, but this was the first time I'd been able to accomplish it alone.

That night, I went with Germano Celant to a party at the Portuguese pavilion for Julião Sarmento. And though I love Julião and his work, and we had a good talk (he was very sweet about my award), afterward the evening began to turn into another one of those gallery receptions where, as I'd complained in *The Onion*, I was standing around with a glass of plain water, pretending to be interested in the small talk I was forced to make with various strangers. I think people who drink wine have the advantage on me at these receptions— probably the wine makes these empty conversations seem more amusing.

That was when I saw Paolo.

He was on his own this time—no Maura in sight. I, however, was not on my own: Michael Stefanowski was with me at the Biennale. He was across the crowded room at the moment, but as Paolo headed toward me with a big smile, I was acutely aware that at any moment, Michael might turn and see us.

What might he see, exactly?

Once again Paolo took my hands in his and stared at me with awe. "Your piece was so amazing," he said. "I was there all four days—I couldn't stay away. Big congratulations on the prize—you totally deserved it."

I thanked him, looking for the message behind the message.

It came. "I need to talk to you," he said.

"But we're talking now," I said.

"I want to sit down with you."

It was a really crowded party. There were some chairs, and people were sitting in them. Then Paolo spotted an empty armchair in a corner of the garden. He led me over to it and motioned for me to sit with him. Just then a guy came up and said, "Sorry, this chair is occupied."

"I'll pay you for it," Paolo said. "How much do you want? I'm serious."

The guy shook his head and walked away. Then Paolo pulled me down into the chair with him. "I want to hold you," he said. "I want to kiss you—everywhere."

Michael still hadn't seen us, but it wasn't exactly as if I was an inconspicuous figure at this party. "I really can't be doing this now," I told him. I stood up.

He heard the urgency in my voice, and nodded. But a little while later, he joined a line of people who were congratulating me, and when his turn came to shake my hand, I felt a piece of paper in my palm. Which had his phone number on it. And then we started calling each other. Oh God, did we start calling each other.

⌒

A couple of months later, I was in New York, discussing strategies for the future with Sean Kelly. I was staying at Sean and Mary's apartment. And Paolo, who'd gotten an artist grant, also came to New York.

We met at Fanelli, the old café at Prince and Mercer in Soho, at lunchtime. We had coffee—who was hungry?—and stared into each other's eyes. Then we went to the apartment Paolo was borrowing from his friend John McEvers and made love for a long, long time.

For the next few days, our menu was exactly the same: coffee at Fanelli's, holding hands and gazing into each other's eyes, back to the apartment. All secret—that was part of the charge. Every morning, as I left the Kellys', Sean and Mary would ask, "Where are you going?" And I would say, "Oh, I have these friends who are refugees from ex-Yugoslavia, and I'm having lunch with them, and then they want me to meet some of their refugee friends."

After a couple of days, Sean said, "Can I meet some of these refugees?"

Stefanowski was in Germany. We'd planned that after I returned to Amsterdam, the two of us would go to the Maldives for vacation. I returned to Amsterdam, and Michael and I went to the Maldives, and it was a disaster.

We were on a little dot of land called Cocoa Island, so small that you could walk around the whole island in twelve minutes. It was famous because Leni Riefenstahl had snorkeled there, and it was absolutely gorgeous, and I was miserable. When Stefanowski went snorkeling, I would run to the island's single landline phone to call Paolo. Other times, I would just walk the beach in circles, desperately missing him.

I noticed a peculiar thing: because tourists had taken all the island's seashells away, the hermit crabs were using discarded plastic sunscreen containers instead of shells for their homes. I felt so bad for them (and for myself) that I took a two-hour boat trip to a nearby island and bought bags and bags of shells at the market to bring back for the crabs. When I got back, I scattered the shells around the beach and watched for ten days to see if they would change their habitat, but they liked the plastic better.

From the Maldives, Michael and I went to Sri Lanka for an Ayurveda retreat. Sri Lanka was so beautiful—I told Stefanowski I wanted to stay for another two weeks. But he had to go back to work in Germany. The minute he left, I called Paolo.

He was still with Maura at this point, so he told her a story. He wanted to think about life, he said—he was just going to ride his motorcycle around for a few days, to clear his head. What he really did was ride his bike to the airport and fly to Sri Lanka, where he spent three beautiful days with me.

When Paolo returned home, his heart was no longer with Maura; their relationship went downhill quickly. One day he cut out his horoscope from the newspaper—it said he should break old ties and find himself—and left it on the kitchen table. Then he packed his suitcase and came to Amsterdam.

10.

It's just after the Bosnian war in Sarajevo—there's no food, no gasoline, no electricity. People are sitting in a café, starving, just drinking water and talking. Just then, a Bosnian guy pulls up in a Mercedes Cabriolet, the latest model, and gets out, leaving the engine running. He's wearing an Armani suit and a big Rolex. He enters the café and says, "I'm buying—the drinks are on me." Everybody's impressed. They ask him, "Where'd you get all this money?" He says, "The best business to run during a war is a bordello." Someone asks, "But how many girls are working for you?" And he says, "At the moment, I'm keeping the business small—just me."

After the Biennale came an intense period of travel: doing my workshops and teaching in Europe and Japan, bringing my exhibitions to museums in Munich, Groningen, Hannover, and Ghent, among other places. During the mid- to late 1990s I worked on and produced a number of different transitory objects. I wrote at the time that I wanted my work to function as a constant mirror for the users of my objects—so they wouldn't see me in the work, but rather themselves.

In that light, I was especially proud of my first two commissions in Japan. *Black Dragon* was a piece I installed in a Tokyo shopping district, consisting of five sets of pillow-shaped blocks of rose quartz, mounted in vertical groups of three on a bare concrete wall. A plaque invited visitors—men, women, and children; families were encouraged to participate—to turn away from the busy street and press head, heart, and hips against the pale-pink, soft-looking blocks "and wait." For what? The instructions on the wall said that the participants should stand in this position as long as they wanted, in order to empty their mind. From afar, the participants looked as though they were just standing facing the wall.

Black Dragon, site-specific project, rose quartz,
Tachikawa Monument, Tokyo, 1994

And in the Okazaki Mindscape Museum, an institution dedicated to examining everything the human mind can't explain—the origin of life, black holes, etc. (it was an earthquake-proof building completely made of glass—I installed two copper chairs: a normal-size one for humans, with a piece of black tourmaline on the back, and a seatless, soaring (fifty-foot-high) chair for the spirit.

Yet for all my spiritual explorations, I still had important lessons to learn.

In 1999, Lama Doboom Tulku, the director of Tibet House in New Delhi, the world center for the teachings of His Holiness the

Dalai Lama, invited me to participate in a festival of sacred music in Bangalore. This was to be a big event, encompassing five different Buddhist traditions—Theravada, Mahayana, Vajrayana, Hinayana, and Bön—as well as many other cultures: Jewish, Palestinian, Zulu, Christian, Sufi.

The Dalai Lama, who felt that music unites everybody, wanted me to choreograph a piece with many monks from these five Buddhist traditions, all singing one song together. I was brought to the Gaden Jangtse Thoesam Norling Monastery, in the town of Mundgod in southern India, and given 120 monks to work with: twenty from each tradition, including—this was revolutionary, and a first—twenty Mahayana nuns.

For the song, I chose the Heart Sutra, a prayer common to all Buddhist traditions. For the choreography, I decided to arrange the monks on movable benches of various heights so that they would form a human pyramid. And in order to have the 120 monks ready to sing when the curtain rose on them, I had to train them to get into position in less than thirty seconds.

I worked with them for a month, and they were impossible. They couldn't ever remember their positions; they were always laughing and giggling. But finally, finally, we shaped the routine to perfection. The monastery even built special wheeled benches for me. All was in readiness.

It was time to head to Bangalore, a five-hour drive, to organize the setup for the show. Doboom Tulku and I were walking to our car when the abbot of the monastery came out to say good-bye. "It was so great that you could come here!" he said. "We really enjoyed your collaboration—but we have a problem."

"What's the problem?" I asked.

"We can't do the pyramid," he said.

"What?" I said.

My God. I babbled something about the solid month of training, the special benches with wheels . . .

Top: *The Family A* (color chromogenic print from series *8 Lessons on Emptiness with a Happy End*), 2008; bottom: *The Family III* (color chromogenic print from series *8 Lessons on Emptiness with a Happy End*), 2008

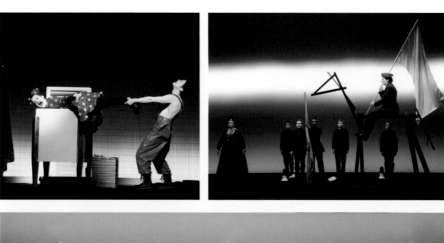

The Life and Death of Marina Abramović by Bob Wilson (theatrical performance),
Theater Basel, Switzerland, 2012

From left to right: Christopher Nell, Anohni, Robert Wilson, Queen Beatrix of the Netherlands, me, Willem Dafoe, and Svetlana Spajić, after a performance of *The Life and Death of Marina Abramović*, Amsterdam, 2012

From left to right: Thomas Kelly, Mary Kelly, me, Lauren Kelly, and Sean Kelly, at the opening of *Generator*, New York, 2014

HAPPY HOLIDAYS AND HAPPY NEW YEAR

ABRAMOVIC LLC

MAI

/ LYNSEY / / VICTORIA / MARINA / GIULIANO / / LEAH /
/ POLLY / / MARIA / / CHRISTIANA / / SIDNEY

photograph Brigitte Lacombe © 2013

Top: Abramović LLC and MAI holiday card, 2013
Bottom: The Abramović LLC holiday card, 2014

We wish
a less exhausting
2015

ABRAMOVIC LLC

Front page of *The Australian*, June 12, 2015

Hans-Ulrich Obrist and me during a planning
meeting for *512 Hours*, New York, 2013

Lynsey and me on
the set for *512 Hours*
(performance, 512 hours),
Serpentine Gallery,
London, 2014

Photograph © Marco Anelli

Woman Massaging Breasts II (color chromogenic print from the series *Balkan Erotic Epic*), 2005

When I told Annie Leibovitz that the first *Playboy* centerfold to appear in ex-Yugoslavia featured a red tractor with no girl, she said, "Let's put a girl on it," 2015.

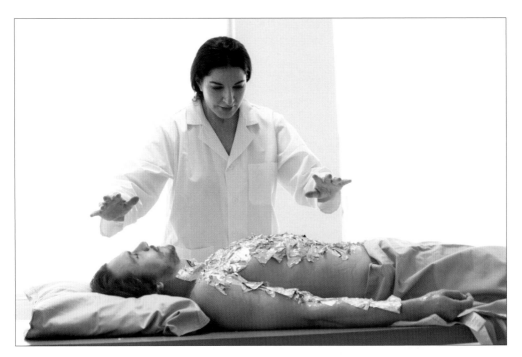

RAHI REZVANI. All rights reserved ©Rahi Rezvani. All manners of reproduction or communication of this work/ reprinting of text or pictures, recitation, performances and demonstration are only admissible within the scope of legal regulation.

Top: With James Franco during *Iconoclasts*, 2012; bottom: Brigitte Lefevre, director of the Paris Opera Ballet, commissioned a new production of *Boléro* in 2013. The concept and scenography were created in collaboration with choreographers Sidi Larbi Cherkaoui and Damien Jalet and me, with lighting design by Urs Schoenebaum and costumes by Riccardo Tisci.

Maria Stamenkovic Herranz performing during Givenchy's first
New York Fashion Week show, September 11, 2015

Marina Abramović and Igor Levit, *Goldberg*,
Park Avenue Armory, New York, December 2015

"Yes," the abbot said. "But you see, this idea of a human pyramid can't work for us. In Tibetan Buddhism, nobody can be at the top."

I recovered some of my composure. "Excuse me," I said, "but I've been here for a month. We've been working so hard every day. We created this entire thing. Why didn't you tell me this the first day?"

"Ah," he said. "You're our guest, and we would never offend you."

And that was that.

On the drive to Bangalore with Doboom Tulku, I was weeping with frustration, fury, exhaustion—and the lama was laughing. Tibetans love to laugh. Through my tears I stared at him and said, "What's so funny?"

"Ah," Doboom Tulku said. "Now you are learning detachment."

"But I worked all this time," I said.

"You've done your best. Now let it go," he said. "Things will happen as they happen anyway. Remember the story of the Buddha—he received his enlightenment, but only after he had given up completely. Sometimes you do everything you can to achieve a goal, and then it doesn't happen because the cosmic laws go a different way."

So I arrived in Bangalore. I didn't have my wheeled benches; I had nothing to do. I arranged the lights on the stage, and then the buses arrived with the 120 monks, and the concert started. The monks sat wherever they wanted to sit. They sang the Heart Sutra. The curtain closed. And His Holiness the Dalai Lama came up to me and held me in his arms. "You've done a wonderful thing," he told me. "We are so happy; everybody is happy."

⌒

While I was in Mundgod, I had also begun making videos of monks and nuns for a big new piece I had in mind. My plan was to film 120 monks and nuns chanting individually, then to assemble all the separate videos into an enormous grid, visually and sonically overwhelming, showing all of them chanting at once. This huge piece, which would eventually take five years to assemble, would be called *At the Waterfall*. A year after the Bangalore festival, I went back to India to finish my recording at several other monasteries.

After I returned to Amsterdam, ten of the monks I'd been working with came to visit Holland, and, in gratitude for their hospitality to me in India, I invited them to stay at Binnenkant 21. My house was more beautiful than ever by now, and I was happy to host them. They all slept in sleeping bags on the floor of my big studio, and we had a wonderful time. By now I'd learned what to expect when Tibetan monks stayed with me: they'd wake up every morning at four, meditate for an hour, then brew the disgusting yak tea that made them so happy. Each morning, very early, the smell of this yak tea would waft up to my bedroom, along with the sound of their laughter—sheer pleasure at the bubbling of the milk.

They toured the city, they attended some symposiums, and then the time came for them to return to India. The day before they left, they told me they'd like to make a special *puja*, to clean every evil spirit from my house. The preparations were elaborate. They made cakes, lit incense everywhere, rang bells, said prayers continuously for four hours. They left early the next morning with big thank-yous and happy smiles all around.

Literally one hour later, my doorbell rang. It was the former drug dealer and his wife. "Can we have coffee with you?" he asked. "We have to tell you something." Sure, I said. We sat down and had coffee. After a little small talk, his wife looked at me. "We've decided to leave the house," she said. As beautiful as their place was, she told me, it just stirred up so many memories of her husband's past. They wanted to change everything. They had some money; they planned to buy a boat and live on it. So they said they would give me back the contract we'd signed. The entire house was now mine. I could easily rent the floor they'd lived on—it was separate from the rest of the house—for enough to pay my mortgage every month. Which is exactly what I did.

All this, one hour after the monks had left.

⌐

The Dayton Agreements had ended the Bosnian war several years before, but what had once been Yugoslavia was in shambles. Life in Belgrade was still hard. And my father, who'd had it with the country he used to love, wanted to get out.

Vojin's wife, Vesna, the blond judge, had a son with her first husband, and the husband and the son had moved to Canada. Now (it was early 1998) my father and his wife also wanted to move to Canada. Vesna, the gorgeous miniskirted blonde I'd once seen kissing my father on a Belgrade street, had developed terminal stomach cancer, and wanted to see her son before she died. Vojin, too, was in poor health: he'd always been thin, but now he had lost an alarming amount of weight. And my father, who'd never asked me for money, asked if he could borrow 10,000 euro. This was a huge sum for me, but I put it together and sent it to them. He never said a word of thanks. They went to Canada, spent two weeks there—and came back. I'll never understand why.

They should have stayed. Soon afterward, hostilities broke out between Serbia/Montenegro and Kosovo, and by the spring of 1999, NATO was bombing Belgrade, where my mother, father, and brother were all still living.

Velimir was six years younger than me, and we had always lived our lives in parallel, rarely intersecting. He was uncommonly intelligent and talented: he wrote his first book, a volume of poetry called *Emsep* (the title was the Serbo-Croatian word for "poetry" spelled backward), when he was fourteen, and it was published by Nolit, a big Serbian publisher. One poem from the book, in its entirety:

Building the abyss under the bridge
is the task of the most advanced builders

He went to the film academy in Belgrade, then got a doctorate in philosophy, with a specialty in the time-space studies of Leibniz.

He was brilliant and accomplished, but he was a very complex and difficult man. Though he had gotten all the love from my mother that she never would give to me, he still hated her. He got married to a woman named Maria, a nuclear physicist and the director of the Nikola Tesla Museum in Belgrade. They had a beautiful daughter, Ivana. Then Maria was diagnosed with breast cancer.

When the bombing in Belgrade began, Maria told Velimir that he had to take their daughter and move to Amsterdam—with me—until the hostilities ended. She said that she needed to stay to continue her chemotherapy treatments. I wasn't asked about this; I was informed. And it was even more complicated than that, because now I was living with Paolo.

I was in love. Not only was he smart (and seventeen years younger!), he was an accomplished artist, though much slower working than me: his love for his motorcycle somehow connected to his desire to make sculptures related to tires and other forms of rubber.

But neither my art nor his was the focus of the relationship. Paolo was interested in me as a woman—*his* woman, he called me. He told me he wanted to be with me for the rest of his life. And he loved to cook. He cooked like a dream, and he wanted to feed me. This was a man, I felt, who could really take care of me.

Unlike my brother, who needed to be taken care *of.*

I met Paolo's friends, Bruna and Alberto, in Rome and liked them very much. Often, when I was in town, I would spend time with Paolo's sisters, Angela and Barbara, but most of all I loved his father, Angelo. I could spend hours talking with him. He knew so much about Italian history, art, architecture. I talked to him on the phone just one week before he passed away. Once, for his birthday, I had given him a watch, and I found out when he died that he had instructed his wife to bury him with it.

At that time, when the Kosovo war started, I was in Japan, working on another new commission, *Dream House*, for the Echigo-Tsumari Art Triennale 2000. In a mountain village north of Tokyo (Uwayu, in

Matsunoyama Tokamachi City, Niigata Prefecture), I was refurbishing a traditional wooden house, over a hundred years old, into a kind of inn, with big copper bathtubs and beds with quartz pillows. There were to be four different bedrooms, one red, one blue, one green, and one purple. Visitors would bathe in the tubs, then put on special sleep suits and sleep in the beds. The sleep suits, which would also come in four colors, to match the rooms, would contain magnets, in small pockets, to make the blood circulate faster and facilitate dreaming. Afterward the sleepers would write down their dreams in the house's dream book. I believed strongly that the minerals in the tubs and the beds would exert their powers, connecting the energy of the earth with the energy of the human body and creating profound dreams.

The piece sprang from the question I've always asked, and am still asking: What is art? I feel that if we see art as something isolated, something holy and separate from everything, that means it's not life. Art must be a part of life. Art has to belong to everybody.

And life—even in 1999—was moving too fast for the human spirit to absorb. "I want you to dream," I'd written in my proposal for *Dream House*. "You must dream in order to face yourself."

The local villagers took care of the Dream House, which between July 2000 and November 2010 around 42,000 people would visit. About 2,200 people would stay overnight during the same period. On March 12, 2011, a massive earthquake centered in the northern part of Nagano prefecture caused severe damage to the house, leading to its closure. Following a large-scale project of restoration, it was decided to reopen the structure on the occasion of the Echigo-Tsumari Art Triennale 2012, and we published the *Dream Book* simultaneously in commemoration. One of the many dreams recorded in the book:

BLUE-8
The passage of time vacillates and I'm living ten minutes further into the future than everyone else. I'm waiting and waiting for

everyone to get through those ten minutes that they're wasting. (August 6, 2008)

I finished refurbishing the Dream House, then I returned to Amsterdam to face my brother.

Velimir arrived with just one suitcase, for his daughter and himself. After a while I noticed that both he and little Ivana always wore the same clothes. I asked my brother what had been in the suitcase he brought. He looked at me. "Just books," he said.

I went out and bought Ivana everything she needed, along with five suits for Velimir. Not long afterward Paolo and I hosted a dinner for New Year's Day. Just before the guests arrived my brother walked in wearing stained pants and the same dirty T-shirt he'd arrived in. "Please," I said, "I'm having people over. Could you wear one of the nice new suits I bought you?" He returned in one of the new suits— with a big price tag hanging down that said DISCOUNT—30 PERCENT OFF.

Things between Velimir and me were uneasy at best. Accepting the hospitality of his well-known sister in her beautiful house in Amsterdam was simply too difficult for him. As was being the in absentia husband of a sick wife and the father of a little girl. An amazing little girl. At ten, Ivana was really like an adult, a wise old soul in a child's body. When I got back to Binnenkant 21 from Japan, I found little toys and tchotchkes that she'd bought on the street placed all over the stark white interior of my big house. I asked her to put all her toys in her own room. Then she looked in my eyes and said in a very serious voice, "Don't you know that small children are afraid of empty spaces?"

Wow.

My niece was astonishing. She learned Dutch in less than three months and went to a Dutch school with no problem. I knew that the transition was very difficult for her: new country, new language, no friends, no mother. But I never saw her crying except once, in the privacy of her own room, for no one to see.

Postcard from my brother, 1999

My brother, on the other hand, was doing his best to play the part of the typical Balkan male. It wasn't just that it was hard for him to be a guest; he also had been brought up in a culture where the women waited on the men hand and foot. Literally. My mother used to bring him his food in bed when he was young, and even when he was not so young. Is it any wonder that at the beginning of his stay in my house, Velimir wouldn't lift a finger? I would serve him his dinner, and then, as Paolo and Ivana and I cleared the table, I would wait in vain for my brother to do anything to help. "You don't have to wash your dishes," I told him, "but can you just take them to the kitchen and leave them by the sink?" He would just look at me.

Velimir once sent me a postcard of a Montenegrin man going on vacation with his mother and sister. It was a joke that wasn't a joke. (Nowadays the sister and mother would walk in front because of minefields.) This was truly Velimir's view of women's role in the world. I was delighted to have escaped this fate.

The main image I retain from the first days of my brother and niece's stay—and they lived in my place, on and off, for three years—is of Velimir sitting in an armchair, constantly watching the

My brother, Velimir, and my niece, Ivana, at my house
in Amsterdam after the bombing of Belgrade, 1999

war coverage on CNN and moaning, "They're bombing Belgrade and
my wife is dying."

I also associate those days with another unpleasant memory: my
father's wife had died, and Velimir informed me that before he left
Belgrade, Vojin had invited him over to talk. During this talk, our father showed him that he had forged the signatures of my brother and
me on his will so he could disinherit us and leave all his money and
property, what there was of it, to his stepson—who lived in Canada
with his own father. Possibly his late wife had talked him into this.
Velimir said nothing, just walked out of the apartment. The whole
thing made me terribly sad.

My house was big, but not big enough to keep Velimir and me
from clashing. Ivana was often in the middle. When I threw her a
birthday party—she had no friends in Amsterdam, so I invited all the
kids from the neighborhood—my brother accused me of doing it for

public relations, to show I was "being nice to the poor refugees." And when I made plans to build a permanent bedroom for the little girl, he blamed me for trying to undermine his authority.

That was something he was quite capable of doing himself. Once, I returned from a work trip to find Ivana alone in my house—a ten-year-old kid alone in a six-floor house in Amsterdam for two weeks. I phoned his sick wife, and she came from Belgrade and picked the little girl up.

I loved Ivana. But I could not look after her. I had to work. And over the three years he lived in my house, my brother kind of went crazy. Eventually his wife called me and said, "I have four months to live; please take care of her." That was many years ago, and I've done my best ever since to stay close to this girl, now a brilliant young theoretical physicist at the Max Planck Institute for Plasma Physics. Her study of a "toroidal magnetic confinement nuclear fusion device" called Wendelstein 7-X—essentially an energy-producing artificial sun created in a laboratory—is nothing less than breathtaking.

⌒

The voice on my answering machine was weak, almost inaudible. It was my father, calling from Belgrade.

He wanted to borrow money. Again.

The death of his wife had devastated him—I really believe she was the love of his life. He was living alone now, and his mind was starting to go, along with his body. He'd recently fallen and broken his hip.

Hearing the frail voice of this man who had once been so strong, who had fought the Nazis in the mountains and survived the Igman March, gave me a twinge of sadness. But what I mostly felt was anger. He had never thanked me for the money I'd given him. Then he had forged my signature and disinherited me. Now he was asking for more money?

Fuck him. I never called him back.

It was the night of August 29, 2000. The next morning I flew to India with Michael Laub to start a new theater production. I arrived in the evening and went to bed, exhausted. At four in the morning, a flash of light made me jump out of bed. It wasn't lightning—this strange light had gone through me, like electricity. I sat on the bed, confused—and sat and sat, unable to get back to sleep. In the morning I got a phone call saying that my father had died, at exactly that moment.

I'll never forgive myself for not calling him back. But neither my brother nor I went to his funeral.

A while later, an old Serbian general, another former partisan, brought me an ancient pigskin bag, a small valise that, he said, contained the things my father had treasured most in the world. Just to look at this old case was heartbreaking—I had it for a full year before I could bear to open it.

Finally I opened it.

There weren't many things inside. I found the photographs of my father and Tito that Vojin had cut in half. One snapshot of my brother and me as children. All his medals. And then I reached inside a small inner pocket and pulled out . . .

A little wooden pencil sharpener.

This was the most heart-crushing of everything that I found in this bag.

What is life? I thought. *It comes and goes like that, and that's it. And what's left? A pencil sharpener.*

And so I made a piece in memory of my father, a video called *The Hero*. For the location I chose the countryside in the south of Spain and asked my dear friend and the director of the NMAC Foundation Jimena Blázquez Abascal to produce it. In this video I am sitting on a white horse, just as my father so often did, and holding a large white flag that flutters in the wind. I just sit there for an indefinite amount of time, staring into the distance, while in voice-over, a woman sings the Yugoslavian national anthem from the time of Tito. Which, by the way, is now forbidden in ex-Yugoslavia—Tito has gone from being a national hero to a national enemy. The video is in black-and-white, to emphasize the past and memory. And when the video plays on a screen in a gallery or a museum, there is a vitrine in front of the screen containing the pigskin bag, with its photographs and medals and pencil sharpener inside.

Why a white flag? My father never surrendered to anything. But he is dead, and white is also the color of death. We must all surrender to change, and death is the biggest change of all.

The Hero, silver gelatin print, 2001/2008

Before my father died, I, too, underwent a change—in my relationship with Ulay. Though we had now been apart for nearly as long as we'd been together, reconciliation was elusive, to say the least. I had agreed to let him control our archive—hundreds of photographs and negatives, as well as hundreds of hours of videotape—and I had frequent cause to regret my decision. He would sell our work, sometimes to people I didn't like, sometimes at a discount that I hadn't agreed upon, and my share of the proceeds would mysteriously never arrive. He would show the work in crappy galleries. I resented all of it, deeply.

One day Ulay called and made an appointment—he wanted to talk business. He came over and said he wanted to sell me back everything, because he needed the money to assure the future of his daughter.

He really did need the money. He was doing very little work of his own at this point, and he had a wife and child to support. But where was I going to get the money to buy our archive? Sean Kelly had an idea.

In the early 1990s, he had introduced me to a wealthy Swedish collector, Willem Peppler, who became a great fan of my work, and a friend. Peppler had even helped to underwrite *Balkan Baroque* at the Biennale after Montenegro pulled out. Now, on Sean's advice, I asked the Swede if he would lend me the money to purchase the archive, and he quickly agreed to loan me the entire sum, without interest, if I would give him one work for free.

It was a lot of money—300,000 deutsche marks—but it gave me control over all aspects of the work: reproduction, exhibition, and sale. Besides receiving the lump sum Ulay would net 20 percent of my share anytime any piece of the Abramović-Ulay archive was purchased.

My freedom was worth it.

⌒

After the fiasco at the Bangalore festival, I was sure I would never again be invited to work with Tibetan monks. But two years later, Doboom Tulku wrote to me saying that everyone had been so happy with my first collaboration that he and everyone else at the Tibet House wanted me to do another. The world is full of surprises.

This time they asked me to choreograph a program with just twelve monks, singing and dancing and wearing ceremonial costumes, for an ethnic festival at the Kulturen der Welt, the big cultural center in Berlin. In a monastery the ceremony they wanted me to stage usually takes place over a period of ten to fifteen days; the program in the festival was to last fifty-five minutes. So I had to teach these twelve monks to change costumes as fast as they could, to place themselves correctly in the spotlight, to reenact their ceremony in a restricted space on the stage, and to do everything they normally do in two weeks in fifty-five minutes.

With Paolo, Doboom Tulku, and two friends, Alessia Bulgari and Giulio di Gropello, I went to the Krishnamurti Ashram in southern India, where I was given twelve monks to work with and all the facilities I needed. We trained and trained and trained until we got everything perfect, and then we did a general rehearsal in front of an audience in the village nearby. It was beautiful and it went really well.

Now there were three weeks until the festival. But I told my translator I wanted the monks to come to Berlin at least five days early to rehearse, because I knew that over a period of three weeks they would forget much of their training. And precise timing was crucial for this piece. The monks agreed.

I flew back to Berlin, and on the appointed day I went to the airport to wait for the monks. Doboom Tulku and my translator were with me. The plane landed, and twelve monks came out—and they were twelve monks I had never seen before in my life. I said, "Who are these guys? Where are my monks?"

"Oh, but your monks didn't have passports," their escort said. "So they just got new monks."

Doboom Tulku was laughing and laughing. "Ah, another lesson in detachment," he said. "It will happen anyway."

Easy for him to say! For the next five days I went crazy training these guys from knowing absolutely zero about performing to kind of being able to do the performance. Everything went pretty well at the festival, and a few more gray hairs were added to my head.

Directing a group of Buddhist monks for a performance
at Haus der Kulturen der Welt, Berlin, 2000

I loved my house in Amsterdam, but the truth is, I had grown tired
of the city. And Paolo, who spent part of his time in Rome, where he
lived with his sister, and the rest of his time in Amsterdam with me,
hated Amsterdam. Every time he came there, he felt unwell—he said
the city made his blood pressure drop because it's below sea level,
and besides, it was always raining, and he couldn't stand it. He was a
Roman, after all.

We thought about moving to Rome. For me Rome is interesting as
a holiday destination, but whenever I'm there I feel I am walking on
the cadavers of many civilizations—somehow it just seems suffocating. So we talked and talked and talked, and it turned out that what
Paolo wanted more than anything else was to make a bigger move.
"Let's go to America," he said, passionately. "Let's try a new life. Let's
change your place, let's change my place—let's *do* something." And
I was in love. So I decided to put into practice some of the Buddhist
detachment I had learned: to sell my house and move to New York.

I was scared to go there, which struck me as the most compel-
ling reason of all to move. I had been to the city many times; I had
performed and shown my work there. But I had made my career in

Europe. I wondered if my work could jump across the Atlantic and flourish in the most demanding city in the world.

Although I was afraid, I had a plan for a new performance to propose to Sean Kelly in New York.

Since our not-so-accidental meeting, Sean's business had grown, as had our friendship. And in the meantime, he had opened a beautiful new gallery in Chelsea. Sean said he'd found a great place for Paolo and me, on Grand Street in Soho, right across the street from his loft. It was a co-op loft, big and airy, with lots of windows. I trusted Sean's taste implicitly. So I told him to make an offer, and I put the Amsterdam house on the market.

Binnenkant 21 had come a long way in the thirteen years I'd owned it. I had turned it into the kind of house that made everyone who walked into it feel good the moment they stepped over the threshold. The words of the banker who had given me the first mortgage in 1989 proved to be prophetic: turning an investment of 40,000 guilder into $4,000,000 turned out to be an amazing real-estate deal indeed. The one low note in this exciting change would be losing my assistant, Declan Rooney. A former student of mine, he would not make the move to New York, but he came over until I got settled. He returned to his life in Ireland and eventually went on to work with my friend Michael Laub.

In 2000, before Paolo and I moved to New York, I was visiting the city, and Klaus Biesenbach—who himself had started to commute to New York from Berlin in 1996 to work as a curator at MoMA PS1—invited me to his birthday party. He had a tiny little place, just one bedroom, and he invited four people: Matthew Barney, Björk, his dear friend Susan Sontag, and me. We all sat on the bed and watched my favorite movie, Pier Paolo Pasolini's *Teorema*.

I'd been obsessed with this film from the first time I saw it in the 1970s. In it Terence Stamp plays a mysterious man called The Visitor who arrives at the home of a haute-bourgeois Italian family and seduces everyone in the house—the mother, the father, the son, the daughter, and the maid—and brings them out of their depression and complacency into a state of religious revelation. It's a complicated story, touching on many big subjects: not just sex and religion, but politics and art itself. For a while Klaus and I had talked about re-making the film.

At the time, Björk was pregnant, and—it was the first time I met her—very eccentric. She brought with her a kind of cardboard bag with a red telephone inside. (Another time I saw her at someone's party wearing a birdcage, with no bird inside, around her neck.) After the movie was over, she and Matthew and Klaus started talking on one side of the bed, and on my side I started to talk with Susan, and we just talked and talked. I liked her very much. She knew my country well, having lived in Sarajevo during the Bosnian war, when she directed a production of Beckett's *Waiting for Godot* in a candlelit theater, winning the affection and gratitude of many in that besieged city. And she had so much of a Russian soul herself.

After the party we shared a taxi, and then we traded telephone numbers, and that was it. I was too shy to call her, and she never called me. Two years passed.

Now, in the fall of 2002, Paolo and I were living in the city. And in November, at Sean Kelly's Chelsea gallery, I performed the new piece I'd been planning, *The House with the Ocean View*.

It was a very ambitious work. I started with an entirely different idea. In India I had met a guru named Pilot Baba, so named because he was a former Indian Air Force airman and Prime Minister Nehru's hand-picked pilot. Once, the story goes, Pilot Baba was flying Nehru to Pakistan when he had a spiritual experience: he saw a giant hand in the cockpit pushing him back. He turned the plane around and re-turned to Delhi. All the other aircraft accompanying them were shot down by the Pakistanis. Pilot Baba had amazing abilities. In particu-lar, he could slow down his breathing to a point that enabled him to be buried underground or to stay underwater for days at a time.

My idea was to bring Pilot Baba to a warehouse in New York City, where I would lie naked on a bed of ice and he would sit in a tank filled with water. After a half hour or so my Western body would reach its

limits and I would have to get up, but Pilot Baba would remain underwater for much longer, maybe twelve hours. I would invite one hundred of the most influential human beings on this planet—people who
make the greatest contributions to science, technology, and art—to
observe the piece. No photography would be allowed. These important people would just witness the event, and of course they would be
shocked by it, since there was no rational explanation. They would
then return to the world with the memory of this piece in their minds,
and see how it influenced their lives and their work.

But Pilot Baba didn't want to come to New York. He had no interest at all in impressing the Western world. Gurus and swamis lose
their powers if they perform their miracles for any other reason than
the spiritual. So I had to think of an alternate idea. By now I had done
several retreats in India, and I had learned important lessons. Could
I bring some of these lessons into my art? I wanted to incorporate my
own mindfulness into the new piece, but I also wanted to include the
public.

I designed the installation. Three large, walled platforms would
be mounted side by side on the wall of Sean's gallery, about five feet
from the floor. The fourth wall of each platform, the one facing the
public, was open. I would live on these platforms for twelve days, consuming only filtered water and performing all bodily functions—
showering, peeing, sitting, sleeping—in full view of the public. One
platform would hold a toilet and a shower, one would have a chair and
a table, and one would have a bed. Each platform would be connected
to the floor by a ladder—only the ladders would have sharp carving
knives, blades up, in place of rungs. I could step from one platform to
the other through openings in the side walls.

The catalogue copy for the piece explained it further:

THE IDEA

This performance comes from my desire to see if it is possible
to use simple daily discipline, rules, and restrictions to purify
myself.

Can I change my energy field?
Can this energy field change the energy field of the audience
and the space?

Conditions for Living Installation: Artist

Duration of the piece	12 days
Food	no food
Water	large quantity of pure water
Talking	no talking
Singing	possible but unpredictable
Writing	no writing
Reading	no reading
Sleeping	7 hours a day
Standing	unlimited
Sitting	unlimited
Lying	unlimited
Shower	3 times a day

Conditions for Living Installation: Public
use telescope
remain silent
establish energy dialogue with the artist

Clothes
The clothes for *The House with the Ocean View* were inspired
by Alexander Rodchenko.
The colors of the clothes were selected in accordance with the
principles of the Hindu Vedic square.
The boots are the ones I used to walk the Great Wall of China
in 1988.

It was just after September 11: people were in a sensitive frame of
mind, and the crowds who came to see the piece would stay for a long
time, sitting on the gallery floor and watching, thinking about what
they were experiencing, immersed in it. My viewers and I felt each

The House with the Ocean View (performance, 12 days), New York, 2002

other's presence intensely. There was a shared energy in the room—and a thick silence, broken only by the sound of a ticking metronome I kept on the table in my sitting room. One of the viewers was Susan Sontag, who started coming every day. But I had no idea she was there, in part because the gallery floor was unlit, but also because up on my platforms I was doing everything—sitting, standing, drinking, refilling my glass, peeing, showering—with (as a performance transcript shows) trancelike slowness and mindfulness:

FRIDAY, NOVEMBER 15: DAY 1

Wearing white

Sitting on the chair

I sit on the chair, shake out my shoulders and push my hair back from my face and forehead with both hands. I shift first my left and then my right buttock back until they touch the back of the chair and I am sitting up perfectly straight. The back of my head is touching the quartz pillow headrest. . . .

I take a deep breath and my chest rises. Then it falls. I remain sitting still. The metronome is on the left-hand side of the table and it is ticking. The glass is on the right-hand side of the table and it is full. My feet are flat on the floor and spaced hip-width apart. My back is straight against the chair. I look at the audience. My head does not move, only my eyes. I blink. My mouth is closed. I blink again. When I take deeper breaths my chest rises and falls. The rest of my body is motionless. After I have been sitting for a long time I have to straighten my back up.

Each day, my routine consisted of moving between the three units: the bath, the sitting room, the bedroom. It was very important that every activity I performed be on the highest level of consciousness, whether it was taking a shower, peeing, sitting in the chair and drinking water, lying on the bed resting, or—especially—standing at the edge of one of the platforms, above the knife ladders, for as long as possible.

This was the only time my mind really couldn't shift anywhere, because I could fall and cut myself badly. During these moments I would always try to catch the eye of one of the dimly lit visitors in front of me. This locking of gazes usually lasted a long time, creating a very intense communication of energy. Yet it sometimes happened during these moments that I started feeling a strong urge to pee.

And so, without breaking this gaze, I would step across the gap to the bathroom unit, turn to my right (still looking at the visitor), and take the toilet paper from the shelf with my right hand. I would put the toilet paper down on the corner of the shower tray. I would then lift the lid of the toilet with my left hand and push it back until it was upright. As I turned toward the front, I would lift my shirt and unfasten my trousers. I would pull my trousers down slowly, to just above my knees, and sit on the toilet. I would put my feet close together in front of me and lay my hands in my lap. I would sit up straight and wait for the pee to come. It would take a while, during which time a silence would fall. Still holding the visitor's gaze, I would then take exactly four squares of toilet paper and fold each piece precisely in a triangle. Then—still holding the gaze—I would wait until the pee came intensely. I would wait for the last three drops, then wipe myself and pull my trousers back up. I would open the water tap to fill the bucket. Still holding the gaze, I would intuitively feel when the bucket was half full, then use it to flush the toilet.

All this was to show that there was no difference between standing on the platform above the knives and peeing—that peeing was as important as anything else. All the shame of the act was gone, and the person holding my gaze understood completely.

The only time I had privacy throughout the entire performance was the few seconds it took to dry my face after I showered.

Over the twelve days, many were deeply affected by this piece. I felt, in a small way, as though this biggest of cities had begun to take me in. People left all kinds of things for me in the gallery: scarves, rings, letters. There were three big boxes full of stuff I'd been given. After the piece was over I was looking through the boxes and I found a cloth napkin from a restaurant, and on it was written, "I really like this work; let's have lunch—Susan."

That was when Susan Sontag and I started to be friends. And as a first gesture of friendship, she gave me a book to which she had written the preface. It was *Letters: Summer 1926*, the story of the Rilke-Tsvetaeva-Pasternak correspondence—the same book, given to me by my mother, that had inflamed my imagination when I was fifteen. Susan adored conversation. She loved to invite people to her apartment to talk, always in her kitchen and always one-on-one: she and I agreed that three people talking is not really a conversation. I usually visited her in the afternoon, because I am not a late person: three P.M. was one of my favorite times to go see her.

Her fridge was almost always empty. One day I said to her, "I am going to bring you something." She said, "Bring me something sweet." So I went to Le Pain Quotidien and got her a lemon pie. It was a big, wonderful pie. I told her, "When I was a child in my grandmother's kitchen, she would make chocolate cakes, and I never liked the cake, just the icing." She said, "Let's do the same."

Susan cut the pie in half, gave me a spoon, and we just ate the filling and left the rest. It was so great! She had taught me such an important lesson about freedom—why can't we do this when we are grown up? Clearly we could.

Her cancer was something we never talked about. She had been told years before that she had only a short time to live, yet she had lived. Surely she would keep living for many years to come.

Alessia Bulgari and me, New York, 2009

A few months after *The House with the Ocean View*, I was in southern Sri Lanka with Paolo, Alessia, Laurie Anderson, and Lou Reed to witness Buddhist monks perform these very special rituals that involved walking on fire, stabbing themselves with swords and knives, and hammering nails into their heads—without any damage. The ceremony began at four in the morning and by then an enormous crowd had gathered. I couldn't believe my eyes as I watched these priests and monks casually stroll across a forty-foot stretch of hot coals that would've melted my camera had I gotten too close. And there, in the middle of this whole scene, was Lou doing tai chi, completely undisturbed. But watching the priests perform these rites reminded me just how limited Western culture is in understanding the true limits of the body and mind.

While still in Sri Lanka, I got a call from Sean Kelly, passing along a strange request: the producers of *Sex and the City* were asking if I wanted to play myself on the show—performing *The House with the Ocean View*. At the time I had never seen *Sex and the City*, and I was not an actress, so I said no. For a fee, I gave them permission to reference the performance, which they did.

Later, after I returned to Amsterdam, I went to my favorite little vegetable shop, which had the most expensive strawberries in the city—and to my amazement, the owners gave me a free box of strawberries. They had never been so nice to me. When I thanked them for their generosity, they explained that they were giving me this gift because I (or at least an actress playing me) had been on *Sex and the City*. Strangely enough, that was the first time I felt accepted by the general public. I was so shocked how fast my performance had been consumed by the mass media. Yet despite my fasting and serious intent to change consciousness in *The House with the Ocean View*, the performance and I were mocked.

⌐

In 2003 I returned to Belgrade—because, in a certain sense, I'm always returning to Belgrade. But I wanted to see my mother, who was now eighty-two, and I also wanted to re-create an old piece of mine, with a new twist.

First, Danica.

She was still in her socialist apartment building; I stayed in a hotel. When I went to see her I brought a big, beautiful bouquet of roses. I kissed her and handed her the flowers with a smile. She accepted them with a little nod—then promptly put them between newspapers and pressed them with heavy books.

I was shocked. "Why did you do this?" I asked.

"I had to, of course," she said. "Can you imagine, if we put them in water, all the bacteria that would develop?"

Nothing had changed.

One morning I phoned her and said, "Let's have breakfast together." I bought food and took it over. "Don't move; I'll do everything," I told her. I went to the kitchen to get out the dishes and the pots.

"No, no, no—you can't; you don't know where anything is," she said.

"Mama, every single kitchen is exactly the same," I said. "The dishes are up here; this shelf is for cups. I'll find everything."

"No, no, you can't take them out of the cupboard."

"Why can't I take them out of the cupboard?"

"Because they're dirty," she said.

"Excuse me," I said. "Why would you put dirty dishes in the cupboard?"

"No, no, no—they were clean when I put them there, but while they're sitting there they become dirty."

I just shook my head.

Along with her cleanliness OCD, my mother had an obsession with plastic bags—she refused to ever throw a single one out. She would wash them and reuse them, then wash them again, over and over until the printing on them became illegible. If it was raining and she was going out, she would take her umbrella—which already had its own cover—and put it in not one but two plastic bags: a very thin, transparent bag over the umbrella cover, and then a heavier bag over that. Only then could she go out. This was a ritual that nobody could change.

One day during my visit it began raining just as we were about to go out. And as she got her umbrella, I remembered the ritual and decided I couldn't fight her anymore. I just gave up. I went to the kitchen and got two plastic bags, the thin one and the thick one, and handed them to her—and she started laughing. That was the only time she understood the irony of all this. And it was the only time we ever had a laugh together.

⌐

The new piece, a multi–video screen projection, spoke to my hopes and fears (mainly fears) about the country of my birth. Soon after I arrived in Belgrade I met with an elementary school music teacher and found out he had written a song honoring the United Nations. I decided to use this song. My intentions were, frankly, sarcastic—I thought the U.N.'s relief efforts during the Kosovo war had been bullshit. But the teacher's song was a sincere hymn of praise, and in the first video I made, I conducted a choir of eighty-six schoolchildren performing it, all dressed in black, as if they were going to a funeral. As they sang hopeful lyrics like, "United Nations, we love you; United Nations, you help us; United Nations, you bring us the future," I stood in front of them wearing two model skeletons attached to my body, one in front and one in back.

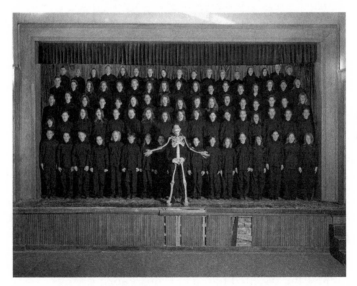

Count on Us (Chorus), color chromogenic print, 2003

The next video referred back to my old piece *Rhythm 5*, from Belgrade in 1974, in which I lay inside the flaming star, the symbol of Communist Yugoslavia, and passed out from the flames. Almost thirty years later, in the very different Belgrade of 2003, I lay inside a star once again—only this time, instead of flaming wood, the star was made up of these same eighty-six schoolchildren, still dressed all in black. And lying in the center, I wore another skeleton costume.

Hollywood budgets allow about thirty-five takes per scene. My budget allowed me one take. And the first take was a disaster: the kids just couldn't settle down. For the second take, they got organized— and then one boy farted, and the rest of them just lost it. Thank God, the third take was perfect.

Count on Us (Star), color chromogenic print, 2003

To create a sense of innocence and beauty, I chose a boy and a girl to sing two songs from my childhood. I selected the two children with the best voices in the choir, and filmed them in a low-angle shot, against the background of a red curtain, to create a heroic image that recalled the Young Pioneers of the Tito period. The boy sang a song about love, and the girl sang about death—the story of a little yellow flower, alive and beautiful now, but doomed to die as soon as spring is over.

And the last video touched on my obsession with Nikola Tesla, the Serbian scientific genius, whom I loved for the mixture of science and mysticism in his work. At the time of his death in 1943, he was working on a system for transmitting electricity over great distances without wires—an idea that spoke to my continuing fascination with transferring energy of all kinds. He also dreamed of drawing free energy from the earth. In her capacity as director of the Tesla Museum, my brother's wife, Maria—who by now was dying of lung cancer—let me use a huge static-electricity generator to light a neon tube I held in my hands by passing 34,000 watts through my body.

Count on Us (Tesla), black-and-white chromogenic print, 2003

I called the whole piece *Count on Us*. The accompanying text read:
Yes, we had a war.
Yes, we are in an economic disaster.
Yes, the country is in ruins.
Still there is energy and there is hope.

⌒

In 2004 I created a new version of my theater piece *Biography* called *The Biography Remix*. Michael Laub directed, inventing a very original way to present both my work and my life, and my students from Braunschweig joined me in re-performing the works featured in the original play. There was also an impressive new addition: Ulay's son, Jurriaan, now in his early thirties and bearing a striking resemblance to his father, portrayed him in *Rest Energy*, *Pieta*, and *Incision*. "I wanted to play my father because I never knew him," Jurriaan told me. It was sad and dramatic at the same time.

And dramatic for me as well. At the final performance, in Rome, Ulay came to see the piece for the first time. There I was on the stage, saying good-bye to Ulay in the bye-bye scene, and there he was in the audience receiving my final farewell; it was the perfect mixture of life and theater.

After the show he came up to me. "I never saw my son naked," Ulay told me.

"You never even saw him born," I said.

⌐

Paolo and I were at my Italian gallerist Lia Rumma's house in Stromboli in the summer of 2004, happy in the sun and among friends. The volcano on the island was erupting, creating a sense of drama and eerie natural beauty. Then Susan Sontag called and said she was going to have a bone-marrow transplant. "Only thirty percent survive this procedure," she told me, "but in my age group, even less."

"Oh, Susan," I said.

"But you know what? If I survive, we're going to have one hell of a big party," she said.

She didn't survive. She died at the end of the year, one cold, rainy day, in a New York hospital. For the past four years, the years of our friendship, I had seen her almost every day. So I flew with Klaus to her funeral in Paris. We sat on the plane barely talking, each of us lost in thought with our memories of Susan.

It was the dead of winter, and it was raining again, and it was a small ceremony at Montparnasse Cemetery. Only twenty or thirty people attended. Patti Smith was there. Malcolm McLaren. Salman Rushdie. Susan's companion Annie Leibovitz. Klaus and I.

It was sad. Funerals are always sad, but this was sad in another way, too. Susan's son, David, had decided to bury her there, in the same cemetery where people like Beckett and Baudelaire and Sartre and Simone de Beauvoir were buried. But Susan and David had had a difficult relationship, and I felt, ultimately, that he had done her an injustice. I thought she deserved a different funeral, one that all the people who loved and appreciated her could easily attend. Paris was too far to travel for almost everyone.

I felt deep sadness at seeing how large Susan had been in life and how tiny this funeral was. And how glum. I've always believed death should be a celebration. Because you're entering a new place, a new state. You're making a major passage. The Sufis say, "Life is a dream and death is waking up." I think Susan had a good life, a fascinating life. Her funeral should have celebrated that.

When I got back to New York, I called my lawyer and told him my plan for my own funeral. It was extremely important, I said, that my funeral should go exactly as I planned it, because, after all, this was to be my final piece.

First came my idea for The Three Marinas.

I told the lawyer I wanted there to be three graves, in the three places I lived longest: Belgrade, Amsterdam, and New York. My body should actually lie in one of the graves—but nobody was to know which.

Second, I said, I want nobody to wear black to my funeral. Everyone is to wear vibrant colors, acid green and red and purple. Also, all my jokes, the good and the bad and the terrible, should be told. My funeral should be a going-away party, I told the lawyer: a celebration of all the things I had done, and of my leaving for a new place.

In the years since, the incomparable singer Antony Hegarty—now Anohni—has become my dear friend and my surrogate daughter. And this friendship has given me another wish for my funeral: I want Anohni to sing "My Way," in the style of the great Nina Simone. She hasn't said yes, but I think she'll be so sad when I die that she'll have to do it for me. I count on that.

11.

Two worms lived in shit, a father and son. The father said to his son,
"Look at the wonderful life we have. We have plenty to eat and plenty
to drink, and we are protected from outside enemies. We have nothing
to worry about." The son said to his father, "But father, I have a friend
who lives in an apple. He also has plenty to eat, plenty to drink, is
protected from outside enemies, and, he smells good. Can we live in an
apple instead?"

"No, we can't," replied the father.
"Why?" said the son.
"Because, my son, the shit is our country."

The House with the Ocean View had been so difficult and demanding
that I was ready for a change of pace. And so when the British curator Neville Wakefield told me he was asking twelve artists to create a work on the subject of pornography, it sounded relatively easy
and fun—at first. Then I looked at a few pornographic movies, which
were a total turnoff. Instead I decided to research Balkan folk culture.

First I examined the ancient origins of eroticism. Every myth and
folktale I read seemed to be about humans trying to make themselves
equal with the gods. In mythology, woman marries the sun and man
marries the moon. Why? To preserve the secrets of creative energy
and get in touch with indestructible cosmic forces.

In Balkan folk culture male and female genitals have a very important function in both healing and agricultural rites. In Balkan

fertility rituals, I learned, women openly displayed their vaginas, bottoms, breasts, and menstrual blood; men uninhibitedly displayed their bottoms and penises, engaging in masturbation and ejaculation. The field was very rich. I decided to make both a two-part video installation and a short film about these rites: I called the pieces *Balkan Erotic Epic.* In the summer of 2005 I went to Serbia to begin the project. It would take me two years to cast the participants, and it wasn't easy. But the Baš Čelik production house, and their amazing production director Igor Kecman, made possible everything that seemed impossible in the sometimes corrupt and dangerous environment of ex-Yugoslavia.

In the film I played the role of professor/narrator, describing each ritual, then having it reenacted. Some of the rites were so bizarre that I couldn't imagine persuading people to participate, so I turned them into short cartoons: for instance, if the woman wants her husband or lover never to leave her, she takes a small fish in the evening, puts it in her vagina, and goes to sleep. In the morning, she takes the dead fish out of her vagina, grinds it into a powder, and puts this powder into her man's coffee.

For the live scenes I enlisted people who had mostly never been in front of a camera before. I crossed my fingers when I put out a casting call for women between the ages of eighteen and eighty-six to show their vaginas to scare the gods in order to stop the rain. And it was equally difficult to find fifteen men who would be willing to be filmed in national uniforms, standing motionless with their erect penises exposed while the Serbian diva Olivera Katarina sang, "O Lord, save thy people . . . War is our eternal cross . . . Long live our true Slavic fate . . ."

I acted in a couple of scenes myself. In one I was bare-breasted, with all my hair combed forward over my face: my head looks as if it is on backward. In my hands is a skull. I hit my stomach with the skull again and again and again, faster and faster and faster, in a kind of frenzy. The only sound is the slap of the skull against my flesh.

Sex and death are always very close in the Balkans.

While I was in Belgrade working on this project, Paolo, who had accompanied me, was making a video of his own: a simple but powerful piece showing a boy playing soccer with a skull in the ruins of the Yugoslav Defense Ministry, which had been bombed during the Kosovo war. To our delight, Paolo's video was selected for the 2007 Venice Biennale—and then the Museum of Modern Art in New York announced it was adding the piece to its permanent collection.

To celebrate this milestone, I made a deal with the collector Ella Fontanals-Cisneros: I gave her a first-edition photograph of me in *Rhythm 0,* and in exchange she chartered a yacht on which I gave Paolo a big surprise party in the Venice lagoon, inviting all our friends and everyone I knew from all the Biennales I'd participated in. He was overwhelmed by all the attention and the many compliments on his video. He really felt he had arrived. And I thought—but I did not say—that it takes much more than one successful piece to arrive.

Balkan Erotic Epic was a way to explore something completely new during the time I had been preparing a huge and complicated performance for the Guggenheim, ironically titled *Seven Easy Pieces.* For a long time I had felt the need to re-create some important performances from the past, not just my own but those of other artists as well, in order to bring these pieces to a public that had never seen them. I first proposed the idea in 1997, soon after *Balkan Baroque,* to Thomas Krens, then the director of the Guggenheim. I wanted to open a discussion about whether performance art could be approached in the same way as musical compositions or dance pieces—and also to examine how performance can best be preserved. After thirty years of performing I felt it was my duty to tell the story of performance art in a way that would respect the past and also leave space for reinterpretation. By re-performing seven important pieces, I told Krens, I wanted to propose a model for the future for reenacting other artists' performances. He loved the idea, and appointed the brilliant Nancy Spector to curate it.

I set several conditions for the show: first, to ask the artist (or, if the artist was dead, his or her foundation or representative) for permission; second, to pay the artist a copyright fee; third, to perform a new interpretation of the piece, always acknowledging the source; and fourth, to exhibit the original performance video and relics.

To a certain degree my idea was motivated by indignation. Performance material and images were constantly being stolen and put into the context of fashion, advertising, MTV, Hollywood films, theater, etc.: it was unprotected territory. I strongly felt that when anybody takes an idea of intellectual or artistic value from someone else, they should do so only with permission. To do otherwise is to commit piracy.

Also, there had been a certain community around performance in the 1970s; by the 2000s, it was completely lost. I wanted to revive this community, and my very ambitious idea was to do it singlehandedly in a seven-day show in which I would perform some important pieces that I'd never seen by other artists from the 1960s and '70s, along with one of my own. I also wanted to create a new performance for the exhibition. Susan Sontag and I had a long conversation about this work: she was very interested in writing something about it. Unfortunately, she died before *Seven Easy Pieces* came to fruition. I dedicated all seven pieces to her.

The pieces I originally chose were Bruce Nauman's *Body Pressure*; Vito Acconci's *Seedbed*; Valie Export's *Action Pants: Genital Panic*; Gina Pane's *The Conditioning, First Action of Self-Portraits*; Chris Burden's *Trans-fixed*; and my *Rhythm 0* and a new piece, *Entering the Other Side*.

Doing my pieces would turn out to be the easy part. Getting permission for some of the others was hell. For example, I really wanted to perform *Trans-fixed*, the famous 1975 piece by Chris Burden in which he was crucified—golden nails driven through his hands—while lying on the roof of a Volkswagen. But no matter how many times I asked, Burden kept saying no. He wouldn't tell me why. Much later, I met him and asked, "Why wouldn't you give me permission?" He said, "Why did you need permission? Why didn't you just do it?" Which made me realize he'd completely missed the point.

To substitute for the Burden, I chose Joseph Beuys's great performance *How to Explain Pictures to a Dead Hare*, in which he sat like a twentieth-century Pietà, his head covered with honey and gold leaf, and murmured softly into the ear of the dead hare he cradled in his arm. But though the Guggenheim sent Beuys's widow (he died in 1986) many letters, she kept saying no.

I flew to Düsseldorf and rang Eva Beuys's doorbell in the middle of a snowstorm. She opened the door and said, "Frau Abramović, my answer is no, but it is cold so you must come in for a coffee."

"Frau Beuys, I don't drink coffee but I would love some tea," I said. I stayed for five hours. At first Beuys's widow kept saying no—she had thirty-six lawsuits against people who'd been stealing her husband's work, she told me. But when I told her about some similar problems I had had—a number of images from my solo pieces and pieces I'd done with Ulay had simply been appropriated by artists, fashion magazines, and other media—she began to understand my intentions. Finally she not only changed her mind, but also showed me old videos from this piece that nobody had ever seen. These videos were a big help in my reconstruction of the piece.

Left: How to Explain Pictures to a Dead Hare, Joseph Beuys, Galerie Schmela, Düsseldorf, 1965; *right*: me re-performing *How to Explain Pictures to a Dead Hare* as part of *Seven Easy Pieces* (performance, 7 hours), Guggenheim Museum, New York, 2005

The difficulty came when we had to find a dead hare for me to perform with. Animal-rights activists took a big interest in this piece. The museum and I had to prove the dead hare had died a natural death the night before it was delivered to the performance. In the end I was given, five minutes before the performance, a frozen dead hare which had been hit by a truck the night before on a Texas highway. As the performance lasted seven hours, the hare started to defrost as I held it, becoming softer and softer, feeling almost alive. At one point, I held the dead hare by its ears with my teeth. It was heavy and I accidentally bit off the tips of the ears. Its fur was stuck in my throat during the whole rest of the piece.

The important thing for me to explain when seeking permission from each of the artists was that my agenda for the reenactment was not commercial. The only reproductions that could be sold, I said, would be of my work. In this way, I was able to get permission not only from Eva Beuys, but from Vito Acconci, Valie Export, Bruce Nauman, and the estate of Gina Pane. Because I couldn't get permission from any lawyer to use the pistol required to perform *Rhythm 0*, I gave myself permission to re-perform *Thomas Lips*.

This piece became more complicated and autobiographical. I added elements that had significance in my life: the shoes I wore, and the walking stick I used to walk the Great Wall (the stick became 15 centimeters shorter over the course of the walk); the partisan cap with a red Communist star that my mother had worn during World War II; the white flag I carried in *The Hero*, the piece dedicated to my father; the Olivera Katarina song that I used in *Balkan Erotic Epic*.

I had originally performed *Thomas Lips* for one hour; now I was doing it for seven hours. Each hour I had to cut a star in my stomach, and each hour I had to lie naked on blocks of ice. It was a very difficult and demanding piece, and the first time I performed it, in 1975, I was still in my twenties. But now, though I was about to turn sixty, I found that my willpower and concentration were stronger than they'd been almost forty years earlier.

The night I finished re-performing *Thomas Lips*, the museum guards threw the blocks of ice onto the street. Later I learned that some Brooklyn artists had collected the ice with my blood and sweat, melted it, and tried to sell it as Abramović Cologne. I got one bottle for free.

Over seven days that November, the community I'd longed for came together again at the Guggenheim. Every evening, from five P.M. to midnight, people came to the museum, watched the performances, went out for dinner, came back with friends. And Paolo was there for me each night, giving me crucial support. The crowds got bigger each day. Strangers standing and watching my performances in the rotunda talked to each other about what they were seeing. Connections were formed.

There were some funny moments during the performances. Acconci's *Seedbed*—in which I lay hidden under a platform and masturbated to sexual fantasies that I spoke aloud while visitors walked over the platform—was the second piece I performed, after the Bruce Nauman. I achieved eight orgasms, and was so exhausted that I needed every bit of my energy, and some more besides, to perform Valie Export's *Action Pants: Genital Panic* the next day.

My performance of Export's piece happened to fall on Veterans Day, and at the time, the Guggenheim also had an exhibition on Russian icons. In *Genital Panic*, I wore crotchless leather pants, with my genitals exposed, and held a machine gun pointed at the audience. This was a very provocative piece, which Export had performed in the early '70s: I never saw it, but I was fascinated by its courage, and intrigued by the relevance of performing it on Veterans Day 2005— many works in the history of art become dated, but this piece had not.

This was also a weekend, and many Russian families came to see the icon show with children. When they arrived, someone called the police. The complaint wasn't about my exposed vagina, but because I was pointing a machine gun at the icons.

In the case of Gina Pane's *The Conditioning*, the part of the piece in which she lay on a metal bedframe over lighted candles had originally lasted eighteen minutes. As I wanted to give my own interpretation to all the pieces, I turned *The Conditioning* into a long-durational work, lasting seven hours instead of eighteen minutes. And, since I never rehearsed any of the pieces I performed (I only had the concept and the documentation material), I didn't realize how difficult it would be to lie over candle flames for seven hours. At one point, my hair almost caught on fire.

Left: *Action Pants: Genital Panic*, Valie Export, Munich, 1968, performance photograph, Munich, 1969; *right*: me re-performing *Action Pants: Genital Panic* as part of *Seven Easy Pieces* (performance, 7 hours), Guggenheim Museum, New York, 2005

The seventh piece, on the seventh day, was *Entering the Other Side*. I stood high above the rotunda on a twenty-foot platform, wearing a blue dress with a giant, circus tent–like skirt whose spiral form (inspired by the Guggenheim itself) covered the scaffolding and draped down to the floor. The Dutch designer Aziz had created the dress from 180 yards of material and generously donated it to me. As I stood there, I waved my arms in slow, repetitive motions. The room was completely silent for seven hours. Because of the rush to put me on the platform in time for the opening, no one had thought to give me a safety belt—and I was so exhausted after performing for seven days, seven hours a day, that I could have fallen asleep standing—and literally fallen—so it was crucial to stay awake and in the moment. Finally, close to midnight, I spoke.

"Please, just for the moment, all of you, just listen," I said. "I am here and now, and you are here and now with me. There is no time."

Then, at the stroke of twelve, a gong sounded, and I climbed down inside the giant skirt and emerged to greet the audience. The applause went on and on; there were tears in many eyes, including mine. I felt so connected to everyone there, and to the great city itself.

⸻

Paolo and I had been together for almost ten years, and the years had been good. The best times were our leisure hours: traveling (we went to India, Sri Lanka, and Thailand, visiting Buddhist monasteries and studying different cultures), going to the movies, making love, vacationing at our house in Stromboli. The hard parts had to do with our very different attitudes about work.

At the beginning of our relationship, just after I won the Golden Lion in Venice, Paolo said to me, "You've achieved the pinnacle—you don't have to prove anything more. Now you can relax! Why don't we just have a good life?" But I didn't know what good life he was talking about—for me, the good life was working, and creating.

He had a different rhythm. When we first moved to New York, I wanted so badly to make it, and I worked so hard. I would wake up at five thirty A.M. and Tony, my trainer, would come to the loft, then I would go to work. Paolo would wake up at eight o'clock and have breakfast, read the newspaper, go to the flea market to look for objects he liked. For the first two years he was just exploring the city—and I was just working.

Then in the evening—it was a very sexual relationship. He really needed to have sex every night, and there were times I just didn't feel like it. It turned into an obligation, and I could not stand it. Simply I was just *tired*.

I loved Paolo, and I knew he loved me. But at the same time, I knew that if I stopped working, our entire household would stop. I was holding everything together—paying the rent, taking care of our lives, keeping it all running. And everything was functioning: it felt perfect to me. But then one day he told me, "We don't need any of this. We can just live simply."

And I knew I couldn't do that. Because to me, we are each put on earth for a purpose, and we must each fulfill this purpose. Yes, I had won the Golden Lion at fifty—and created *The House with the Ocean View* at fifty-five, and *Seven Easy Pieces* at fifty-nine. And soon I would turn sixty, but I knew I still had a lot of work to do.

Living simply is also not in the cards when you're a couple of artists trying to make it on the New York scene. We threw lots of parties in our apartment, for artists and writers and all kinds of interesting people. And as we became known, we began to be invited to many parties. We were walking on red carpets for the first time.

Although Paolo and I had different feelings about work, we were still very much in love. One day we were grocery shopping at Gourmet Garage on Mercer Street, and as we came out into the rain, Paolo put his bags down, knelt on the sidewalk, and proposed. In the spring of my sixtieth year, the answer came easily: I said yes. I truly felt I would've had a child with him if I had been younger.

One day, a few days before our wedding, he went out after lunch and didn't come back until evening. He walked in with a mysterious smile on his face and turned on music. As the sound of Frank Sinatra singing "I've Got You Under My Skin" filled the room, Paolo rolled up his sleeve and showed me the tattoo he'd just gotten: "Marina," circling his left wrist. He held me in his arms and whispered, "Now I have you under my skin."

It was a tiny ceremony, with a judge, held opposite the Metropolitan Museum of Art in the beautiful townhouse of the dermatologist Catherine Orentreich, whose father had founded Clinique. Sean Kelly was the best man, and Stefania Miscetti, Paolo's gallerist at the time and the woman who'd introduced us, the maid of honor. Just a few friends were there: the Kellys, Chrissie Iles, Klaus Biesenbach; Alessia Bulgari, a few others. (A couple of months later, over the summer, Paolo's parents, who hadn't been able to make the trip and who really

Paolo with my name tattooed on his wrist

loved me, gave us another wedding, a very large one, in a beautiful house in Umbria.) It was a brilliant April morning, and it felt like a new beginning.

For my sixtieth birthday, on the other hand, nothing small would do. Since the Guggenheim hadn't paid me anything for *Seven Easy Pieces*, Lisa Dennison, the museum's new director, agreed to let me use the Guggenheim's rotunda for my party. I invited 350 people: friends and colleagues from around the world, including the Kellys, of course; my friend Carlo Bach of illy (which sponsored the party and produced a mug called "Miss 60" featuring a pin-up version of me, given away to the lucky guests!), Chrissie Iles, Klaus, Björk, Matthew Barney, Laurie Anderson and Lou Reed, Cindy Sherman, David Byrne, Glenn Lowry and his wife Susan, David and Marina Orentreich and David's sister Catherine, my new friends Riccardo Tisci of Givenchy (who designed my dress for the occasion) and Antony

Hegarty (now Anohni)—and once more, the sharer of my birthday, Ulay. Now that we had a contract, everything between us seemed fine.

The evening was nothing short of amazing. Ektoras Binikos designed a special cocktail, each glass containing one of my teardrops, and there were many great toasts. Björk and Antony sang "Happy Birthday" to me, and then Antony alone sang "Blue Moon" and Baby Dee's "Snowy Angel," a song that just pierced my heart, and still does.

With Laurie Anderson at Danspace Project Spring Gala,
St. Mark's Church, New York, 2011

My mother, now eighty-five, had been declining physically and mentally for a couple of years, and now, in the summer of 2007, she was in the hospital in Belgrade. In my heart I knew she was dying, even though I didn't want to admit it to myself. The last time I'd seen her, in her apartment, I'd had the feeling that she was sleeping in her armchair rather than her bed. Why? I think she was terrified to lie down—afraid that if she lay down, she would die.

Now she was lying down all the time, immobilized and sinking into senility. Hospitals are such fucked-up, disorienting places that they drive people crazy anyway. She called the masseur I hired for her "Velimir"—in part, I'm sure, because my brother, who lived close to the hospital, rarely, if ever, visited her. My aunt Ksenija took care of her every day; I flew in from New York once a month.

Danica was more and more out of her mind, but she remained ever the tough old partisan. I could see when the nurses turned her that her bedsores were truly awful: the flesh was rotten; her spine was literally exposed. But when I asked her how she was, her answer was always the same: "I'm fine."

"Do you feel any pain, Mama?"

"Nothing hurts me."

"Do you need anything?"

"I don't need anything."

It was more than stoicism: all her life, she (along with the rest of her family) had avoided discussing anything unpleasant. If I brought up politics—and I did frequently—she would immediately change the subject. "Oh, it's very warm today," she would say. Tragedy was off the table. When her younger brother, my uncle Djoko, was killed in a terrible car crash in 1997, my mother never called me to tell me. (She also never told my grandmother, who was made to believe—and never stopped believing until the day she died—that her son had gone on a long business trip to China. Once a month, without fail, my mother and her sister would fabricate a "letter from China" from their late brother and read it to their mother.) Then six months later, I was at the Venice Biennale, and a friend of mine said, "Oh, I saw your mother; she's really not looking well after this tragedy." I said, "What tragedy?" Then I called her. It drove me crazy.

But I think perhaps it was this very avoidance that caused her to seek a richer, deeper life—a life that was outside her terrible marriage.

After an especially difficult visit with my mother that July, I flew back home. Every morning I would call the hospital, though Danica could no longer speak coherently, just to ask a nurse to hold the phone up so I could hear whatever she was saying. Then one day, when I called with the usual request—"Can I hear my mother talking?"—the nurse said, "No. Nobody's in the room."

It was August 3, 2007. Shortly afterward I got a call from my aunt saying my mother had died early that morning. I asked if Velimir knew; Ksenija said no. So Paolo and I flew to Belgrade. Paolo, Ksenija, and I went to the morgue to identify my mother's body. She was lying there, covered with a dark-gray sheet. The mortician came in and said, "We didn't wash your mother's face yet, and we didn't shut her mouth. If you give us one hundred euros we will do this for you."

Oh, my country.

None of us had that much cash with us. So this man pulled the sheet aside. My poor mother had fluids and blood all over her face, and her mouth was wide-open: this was the dead screaming at me. The worst part was touching her hand—the coldness of a dead body is indescribable. I started crying uncontrollably; Paolo held me in his arms. I was so glad he was there for me.

I made arrangements for the funeral. My aunt wanted a church funeral, but my mother had been an atheist and a partisan. So I made a compromise: first we would hold a funeral in an Orthodox church, then everybody would come outside and there would be soldiers shooting rifles. I didn't sleep at all that night. In the middle of the night I called Velimir, whom I hadn't talked to for several years, and said, "This is your sister, our mother is dead—come to the funeral." He arrived at the funeral one hour late and drunk.

Sometimes what the dead leave behind tells us things our dear ones would never have revealed to us while they were alive. After my mother died I went to her apartment to clean up and found a collection of medals she'd been awarded as a national hero. I also discovered a trove of letters and diaries that showed me a Danica I never knew.

With Paolo at my mother's funeral, Belgrade, August 2007

For one thing, she had a lover. My mother! It was in the early and mid-1970s, during the time she was traveling to Paris for UNESCO. The letters were so passionate, so filled with emotion. He called her "my dear beautiful Greek woman"; she called him "my Roman man." My mouth fell open and my eyes filled with tears as I read.

Her diaries were just as heartbreaking. One entry from that same time period read, "Thinking: If animals live a long time together, they start loving each other. But people start hating each other." That shook me to my core, not only for what it said about my parents' lives, but for what it might say about mine.

And how could I account for the detailed list she had compiled of every mention of my work in the press in the late 1960s and early '70s? From which (and also from the books about me that I had sent her) she had edited by carefully cutting out every last nude picture of me—so, I'm sure, she could show me off to her friends without shame. It reminded me of the way my father had cut Tito out of their photos together.

What a profound mystery the human heart is.

After Danica's death her friends told me how when they went out together in a group, my mother had always been the most outspoken and the funniest, the one who told the best jokes. It made no sense to me. I had never, never seen any trace of that in my mother. We had never had a moment that was normal, easy, or relaxing—except twice: There was the incident with the umbrella and the plastic bags. And there was a time, when I was visiting her, when I saw her smiling happily. "Why are you smiling?" I asked her. "Because that woman is dead," she said. She was talking about my father's wife, Vesna.

I read these words at Danica's funeral:

My dear, honest, proud, heroic mother. I didn't understand you as a child. I didn't understand you as a student. I didn't understand you as an adult until now, in my sixtieth year of life, you started shining in the full light like a sun that suddenly appeared behind gray clouds after rain. For ten full months, you were lying motionless in a hospital, and suffering in pain. Whenever I asked you how you were, you said, "I am fine." When I asked you if you were in pain, you said, "Nothing hurts me." When I asked you if you needed anything, you said, "I don't need anything." You never, ever complained, either of loneliness or of pain. You raised me with a strong hand, without much gentleness, so as to make me strong and independent and teach me discipline, never to stop, never to halt myself until the task is completed. As a child, I thought you were cruel and that you didn't love me. I have never understood you until now, when I found your diaries, notes, letters, and memories of war. You never spoke to me about the war. I didn't know of all the medals you had, the ones I found at the bottom of the case in your room.

Right here, standing at your open grave, I wish to mention just a single event from the many of your life. Belgrade was being liberated for seven days, and there were fights for every street, every building. You were in a truck with five nurses, a driver, and forty-five badly wounded partisans. You were driving through gunfire, through Belgrade, towards Dedinje, which was already free, so as to take the wounded to hospital. The truck is shot full of holes, the driver is killed, and the truck is burning. You, chief nurse of the First Proletariat Brigade, jump off the truck, together with the five nurses, and with incredible strength pull all forty-five wounded from the burning truck and lay them onto the pavement. You take the radio telephone and ask for another truck to be sent. The hell of war is burning around you. Another truck is coming. The six of you are getting the wounded in, and four nurses are killed in the process, their bodies filled with bullets flying around them. You and the remaining nurse manage to load all the wounded in the new truck, and break through to the hospital so forty-five lives get saved. Your medal of honor remains a confirmation to this story.

My dear, honest, brave, heroic mother. I love you endlessly, and I am proud to be your daughter. Here at your grave, I wish to thank your sister, Ksenija, for her sacrifice and for taking care of you. She fought for your life until the very end. Thank you, Ksenija.

Today we are only putting your body in the grave, and not your soul. Your soul is not carrying any luggage on its journey. It is bodiless, shines and shimmers in the dark. Somebody once said that life is a dream, an illusion, and death is the awakening. My dear, only mother, I wish your body eternal rest and your soul a very happy, long journey.

⁓

In 2006 I'd traveled to Laos as a visiting artist, under the auspices of an art and education organization called The Quiet in the Land, founded by the curator France Morin. I didn't have a specific piece in mind, but I happened to arrive during a Buddhist holiday, a celebration of water. All the people were gathered along the river, the priests were chanting—and all the little kids were running around with toy guns, playing war games. I was so struck by this contrast, which to me reflected the heavy history of war in that country, especially during the Vietnam War.

While I was there I visited two of the most important shamans of Laos. I also found out that the United States had dropped more bombs on Laos than on Vietnam during the Vietnam War, and that children were still being injured, crippled, and even killed by unexploded bombs. And these same injured and crippled children were playing war games with wooden guns they'd made themselves. I felt acutely how war and violence bring people to spiritual emptiness. But I also found that in monasteries monks had made bells from the big bombshells to ring for meditation, and from the small bombshells they'd made vases for flowers. This reminded me of the Dalai Lama, who said, "Only when you learn forgiveness can you stop killing. And it's easy to forgive a friend; it's so much harder to forgive an enemy."

This is why I dedicated the piece to friends and enemies.

I returned to Laos in early 2008, with Paolo; my niece, Ivana, now eighteen and making her first trip to the Far East; and the great Baš Čelik film crew from Serbia. Once again, the production director Igor Kecman would work wonders, making the impossible possible amid the many restrictions imposed by the Laotian government.

My idea was a big video installation with children, called *8 Lessons on Emptiness with a Happy End*. I recruited a group of very young children, ages four to ten, dressed them in military uniforms, and gave them expensive Chinese toy guns with lasers. I asked them to play war, just as they had with the wooden weapons. And anything I asked them to do they did perfectly, because they understood war so well, even at such a young age. I'll never forget one image from the video: seven little girls lying in a bed, covered by a pink blanket, with their weapons lying next to them. The combination of the innocence of children's sleep and violence was devastating.

To re-create the drama of warfare, performed by children, was the strongest statement I could make. The video's lessons on emptiness were images of war—battles, negotiations, searching for landmines, carrying the wounded, executions—reenacted with kids; the happy end was a massive bonfire in which we burned all the children's weapons in front of the whole village. The children didn't want to burn their weapons, because it was the first time they'd had toys that weren't made of wood. But this was my lesson to them about detachment, and the horror of war. The plastic guns burned so terribly, throwing up a cloud of thick, smelly black smoke that covered the village: it was like burning evil itself.

While we were in Laos, Riccardo Tisci sent us an enormous box containing two haute couture gowns he'd designed. He was creating a big fashion show in Paris for Givenchy, and he wanted Paolo and me to interpret the dresses for him—to alter them artistically. After the show, at the gala dinner, we would present two videos, his and mine, showing what we had done with these dresses.

We altered the gowns in very different ways. Paolo made a big cross and put his dress on it and burned it. I took mine to a waterfall and washed it to death, just scrubbed the hell out of it, like Anna Magnani scrubbing the dress in *Volcano*. When we flew to Paris and showed Riccardo our videos, he was very happy.

At the Givenchy party after the show, I noticed a tall redhead in a black leather dress. With her flaming hair and pale skin, she looked like she'd stepped straight out of one of the Bettie Page pinups that Paolo had been collecting since he was sixteen. "Amazing, right?" I said to him. "Amazing," he said, nodding. Someone said she was a sexual anthropologist. *Perfect*, I thought. Our friend the photographer Marco Anelli was next to me, and I asked him to take a picture of her. She didn't smile.

The next day, it was time to fly home, but Paolo said he wanted to stick around Paris for a couple of days, then go to Italy for a week before returning to New York. To recharge. We kissed. "See you then," I said.

But when I got back to the city, something strange happened. One afternoon I was walking down the street in Soho when suddenly a feeling of overwhelming sadness washed over me. I really felt as though my heart was broken, as if all the energy had just been sucked out of me, and I had no idea how or why. *I'm overworked*, I thought. *I really should spend more time with Paolo—I'm not giving him enough attention.*

Then he came back from Milano, and everything started to get strange.

Paolo was always melancholic, but now he was sadder than I'd ever seen him. He just moped around the apartment, staring at his computer for hours at a time. Or talking on his cell phone in Italian, or texting. And every time I came into the room, he would hang up or close his computer. He started to complain—our friends annoyed him; he couldn't find a gallery that would show his work in New York. He seemed constantly irritated by me, and whatever I did. All the signs were there, but I still didn't know what to make of them.

To make things worse, we'd decided to renovate our place, and we were in the process of moving to a rental on Canal Street while the work was being done. We'd packed up all our stuff in boxes and put them in storage; everything was upside down.

And then Paolo, with the saddest expression on his face, told me that he felt completely in my shadow, and that he wanted to leave for a while and do his own work. In Italy.

So we made love, and then he left, leaving me to handle the renovation by myself. I stayed by myself in this place on Canal for three months, and he never called. Then, out of the blue one day, he showed up again, looked at me, and said, "I want a divorce."

"Is it another woman?" I asked.

He shook his head. "No, no, it's not that," he said.

"Then what?"

"I have to find myself," Paolo told me. "And I can't find myself while I'm with you. I've lost myself while I've been with you."

I took this in for a minute. There was a strange little echo in my mind. Then I said, "You know what? I can't accept this. I want to wait one year. I'll wait for you for one year."

In the meantime, I told him, I would sell our vacation house in Stromboli and give him half the proceeds. We had this beautiful place on that beautiful island north of Sicily; when we married I'd given him half the house as my present. I would wind up selling it for a million euro and giving Paolo half the money to help him find himself, not knowing what he was really spending it on.

But then I knew nothing. And I still loved him; I couldn't help myself. "Come here, baby," I said. We lay down on the bed together, fully dressed. And this was the worst part. "I can't touch you," he told me. Then he got up and left again.

The strangest thing. As everything was falling apart with Paolo, but before I had any idea he was going to leave me, I made this image of myself carrying a skeleton into the unknown:

Carrying the Skeleton, color chromogenic print, New York, 2008

He came back three times over the next few months, but he always left again. Each time was awful. Once, we started to make love and then he just stopped. "I can't do it," he said.

I looked into his eyes. "Do you have another woman?" I asked.

He looked into my eyes and told me he didn't.

I believed him. Maybe I was a fool. But our intimacy was such that I trusted him blindly. He knew how much Ulay had lied to me, and he always said, "I will never hurt you like that." He said it so many times—and he did worse.

That July, Alex Poots, the director of the Manchester International Festival, and Hans-Ulrich Obrist, the artistic director of the Serpentine Galleries in London, invited me to curate a performance event at Manchester's Whitworth Art Gallery. The event was to be called *Marina Abramović Choices*. The idea was to combine long-durational performances, over seventeen days and four hours a day, by fourteen international artists—and to prepare the public, in a completely new way, to view these works. I invited some of my former students and other artists I'd never worked with before: Ivan Civic, Nikhil Chopra, Amanda Coogan, Marie Cool and Fabio Balducci, Yingmei Duan, Eunhye Hwang, Jamie Isenstein, Terence Koh, Alastair MacLennan, Kira O'Reilly, Melati Suryodarmo, Nico Vascellari, and Jordan Wolfson.

Alex and I went to meet Maria Balshaw, the director of the Whitworth. She asked how much space I needed. And I asked her, "Do you want to make something regular and ordinary, or something unique and extraordinary?" She said that of course she wanted to do something unique.

"Then empty the whole museum," I said. "We'll take the whole space."

She looked at me with amazement—no one had ever asked her this before. To empty the whole museum would take three months, she said, and asked me to give her some time to think about it. The next day she said, "Yes, let's do it."

To enter the museum, the public had to sign a certificate promising they would stay four hours without leaving. They had to put on white lab coats, so they could feel they were making a transition from viewers to experimenters. For the first hour they were there, I would give them simple exercises: slow walking, deep breathing, looking into each other's eyes. After I had conditioned them, I would then lead them to the rest of the museum to see the long-durational performance work.

This was the first attempt at a format that would later form the basis of my institute and my Method.

⟶

In the middle of all of this, Klaus Biesenbach and I had begun planning the biggest show of my life, a career retrospective at the Museum of Modern Art. Klaus was very blunt about what he wanted. He was much less interested in my non-performance work—the transitory objects with crystals—than in my performance pieces. He told me that when he was an art-loving kid in Germany, invitations to exhibitions used to come on postcards. And the postcards that always excited him the most were the ones that said on the bottom, *"Der Kunstler ist anwesend"*—the artist is present. Knowing the artist would be *right there* in the gallery or the museum meant so much more than just thinking about going to look at some paintings or sculptures.

Klaus said, "Marina, every exhibition needs a kind of rule of the game. Why don't we have one very strict rule: you have to be present in every single work, either in a video, or a photo, or a restaging of one of your performances."

At first I didn't like the idea. So much of my work would have to fall out, I complained. But Klaus insisted. He had become very strong-willed since our first meeting, almost twenty years earlier! But he was also so smart, and he had accomplished a great deal. I trusted him. And I began to warm to his concept.

The Artist Is Present.

I had an idea. On the upper floors there would be continuous re-performances of my pieces, but in the atrium space, I would do a major new performance, with the same title, where *I* would be present for three months. It seemed like an important opportunity to show a large audience the potential of performance: this transformative power that other arts don't have.

I thought again of the Rilke line I'd loved as a girl: "O Earth: invisible! / What, if not transformation, is your urgent command?" And of the great Taiwanese-American artist Tehching Hsieh—for me, always a true master of performance art, and one who truly represents transformation. Tehching has made five performances in his life, each of them lasting for one year. He followed this with a thirteen-year plan, in which he made art without showing it. If you ask him what he's doing now, he will say he is doing life. And this, for me, is the ultimate proof of his mastery.

With Tehching Hsieh

The new piece took shape in my mind. We were talking about five decades of my career as an artist. . . . In my mind's eye I saw shelves, similar to *The House with the Ocean View*, only in chronological levels—up and down rather than straight across. Each shelf would represent a decade of my career, and I would move from level to level throughout the performance. The idea became very complex. I even designed chairs for the audience, something like chaise longues, with binoculars attached: people could recline comfortably in the atrium, I thought, and watch my eyes and the pores of my skin if they chose.

It was all very exciting—and complicated. There were structural issues with fastening the shelves to the atrium wall, there were security and liability questions. Klaus and I began planning. . . .

All this busyness, and then Paolo left.

I was going mad. I was crying in taxis. I was crying in supermarkets. Walking down the street, I would just burst into tears in the middle of the sidewalk. I talked to our friends and his family about nothing else—I got sick and tired of listening to myself talking about it, and I knew all my friends were sick and tired of listening to me. I couldn't eat, I couldn't sleep. And the hell of it was that I just couldn't understand why he had gone away.

I was a total wreck. But what could I do? I went on.

One day that summer, Klaus and I were visiting the Dia Art Foundation, a wonderful modern-art museum in upstate New York, and we were looking at the wall drawings of Sol LeWitt, who had just died the year before. These are big, beautifully stark graphite grids, extraordinarily simple—which means that their conception was so difficult. And as I stared at these drawings, I began to weep.

It was everything. Paolo, the gorgeous simplicity of these grids, LeWitt's death ... I really wasn't sure. It didn't even matter. Klaus took me by the hand, and we walked on until we came to a Michael Heizer piece: a rectangular hole in the floor with a smaller rectangular opening inside, almost like a conversation pit. We sat on the edge, and Klaus talked to me. He spoke softly, but—this is his way—he was very direct.

"Marina," he said, "I know you. And I'm worried about you. This is the same tragedy in your life, all over again. You were with Ulay for twelve years; you were with Paolo for twelve years. And each time, the umbilical cord gets cut, and *boom*—you're devastated."

I nodded.

"This Michael Heizer piece is reminding me of a very famous image of you and Ulay performing *Nightsea Crossing* in Japan," Klaus said. "Remember? There was a square hole like this in the floor, and the table was in the hole, and you and Ulay sat across from each other.

"Marina, why don't you face the reality of who you are now?" he said. "Your love life is gone. But you have a relationship with your audience, with your work. Your work is the most important thing in your life. Why don't you just do in the MoMA atrium what you did in Japan with Ulay—except that instead of Ulay sitting across the table from you, it is the public? Now you're alone: the public completes the work."

I sat up very straight, thinking about it. *The Artist Is Present* was taking on a whole new meaning. But then Klaus was shaking his head. "Or maybe not," he said. "We're talking about three months, all day, every day. I don't know. I don't know if it would be good for you, physically or psychologically. Let's go back to the shelves."

But the more I thought about the shelves, the more complicated the whole idea seemed. Too complicated. I thought about Sol LeWitt's beautiful simplicity. The whole way home, I kept bringing up the table idea—and Klaus kept shooting it down. "No, no, no," he said. "I don't want to be responsible for you doing that kind of damage to yourself, physical and psychological damage."

"I think I can do it," I said.

"No, no—I won't hear it. Let's talk about it another day."

I called him back the next day. "I want to do it," I said.

"Absolutely not," Klaus said. But by then I realized we were playing a game, and that it was a game both of us had understood from the start.

⌐

Soon afterward I was at dinner at a friend's place, talking to a few people I'd just met about my plans for *The Artist Is Present.* One of them was Jeff Dupre, who had a film company called Show of Force. He was so enthusiastic about my plans for the retrospective that he said, "Why don't we make a film about your preparations?" A few days later Jeff introduced me to a young filmmaker, Matthew Akers. Matthew knew nothing about performance art—in fact he seemed skeptical about it—but was very interested in me and the project anyway.

It happened that I was just beginning a workshop, called *Cleaning the House*, with the thirty-six performance artists who were going to re-perform my pieces in MoMA. And though there hadn't been enough time yet to find the money for the movie, Matthew was so eager to start that he decided to begin filming immediately. He filmed the workshop, and then we decided that he and his crew would follow me for the entire next year to record the preparations for *The Artist Is Present.*

With Matthew Akers at the Sundance Film Festival, 2012

For the next year, I lived my life with a microphone taped to me and a camera crew documenting my every movement. I gave Matthew the key to my house so the crew could come anytime, even six in the morning. Sometimes I would wake up to the sight of a cameraperson standing at the foot of my bed. There were times I wanted to kill Matthew and his crew with my own hands. It was very hard to have any privacy, but this was something I felt I needed to do: I saw this as my only chance to show the general public, who didn't even know what performance art was, how serious it was, and how profound an effect it can have.

And I had no idea at all what tack Matthew was going to take in his film—I knew there was even a chance the piece might ridicule me. It didn't matter. I believed so strongly in what I was doing that I felt he might come to believe in it, too. And in the end, he did.

I went into training. Just to be clear, we were talking about me sitting in a chair in the atrium of the Museum of Modern Art for eight hours a day, every day (and ten hours on Fridays) for three months, continuously and without moving—no food or drink, no bathroom breaks, no getting up to stretch my legs and shake my arms out. The strain on my body (and mind) would be huge: there was no anticipating exactly how huge.

My preparation. Dr. Linda Lancaster, a naturopathic physician and homeopath, created a nutritional plan for me. This was really like a NASA program. Not eating or going to the bathroom was a big deal. The stomach produces acids around lunchtime—the body learns through repetition that it is going to be fed, so if you don't have lunch, your blood sugar level goes down, and you can have headaches and get sick. So a year ahead of the March 2010 opening, I had to start learning to have no lunch at all, and to eat breakfast very early in the morning and a small, protein-rich meal in the evening. I had to learn to drink water only by night, never by day, because peeing during the day would not be an option. Just in case, I had a trapdoor built into the seat of my chair that would allow me to urinate while sitting there. After the second day of my performance I knew I would never need it—I put a cushion on top of it. There was some speculation during the performance about whether I was wearing an adult diaper. I was not. There was no need. I am the daughter of partisans. I had trained my body.

My heart was another question—for the heart, there is no NASA training. I missed Paolo so desperately. I wanted him back, shamelessly, more than anything.

Of course it wasn't just him. It's one thing to be forty when you split with somebody, as I was when my relationship with Ulay fell apart. It's another thing to be in your sixties—you face loneliness in a completely different way. This whole thing was a mix of getting old and feeling unwanted. I felt so isolated, and the pain was just too much to bear. I began to see a psychiatrist. She prescribed antidepressants, which I never took.

I went through all of 2009 without seeing Paolo. As we agreed, we would wait until the first of June to decide if we were to stay together or not. Midway through the year, I found out the truth from a friend in Milan: there was someone else, and it was *that woman,* the one we'd met at the Givenchy show, the sexual anthropologist. They'd been together since the day after the event, when Paolo had decided to stay in Paris. It took me all too long to realize that he'd left me for her in precisely the same way he'd left Maura for me. That he had played me just the way he'd played her. With a dead feeling in the center of my heart, I filed for divorce. It became final that summer. One night soon afterward I went to dinner with the artist Marco Brambilla, whom I'd recently met and who has since become a very good friend. We bonded that night over our stories of heartbreak. As we commiserated, it was clear he was really trying to cheer me up, and even though I don't drink, I had a big glass of vodka to wash away the pain. I needed it.

Marco Brambilla and me in Venice, 2015

Knowing the bad condition I was in, Riccardo Tisci invited me to go on holiday with him and his boyfriend to the island of Santorini, in the Aegean Sea. When I arrived at Athens harbor to catch the ferry, Riccardo was alone. "What happened?" I asked. "He just left me," Riccardo said.

It was the saddest holiday on earth—the two of us just cried and cried. This was the moment Riccardo and I really became close friends. But after he went back to Paris to work, I felt I still needed to heal some more. And so, at the invitation of Nicholas Logsdail, I went to the island of Lamu, in the Indian Ocean off the coast of Kenya.

Lamu was an old Swahili settlement with no roads, but a lot of donkeys everywhere. The atmosphere was kind of post-Hemingway. The sheriff of the island was named Banana; the barista at the café was called Satan. Nicholas's cook was named Robinson. I asked him if his last name was Crusoe, and he said yes, of course. Another artist, Christian Jankowski, was visiting Nicholas, along with his girlfriend. They both tried to cheer me up with jokes; in return I told them the saddest Balkan jokes I could think of. Someday, Christian and I decided, we would make a joke book together.

Then, one day, I decided to go back to work.

The donkeys of the island impressed me. They were the most static animals I'd ever seen—they could stand in the burning sun for hours, hardly moving. I took one donkey into the backyard of Nicholas's house and made a video piece called *Confession*. In it, I first tried to mesmerize the animal with my gaze as he stood opposite me, virtually frozen and with a deceptively sympathetic look in his eyes. Then I began to confess to the donkey all the flaws and mistakes of my whole life, starting from my childhood and extending to that day. After about one hour, the donkey decided to walk away, and that was it. I felt a little bit better.

Confession (performance for video, 60 minutes), 2010

That fall I went with Marco Anelli to Gijón, Spain, to make a new work, a set of videos and photos called *The Kitchen*. The piece was set in an actual kitchen, an extraordinary architectural space in an abandoned convent of Carthusian nuns who had fed many thousands of orphans while the convent was active. Although the work was born as an homage to Saint Teresa of Ávila—who in her writings tells of an experience of mystic levitation in her kitchen—it became an auto-biographical piece, a meditation on my childhood, when the kitchen of my grandmother was the center of my world: the place where all the stories were told, all the advice about my life was given, all the future-telling through cups of black coffee took place.

I was fascinated by the stories of Saint Teresa's levitation, which many witnesses confirmed. One day (one of the accounts said), after she had been levitating for a long time in the church, she got hungry and decided to go home and make herself some soup. She returned to her kitchen and started cooking, but suddenly, unable to control the divine force, began to levitate again. And so, in the middle of cooking, she hovered above the pot of boiling soup, powerless to descend and eat, hungry and angry at once. I loved the idea that she could be angry with the very powers that made her saintly.

The Kitchen I, color fine art pigment print from the series
The Kitchen, Homage to Saint Teresa, 2009

I returned to New York, but I couldn't face Christmas and New Year's alone, and I couldn't stand the thought of being around happy couples during the holidays. So I went traveling again, this time to southern India for a month of panchakarma therapy. Doboom Tulku and my close friend Serge Le Borgne accompanied me, as did Matthew Akers and his film crew.

Panchakarma is a form of Ayurvedic healing, a very old Sanskrit system of medicine that involves a complete detox for twenty-one days, daily massages, and meditation. Every morning you drink liquid ghee to lubricate the internal cells of your body. I went to this place for a month, and I felt so clean. I felt as though all the germs had left my body, including Paolo. Then a funny thing happened.

It took me almost thirty-six hours to get home from India: a long car ride to catch a local plane; the local plane to get another plane; changing planes in London; waiting in waiting rooms; reading magazines; nodding off. Finally I got back to New York, and the next day—I'd gone to the movies—I got as sick as a dog. Vomiting, high fever; terrible. All while Matthew Akers and his faithful crew continued to film me. I realized I still had a hole in my heart from Paolo. But in the middle of it all I remembered something my grandmother had said: "Whatever starts bad always finishes good." So I thought, *Okay, maybe this is the way it has to be—going from total health and cleansing into complete sickness.* Then one morning I was better, and then it was time for *The Artist Is Present.*

12.

AN ARTIST'S CONDUCT IN HIS LIFE:

An artist should not lie to himself or others

An artist should not steal ideas from other artists

An artist should not compromise for himself or in regards to the art market

An artist should not kill other human beings

An artist should not make himself into an idol. . . .

An artist should avoid falling in love with another artist

AN ARTIST'S RELATION TO SILENCE:

An artist has to understand silence

An artist has to create a space for silence to enter his work

Silence is like an island in the middle of a turbulent ocean

AN ARTIST'S RELATION TO SOLITUDE:

An artist must make time for the long periods of solitude

Solitude is extremely important

Away from home, Away from the studio, Away from family, Away from friends

An artist should stay for long periods of time at waterfalls

An artist should stay for long periods of time at exploding volcanoes

An artist should stay for long periods of time looking at fast-running rivers

An artist should stay for long periods of time looking at the horizon where the ocean and sky meet

*An artist should stay for long periods of time looking at the stars in
the night sky*
—An Artist's Life Manifesto: Marina Abramović

The crowds were lining up outside MoMA from the very first day of
the performance, March 14, 2010. The rules were simple: Each person could sit across from me for as short or as long a time as he or she
wished. We would maintain eye contact. The public was not to touch
me or speak to me.

And so we began.

In *The House with the Ocean View*, I had a relationship with the
audience, but *The Artist Is Present* was a whole different story, because now the relationship was one-on-one. I was there, one hundred
percent—three hundred percent—for each person. And I became extremely receptive. As I'd noticed in *Nightsea Crossing*, my sense of
smell was heightened. I felt I understood the state of mind Van Gogh
achieved when he painted his paintings. When he painted the lightness of air. I felt I could see, around each person sitting across from
me, the same little particles of energy that he saw. Very early on I
realized the most amazing thing: every single person sitting in that
chair across from me left a specific kind of energy behind. The person
left; the energy stayed.

Later on, several scientists in America and Russia became interested in *The Artist Is Present*. They wanted to test the patterns in
brain waves triggered by this mutual gaze, this nonverbal communication between two strangers. And what they are finding is that in
this situation, brain waves sync up and make identical patterns.

What I found, immediately, was that the people sitting across from
me became very moved. From the beginning, people were in tears—
and so was I. Was I a mirror? It felt like more than that. I could see
and feel people's pain.

I think people were surprised by the pain that welled up in them.
For one thing, I don't think people ever really look into themselves. We

all try, as much as possible, to avoid confrontation. But this situation was profoundly different. First you wait for hours just to sit in front of me. Now you're sitting in front of me. You are observed by the public. You are filmed and photographed. You are observed by me. There is nowhere to go except into yourself. And that's the thing. People have so much pain, and we're all always trying to push it down. And if you push down emotional pain for long enough, it becomes physical pain.

On the morning of the first day, an Asian woman with a baby sat in front of me. The baby was wearing a little hood on her head. And I'd never seen anybody with so much pain in my life. Wow. She had so much pain, I couldn't breathe. She looked at me for a long, long time, and then she slowly took the hood off the baby, and the baby had a huge scar across the top of her head. Then she and the baby left.

Woman sitting with her sick child, *Portraits in the Presence of Marina Abramović* by Marco Anelli, Museum of Modern Art, New York, 2010

The photographer Marco Anelli, who spent every minute of the 736 hours of *The Artist Is Present* in that atrium, taking pictures of every single one of the more than 1,500 people who sat across from me, got an amazing shot of that woman and her baby. He eventually published a book of all these photographs, and this one image was so powerful that he gave it a full page.

Oddly enough, the image harked back to the beginning of my friendship with Marco, whom I first met in Rome in 2007. All I knew about him at first was that he was a friend of Paolo's, and he kept asking to make a portrait of me. Finally I said, "Okay, I'll give you ten minutes." He arrived exactly on time, with an assistant and a great deal of camera equipment. When I asked how I should pose, he said, "I'm not interested in your face—I'm interested in your scars." He was talking about the scars on my neck from *Rhythm 0*, on my hands from *Rhythm 10*, on my belly from *Thomas Lips*. I was so impressed by this idea—really almost jealous that I hadn't thought of it myself—that Marco and I became instant friends. And when I began preparing *The Artist Is Present*, he was the only photographer I could think of who could dedicate his time to every moment of the piece.

Marco Anelli photographing my scars, Rome, 2007

A year later, this Asian woman saw the book of portraits, and wrote a letter to Marco and me, saying, "I saw the book, and I wanted to tell you that my baby was born with brain cancer, and she'd had chemotherapy. On that particular morning, just before I came to MoMA, I went to the doctor and he said to me, 'There is no hope anymore,' so we stopped chemo. In a way I was relieved that she would not suffer

Portraits in the Presence of Marina Abramović by Marco Anelli,
Museum of Modern Art, New York, 2010

further, because the chemo was so terrible, but at the same time I also knew that this was the end for my baby. So I came to sit with you, and this photograph was that moment."

It was unbelievably sad. I wrote her back. A year passed, and then she sent me another letter saying, "I am pregnant again." We've stayed in touch, and her new baby is okay. Life goes on.

⁓

I had designed a special dress for the piece, floor-length and woven in cashmere and wool, to keep me warm. The show had begun in early spring, and the atrium was full of cold drafts. The dress was like a house that I inhabited. I had it made in three colors: blue, to calm me down; red, to give me energy; and white, for purity. On the day of the premier, I wore the red. It turned out I would need it.

At the end of that first exhausting day, after more than fifty people had sat across from me, bringing all their pain to me, one more came—Ulay.

MoMA had flown him and his new girlfriend—he was about to marry yet again—to New York for the show at my request, out of respect, because after all, he was half of twelve years of the work that was being shown upstairs. I knew he was there. He was my guest of honor. But I never expected him to sit in front of me.

It was a shocking moment. Twelve years of my life ran through my mind in an instant. For me he was so much more than just another visitor. And so, just this once, I broke the rules. I put my hands on top of his hands, we looked into each other's eyes, and before I knew what was happening, we were both in tears.

Very soon after this, he went back to Amsterdam, and that August he discovered he had cancer. And not long after that, he decided to take me to court over the profits from our work. We needed a judge to resolve decisions we couldn't agree upon over the last twenty-six years. So life not only goes on—it also gets very messy sometimes.

The deep emotional pain I kept seeing across the table put my own heartbreak into perspective. But my physical pain was considerable. I had made a simple but huge mistake in planning *The Artist Is Present*: not putting arms on my chair.

Aesthetically the chair was perfect: I like everything to be very simple. But ergonomically, it was hell for me, because after hours and hours the pain in my ribs and my back was just excruciating. With arms on the chair, I could've sat up straight for hours at a time; without them, it was impossible.

I never thought of correcting my mistake, not even for one second. I was too proud. This is a rule of performance: once you enter into this mental-physical construct you've devised, the rules are set, and that's that—you're the last one who can change them. I was also—paradoxically—too committed to the humble look of the piece. Arms on my chair would have changed my presence completely, might have made me look grand.

But now it was as it had been in past performances. I had more pain than it seemed the human body could withstand. Yet the moment I said to myself, *Okay, I'm going to lose consciousness—I can't take any more*—that was the moment the pain completely disappeared.

⁓

There was one thing I was very proud of: I mastered the art of not sneezing.

This is how it works. As you know, sometimes when there is dust in the air, you have an incredible urge to sneeze. The trick is to concentrate on your breathing to the point where you're barely breathing at all—but you have to give yourself a tiny bit of air, because if you stop entirely, then you'll sneeze with full force. It's a matter of willpower: you have to stay right on the edge. What happens as a side effect is that your eyes start to really, really hurt. But then the sneeze has passed—it's not going to happen. Kind of amazing.

It was so funny with peeing—I never had the slightest urge, nothing at all. The same with hunger: I just never thought about food. My NASA training had worked. The body really is like a precise machine, and you can train a machine to do certain things. It's just that we almost never do.

Some people only sat in front of me for a minute; some sat for an hour or more. One man sat twenty-one times, the first time for seven hours. Was I present for every second of all this time? Of course not. It's impossible. The mind is such a changeable organism—in the blink of an eye it can go anywhere. And you have to always bring it back. You're thinking you're in the present, and then you suddenly realize that you are who knows where—deep in the jungles of the Amazon, perhaps.

But it was really important always to come back. Because the central thing was my connection with the person. And the more intense the connection, the less space I had to go elsewhere.

Public figures came to sit. Lou Reed. Björk. James Franco. Sharon Stone. Isabella Rossellini. Christiane Amanpour. Lady Gaga came to the atrium to see the piece, though she didn't sit in front of me. When the young people who were there saw her, they tweeted about it, and many more young people showed up. After she left, they stayed. And all at once I had a whole new audience of young people. The profile of the atrium piece rose to crazy heights: people began to wait in line overnight, sleeping in sleeping bags in front of the museum. And many people began to come who, I'm quite sure, had no interest at all in the art scene: people who possibly had never gone to a museum before.

One day, after two months, a man in a wheelchair arrived at the front of the line. The guards removed the other chair and put him in his wheelchair across the table from me. And I looked at this man, and I realized that I didn't even know if he had legs—the table was in the way. That night I said, "I don't need a table; let's move it out." It was the only time I've ever made a major change in the middle of a piece. Now it was just me and the other person, in two chairs, facing each other. I remembered an old Indian folktale: There was a king who fell madly in love with a princess, and she fell madly in love with him. They married, and they were the happiest couple in the world. Then she died very young. The king was so overcome with sorrow that he stopped all other activity and began to decorate her small wooden coffin. He had the coffin covered with gold, then covered with diamonds, rubies, emeralds. The coffin became bigger and bigger, surrounded by so many different layers. Then around the coffin he built a temple.

That was not enough. He had a city built around the temple. The whole country became this young woman's grave. Then the king was just sitting there, because there was nothing left to do. So he said to his servants, "Can you just remove the walls, the columns, the roof, take down the temple? Take the jewelry away." And finally there was just the wooden coffin again, and he said, "Take this coffin, too."

I always remember that. There is a moment in your life when you realize that you don't actually need anything. That life isn't about things. Taking the table away was so important for me. The wonderfully protective head of museum security, Tunji Adeniji, didn't like it very much—the table had been a kind of buffer between the audience and me, and there were some pretty crazy people around. But I just knew it was the right thing: Make it simple. Increase contact. Remove barriers.

On the first day without the table, the strangest thing happened: as I was sitting there, I felt an excruciating shooting pain in the front of my left shoulder. At the end of the day, when I asked Dr. Linda what she made of it, she said, "Did you see anything wrong in the position of the two chairs?"

It turned out that when the table was removed, Marco had shifted one of his lights to avoid reflection—and that somehow this shift had caused the shadows of the other chair's legs to converge and point directly at my left shoulder, like an arrow. The minute we moved the chair slightly, the pain disappeared. I could never explain this rationally. But then so many important things have no rational explanation.

I went through so many different experiences over the three months of *The Artist Is Present*—every day was a kind of miracle. But this last month was the absolute culmination of that experience, mostly because I had removed the table. The moment it was gone, I felt a powerful connection to everybody sitting there. I felt that the energy of every visitor remained in layers in front of me even after they left.

And people were coming back, again and again—in some cases a dozen times or more. I began to recognize some of the people sitting across from me from previous visits. I was even aware of the people in the line. There was one man who waited day after day, for hours, and every time he got to the front of the line, he would give his place to somebody else. He never once sat in front of me.

The piece brought people together in new ways. I later heard about one group who met on the line and afterward started having dinner together every month or two, because they felt the experience had changed their lives. And the man who sat in front of me twenty-one times made a book for me, called *75*. The preface reads:

In 75, 75 people shared their stories of participating in Marina Abramović's *The Artist Is Present*, her performance piece that ran for 75 days in New York City's Museum of Modern Art. Each person sat silently, face to face with Abramović at least once during the show. Some returned again and again. They were asked to give voice to their experiences in 75 words, and their writings appear in the order in which they were received by me. I created this book as a way of honoring and paying tribute to Marina Abramović for her extraordinary work of art.

—Paco Blancas, New York City, May 2010

And Paco had the number 21 tattooed on his hand, for his twenty-one visits.

There were eighty-six guards in the museum, and all of them came to sit with me. One of them wrote me a letter:

Marina—in advance I want to congratulate you for your great exhibition at MoMA. It was a huge pleasure to work with you. When I sat on the chair with you, it was very different to observe you from my point of work. I don't know why, but I felt scared, my heart was palpitating fast, into the minute that it came back to normal. You are an enormous person. God bless you.

—Luis E. Carrasco, MoMA security

The community that had vanished from performance art had returned, only much bigger and far more inclusive than ever before.

⌒

During this last month, my sitting in the atrium became something different. It's not just that I knew the piece was ending—it wasn't about ending anymore. It was that the performance had lasted so long that it had become life itself. My life seemed to extend from the moment I first sat on the chair in the morning to the recorded announcement that was the last sound of the day: "The museum is closed; please leave the space." Then I would watch the guards usher the people away, and the lights would go dim, and my assistant, Davide Balliano, would come and touch me lightly on the shoulder.

Kneeling under the table at the end of the day during *The Artist Is Present* (performance, 3 months), Museum of Modern Art, New York, 2010

Then I would finally stand up, or just lie on the floor to stretch my back. I would go to the elevator with the two guards who escorted me to the dressing room. I would begin to try to take off my dress, with hands that hurt so badly I could barely move them.

During the final month, as this piece became one with life itself, I started to think intensely about the purpose of my existence. Eight hundred fifty thousand people in all had stood in the atrium, seventeen thousand on the final day alone. And I was there for everyone there, whether they sat with me or not. Suddenly, out of nowhere in the world, this overwhelming need had appeared. The responsibility was enormous.

I was there for everyone who was there. A great trust had been given to me—a trust that I didn't dare abuse, in any way. Hearts were opened to me, and I opened my heart in return, time after time after time. I opened my heart to each one, then closed my eyes—and then there was always another. My physical pain was one thing. But the pain in my heart, the pain of pure love, was far greater.

Chrissie Iles wrote this: "I walk into the arena of the performance. Marina's head is bowed. I sit down in front of her. She raises her head. She is like my sister. I smile. She smiles gently. We look into each other's eyes. She begins to cry. I cry. I think nothing of my life and everything about how the people sitting have affected hers. I want to send her love. I realize she is giving me unconditional love."

The sheer quantity of love, the unconditional love of total strangers, was the most incredible feeling I've ever had. *I don't know if this is art*, I said to myself. *I don't know what this is, or what art is.* I'd always thought of art as something that was expressed through certain tools: painting, sculpture, photography, writing, film, music, architecture. And yes, performance. But this performance went beyond performance. This was life. Could art, should art, be isolated from life? I began to feel more and more strongly that art must *be* life—it must belong to everybody. I felt, more powerfully than ever, that what I had created had a purpose.

The end finally came on May 31, and Klaus Biesenbach was the last person to sit across from me. In honor of the occasion, we had prerecorded a different message: "The museum is now closing, and this performance of 736 and a half hours is at an end." And Klaus was supposed to sit there until the announcement played, but he got so self-conscious and nervous that eight minutes before the official ending, he stood up, came to my chair, and kissed me—and everybody thought *that* was the end. The atrium erupted in deafening applause; it went on and on. What could I do? I stood up. And since we'd prearranged that the moment I stood up, the guards were to take both chairs out, they did—and that was the end.

That killed me. The endurance artist in me, the walk-through-walls child of partisans, had so wanted to go to the very last second, until the end. To have begun exactly when the museum opened on March 14, to finish exactly when it closed on May 31. Instead there was this strange eight-minute gap at the end.

Photograph © Marco Anelli

With Klaus Biesenbach, *The Artist Is Present* (performance, 3 months),
Museum of Modern Art, New York, 2010

Photograph © Marco Anelli

At the end of *The Artist Is Present* (performance, 3 months),
Museum of Modern Art, New York, 2010

But as I've always said, once you enter the space of performance, you must accept whatever happens. You have to accept the flow of energy that is behind you and below you and around you. And so I accepted it.

That was when Paolo appeared by my side.

I had known—had been told—he was in the atrium during the final month; I never saw him. Unlike Ulay he never had the courage to come and sit down across from me. But now here he was, standing in front of me, and I couldn't help myself. Time stopped again. We kissed and stayed in an embrace, and then he whispered something in my ear, first in Italian and then in English, that I'll never forget: "You're incredible; you're a great artist."

Not "I love you." *You're incredible; you're a great artist.*

I needed more. I kissed him good-bye for the second—and, I thought, last—time.

The next day, MoMA and Givenchy threw a huge party to celebrate the end of my performance. It was surreal for me to go from complete seclusion into the hot center of the limelight. For the occasion, Riccardo made me a long black dress and a long coat made out of 101 snakeskins—I hope they died natural deaths!

I arrived at MoMA with Riccardo and walked onto the red carpet. I felt so happy—I felt I'd accomplished something truly important in my life. I was surrounded by hundreds of people: my friends, artists, film stars, luminaries of the fashion world, socialites. It was like entering another universe. Everybody was congratulating me. What I didn't notice at the moment was that Klaus, very upset, had already had a few drinks. In the thrill of the moment, I had paid too much attention to Riccardo and not enough to him. And for Klaus it was very important to celebrate this moment with me, the celebration of the show he had named and curated.

During the dinner there were speeches: MoMA head Glenn Lowry, Sean Kelly, and Klaus all stood to give a speech. By this time, though, Klaus was clearly intoxicated: his speech was disruptive and repetitive. I didn't know what to do. (I later found out that Patti Smith had written a little note and sent it to Klaus's table—"The speech was great—it was so punk.") Afterward, there was a long silence; I felt I had to say something. So I stood and tried to lighten the atmosphere with a long-durational joke: How many performance artists does it take to change a lightbulb? The answer: I don't know—I was only there for six hours. Then I talked about how hard this show had been to create, and how much work Klaus had put into it. And in the process of making this speech, I totally forgot to mention Sean Kelly and his huge contributions to my career. When I got back to my table, Sean said, "Thank you for mentioning me"—and got up and left.

Oh my God.

After the party, I went home alone. This was supposed to be the happiest moment of my life, and I felt so miserable. I had hurt two people I really cared for, Klaus and Sean, and they had put me down. In a certain way it was about their egos—they didn't realize how totally exhausted I was, and I needed them to be happy for me. But there was no getting around it: I had really screwed up.

At seven the next morning, the telephone rang. It was Klaus. He was completely clear, and he was so mortified by his behavior that he considered resigning. I told him he was being ridiculous, that things happen, and we should just forget it and move on. I called Sean to apologize, but he wouldn't talk to me. Later that day I spoke to Glenn Lowry. He told me he'd told Klaus just to take a little rest and everything would be okay.

The day after, I went with a few friends—Alessia, Stefania, Davide, Chrissie, Marco, and Serge—to my house upstate to relax, to swim, to enjoy the countryside. I needed time before returning to normality. Ten days later, I called Sean again. This time he took my call. I told him how sorry I was, and he accepted my apology.

⁓

I had put a great deal of money into renovating our Grand Street apartment. It was so beautiful. But when Paolo left me, I just sold it and threw out everything we had used together—the sheets, the towels, even the dinnerware. All I kept were a few objects, things I'd owned before we were together. The only way to deal with that kind of pain, I knew, was to make a clean sweep.

I made a small profit on Grand Street, and the sale of my Amsterdam house (and the rise of the euro against the dollar) continued to sustain me. I bought a new place on King Street in Soho. And I put a down payment on an old brick building in upstate Hudson, New York, a run-down former theater. I wasn't sure what I would do with it, but I followed my intuition and bought it anyway. It seemed I had a gift for real estate! And a few miles away, at a bend in the Kinderhook Creek, I'd found a folly of a house, shaped, amazingly enough, like a six-pointed star.

The architect Dennis Wedlick had designed the house in the 1990s for a Bangladeshi heart surgeon who wanted every member of his family to have the exact same space: this was how the concept of a six-point star evolved. But shortly after the place was built, the surgeon's wife developed problems walking, and since it was too difficult to readjust the house for wheelchair use, the surgeon had to put it on the market. And there it sat for four years—this house was simply too strange for American tastes.

But not for mine. It took me all of thirty seconds to decide to buy it, especially when I discovered the stream crossing the land. The water was a living force, breaking into little rapids as it passed over the rocks, and the sound of its steady rush was profoundly relaxing. I decided later to have a small hut built above the riverbank for short retreats, a place where I could find serenity without going to India. When I was at Star House, I never felt I was only two and a half hours from New York City. Here I knew I could think and create.

And so I learned to drive. At sixty-three! I had been a passenger my whole life: Ulay had driven our van around Europe; once, when he tried to teach me to drive in the Sahara, I veered off the road and we were stuck in the sand for an entire day. After this he gave up. As a city-dweller, I took cabs and subways. If I was going to live in the country, though, even part-time, it was imperative that I learn to get around by myself.

I looked in the telephone book for a driving teacher who taught disabled people. When I called, I asked the man who answered the phone, "What is your expertise?"

"I can teach people in wheelchairs," he said. "People with one leg, with one arm; people who are unable to turn their neck."

"Can I make an appointment?" I asked.

When I arrived he looked at me and asked, "What's wrong with you?"

"Everything," I said.

His car, with dual controls and a 360-degree mirror, was like a spaceship. But the most important thing this man had was the patience to teach me to drive.

Then Paolo called.

It was the summer after *The Artist Is Present*, and—I knew for certain; we had friends in common—he had been separated from that woman for six months. He called, and then he took the train up to Hudson, and I met him at the station in my shiny new Jeep. I was so proud: he'd never seen me driving. We had lunch, then we went back to Star House and made love for three days, with all the passion we'd known at the beginning. It was three days of pure paradise. And then we were together again. I felt the worst was behind us.

In September I went to Paris for the Givenchy show. We were still filming post-shots for Matthew Akers's documentary: Matthew was interested in showing my relationship with Riccardo Tisci, along with the side of me that was not an artist, the woman who was so ashamed of her desire to dress in high-fashion clothes, the one who remembered the petticoat her mother never gave her.

So I went to see the Givenchy show. And there she was, the sexual anthropologist, sitting in the audience just across from me. At five foot ten, with her dead-white skin, red hair, and cold face, she was impossible to miss.

Afterward I went over and—we had never been properly introduced—presented myself, with complete confidence. Paolo was now back with me even though we were divorced. I was in love, and my heart was light. I was so happy; I wanted to forgive everyone. I wanted everyone to be friends. And so when she said, "Let's have coffee," I smiled and said, "Of course."

But when I told Paolo, he was terrified. "Don't see her, please," he said. "Please. It will destroy everything we've built up again."

"Don't be silly," I told him. And then I went to meet her.

She had a lot of things to tell me. She said that while I was in the bathroom at the 2008 Givenchy show, Paolo had gone straight up to her and said, "You are the most beautiful woman in the world; can you give me your number?" She gave him her number. And while I went trustingly back to New York, he stayed with her in Paris for several days. For days, she told me, they did nothing but have every kind of kinky sex; they lived on oysters and champagne. Paolo was totally possessed by her, she said. She told me she was learning his body, discovering ways to increase his pleasure by using certain instruments to extend his orgasm.

I listened in disbelief. I thought of the times he'd come back to New York and told me there was no other woman. The times he'd looked in my eyes and said, so sadly, "There's something broken in me."

She went on. "He was never in love with you. All he wanted from you was your money. This is a man who has never worked," she said, scornfully. "But I want to have children; I want him to work," she said. As though Paolo and I weren't back together. As if I didn't exist.

I could see she was furious, but now I was furious, too. "He's back with me now," I said.

"He's addicted to me," she told me, coldly. "He will always come back."

Looking back now, it was a cruelly accurate prophecy.

She had planted this evil seed, and it began to grow and fester.

Paolo had been right to fear her. I went back to him, but we fought like crazy. We went to Rome for a while to try to work it out. He'd tried to introduce that woman to his parents, but they refused to meet her. They really loved me—especially his father, Angelo—and they wanted to do everything they could to get us back together. We kept fighting.

I took some days off and went with Marco Anelli to the hills south of Rome to do a photo and video project called *Back to Simplicity.* I was in so much pain that I had to make some kind of contact with innocent life, so Marco photographed me with newborn baby lambs and goats. It helped me feel better, but the relief was temporary.

When Paolo and I returned to New York, he stayed in a separate apartment—his decision. There were sweet moments, moments of hope, yet we continued to fight. We went to a psychoanalyst together, and it didn't help—things got worse and worse and worse.

I felt the psychoanalyst was taking Paolo's side. I felt she was saying that everything he did was right, and everything I did was wrong. That I had been guilty of pushing him away in the first place. That I worked too much, I didn't pay him enough attention, and this was why he cheated on me and left. There was some truth in all this, and it hurt.

Did he see that woman again during this time? I'm certain he didn't. I heard through friends that she was falling apart, she was missing him so badly. As bad as things were between Paolo and me, I took satisfaction in that.

That Christmas I invited a few friends to celebrate with us at Star House; it was a warm, wonderful occasion. And in the middle of it, Paolo came up to me, looking like a lost dog. "I'm missing her again," he told me.

I felt as though he had kicked me in the stomach. To have left me in the first place was bad enough. But to have come back without really meaning it was the cruelest thing he could have done to me.

If you can believe it, we stayed together for nine months after that.

With Serge Le Borgne in the institute's building on the set of a video
being filmed for the Kickstarter campaign, Hudson, 2013

I first met Serge Le Borgne in Paris in December 1997 after he e-mailed
me saying that he was opening a gallery there and wanted to work
with me. Paolo and I were in Paris at the time, we went to check out
the space, and Serge and I almost instantly became friends. From the
beginning we understood each other without talking. I have very few
people in my life whom I can sit with all day without saying a word,
and he is one of them. Also—and quite inexplicably—he has happened
to be present at many of the most difficult moments of my life.

The September after *The Artist Is Present*, I again went to Serge's
gallery in Paris to tell him about my dream for an institute. He looked
me in the eyes and said something I'll never forget: "What you're trying to do is important—more important than me having a gallery in
Paris. I'm going to close my gallery and come work with you."

And he did. Six months later he came to New York to become
artistic director of the Marina Abramović Institute. All we had to do
now was create it.

We had many meetings with lawyers, signing many documents
to establish the organization and give it nonprofit status, and then we
wrote our mission for the institute. The Marina Abramović Institute
(MAI), we wrote, would serve as my legacy, an homage to time-based

and immaterial art. MAI's mission was to change human awareness through productive unions between education, culture, spirituality, science, and technology. The institute would include performance, dance, theater, film, video, opera, music, and any other form of art that might be developed in the future.

In September 2011, Klaus and I took the *Artist Is Present* retrospective to the Garage Museum of Contemporary Art in Moscow. This was the biggest exhibition I'd ever done in my life. The museum was in an old factory where railroad engines had once been manufactured; the architect for the exhibition literally built a space for every work I've ever made. When I saw all my work, in such a huge quantity, I felt so depressed. I thought, "This is it; I can die now."

The split with Paolo also colored my mood deeply. I called Chrissie Iles, who was seeing him regularly, to ask how he was. "He's doing well," Chrissie told me. "In fact, he's doing so much better without you."

Did she mean to hurt me by saying this? "Maybe if I died, he'd be doing even better," I said, and hung up.

Chrissie immediately called Sean—who was about to leave for Moscow to help me prepare the Garage show—and told him I was planning to kill myself. The next night, I returned to my hotel at around 11 P.M. to find Sean sitting in the lobby, looking very serious. "Did you just get here?" I asked him.

"Yes, and I'm waiting for you," he said. "We're going to your room. Immediately."

"Why?" I asked.

"Let's go," Sean said. "Now."

So we went to my room, and he started going through all my things, checking the medicine cabinet, the drawers, the closet, clearly looking for whatever I might use to kill myself. But I told Sean, and people should know this about me: I despise suicide. I think it is the worst way to leave life. I believe passionately that if you have the gift to create, you are not allowed to kill yourself, because it's your duty to share this gift with others.

My relationship with Chrissie was never the same again because of this and for a number of other reasons.

⁓

When I think back on all that happened between Ulay and me, and Paolo and me, I often wonder what I contributed to each split. And I can't help believing that the need to be loved and taken care of that my mother never satisfied was a hurt I brought to every man I was ever with—and something that they couldn't fix.

13.

It's just after sunset. I'm sitting on the beach, alone. There is nobody around and I'm looking at the horizon, where sky and ocean meet. Out of nowhere, in front of me passes a big black dog from the right. When he reaches me he turns away and goes straight to the sea and starts walking on the water, toward the horizon. When he reaches the horizon, he starts walking parallel to it, to the right. Everything seems normal and natural to me, the fact that this dog is walking on water. Then, a strong white light comes from the sky and hits the dog. In front of my eyes he disappears into that light. I feel that I am witnessing something extraordinary. Then I woke up and the reality of the dream was stronger than the reality of the day.
  —*India, January 10, 2016*

My professional life changed completely after *The Artist Is Present*. For four years I'd been working with only one assistant, Davide Balliano, a young and very talented artist. Davide had told me he would stay with me until I finished the MoMA performance: He had learned a lot from me, he said, but he wanted to leave and do his own work. Before Davide left, he brought another, much different, Danica into my life for the next three years. My new assistant may have shared my mother's name, but the similarities stopped there—in fact, she grew up in Texas, not Yugoslavia. Danica interned at MoMA during *The Artist Is Present*, so it was a natural fit to join me as I moved from one phase of my career to the next.

With my assistant, Davide Balliano,
during *The Artist Is Present*, New York, 2010

In the years after the show I found myself with over a hundred e-mails pouring in every day, making all kinds of requests: for interviews, exhibitions, collaborations, lectures, and special projects. I was simply unable to deal with it all by myself. With more money coming in—seven galleries were now selling my work, and a recent show at Sean Kelly's gallery had done very well—I decided it was time for a bigger office, and a bigger office staff. I rented space in a commercial building in Soho and started interviewing candidates.

Around that time, my Italian gallerist, Lia Rumma, sent me an e-mail saying she thought she had somebody who could help me. If I liked him, Lia wrote, he would be someone for the rest of my life. His name was Giuliano Argenziano; he was from Naples, and he'd been living in New York since 2008, working at an art gallery on the Lower East Side.

Giuliano was very energetic and very smart—his English was delightfully accented but perfect, and he had a wicked sense of humor. He had trained as an art historian, but he had grown so disgusted with the egos and the power games of the art business that he'd been on the verge of leaving the art world completely to start his own catering company when Lia contacted me. I said, "Let's try each other out for one month." It's now been more than four years.

With Giuliano Argenziano, backstage at *Charlie Rose*, New York, 2013

In the past I'd always worked with young artists who eventually left to go out on their own. In Giuliano I'd finally found someone who didn't want to be an artist, someone who could work with me forever. I made him director of Abramović LLC, then we interviewed more people and finally settled on five: Sidney, Allison, Polly, Cathy, and Hugo.

As things progressed with MAI, Serge and I rented another office to keep MAI completely separate from my own work under the auspices of Abramović LLC. We also had to search for a new team. Serge wanted to work with very young and motivated people who believed in the mission of the institute, and we found them in Siena, Leah, Maria, Christiana, and Billy, along with another rotating team of collaborators.

The first thing I did was to take them all to the countryside to do a workshop to understand my method: as an introduction I gave them the exercise of sorting and counting piles of rice and lentils. After six hours I told them they could stop, and all of them did—except Giuliano, who wouldn't give up until the last grain. It took him seven and a half hours.

Working with Allison Brainard at my apartment in Soho, 2013

My office is more like a family than an office: everybody who works for me is really in my life. People take holidays when they need them; they go home when they finish work. They're all responsible for their own jobs. Fortunately I forgot all the lessons a Communist dictatorship tried to teach me.

⌣

After the MoMA performance, Matthew Akers and Jeff Dupre filmed and edited *Marina Abramović: The Artist Is Present* for another year. We went to Paris and Montenegro, to Belgrade, to my mother's grave; they interviewed my brother, my aunt Ksenija, Riccardo Tisci in Paris. In the end, we had more than seven hundred hours of material: three editors worked on it full-time for months. Roman Polanski once said that in order to follow the story in a film, you have to cut 70 percent of the good stuff. Matthew and Jeff's editors cut 70 percent—and then the film was finished, ready to send to festivals.

We showed it at Sundance, then at the Big Sky film festival in Montana, then at the Berlin Festival. After the screening in Berlin, I returned home. A week later I heard the film had won the Best Documentary award there. Matthew, who'd been at Big Sky, had to jump on a plane with only the clothes he was wearing to get to Berlin on time. My friend Francesca von Habsburg bought him a suit—which Matthew changed into in the bathroom to receive the award.

In the end, the film received six prizes, including the Independent Spirit Award, the Audience Award—Best Feature Film at the Sarajevo Festival, and an Emmy. I was very proud of the film and the filmmakers, and prouder still that Matthew, who'd begun as a skeptic about performance art, had become a passionate fan, and a friend.

Something else changed after *The Artist Is Present*: I became a public figure. People started recognizing me on the street; often, when I went into a shop to buy a cup of coffee, a smiling stranger would insist on paying for me. And then there was the other side—I began to be heavily criticized in the media for being a star, and for hanging around with stars. But I didn't ask for this. The perception is that an artist has to suffer. I've suffered enough in my lifetime.

⌒

I first met Bob Wilson in the early 1970s, when he gave a lecture and demonstration at a theater festival in Belgrade. His approach to the theater—the way he dealt with time and movement, the way he created mesmerizing images with stage lighting—fascinated me. From the moment I heard him speak, I wanted to work with him. And now, thirty-seven years later, I had an idea for him.

Bob had already picked up on the fact that I knew about presence and how to be in a space when he sat across from me at MoMA during *The Artist Is Present*. Up to this point, I had staged my life, in *Biography* and *The Biography Remix*, in five different ways for five different directors. Now, in my early sixties, I wanted to create a big piece that would not only tell my life story but also the story of my death and funeral. This felt very important because I knew I was entering the last period of my life.

I put death in my work very often, and I read a lot about dying.

I think it's crucial to include death in your life, to think about death every single day. The idea of being permanent is so wrong. We have to understand that death can appear at any moment, and being ready is essential.

These were the ideas I discussed with Bob Wilson. I told him I could think of no one better to direct the piece than him.

When Bob looked at videos of my earlier autobiographical pieces, he said, "If I do this work I'm not interested in your art—I only want to work with your life." And he had a unique take on my life. "I like your tragic stories," he told me. "In a certain way they're so funny. There's nothing more kitschy than showing the tragic as tragic—I feel we have to stage your life comically to reach the public's heart." I thought instantly of the Dalai Lama's almost identical wisdom.

We decided to call our piece *The Life and Death of Marina Abramović*.

I gave Bob a lot of my material to work with—piles of notebooks, images, films and videos. And when he was going through all of it, he came upon *The Biography* by Charles Atlas, where I was suspended in the air with dogs and raw meat on stage below me, and thought: maybe we could lift out that idea of the dogs and put them on stage.

Of course, I wanted real meat, raw meat like in *Balkan Baroque* at the Venice Biennale, but Bob couldn't stomach the idea: "No, no, no. Plastic meat! And I will light it red, more delicious-looking, more bloody, and it will be totally artificial."

One of Bob's first ideas was that I should sing onstage. The thought terrified me. I had never sung in my life—I've always been tone deaf. I took some singing lessons, but it was hopeless. Bob said to me, "Study Marlene Dietrich. Look at her; learn from her. Just stand there and kill them with your eyes."

I approached Anohni to write a song for me to sing. She hesitated, unsure how to write for someone else when she usually works from a very personal place. She had a conversation with Lou Reed while mulling over the invitation: Lou told Anohni that it hurt him so much to see me suffer in my performances and that she should ask me why

I cut myself. And that unlocked something for her. "I realized that was exactly how I felt," she told me. It transformed her idea of how to approach the material and made it very personal. And from that she wrote the first song for the piece, "Cut the World":

With Anohni in London, 2010

For so long I've obeyed that feminine decree
I've always contained your desire to hurt me
But when will I turn and cut the World?
When will I turn and cut the World?
My eyes are coral, absorbing your dreams
My heart is a record of dangerous scenes
My skin is a surface to push to extremes
But when will I turn and cut the World?
When will I turn and cut the World?
But when will I turn and cut the world?
When will I turn and cut the World?
But when will I turn and cut the World?
When will I turn and cut the World?

Working with Bob was a nightmare. At the same time, though, it was a very important experience for me. He never wanted to imagine anything in rehearsal—we had to prepare in full costume, with makeup and lighting. In one scene I was suspended fifteen feet above the stage: I remember hanging there forever while Bob, speaking very slowly, had the lighting director adjust colors: "Ten percent blue, twelve percent magenta, sixty percent red . . ." Meanwhile I hung there thinking, *He could've just hung a goddamn doll up here while he tinkered with the lighting, but no, he had to do it the Bob Wilson way.* This was his version of a durational piece!

The rehearsals were extremely emotional for me. Onstage I had to revisit all the terror and sadness and shame of my mother and father's fights: during the story of my father breaking the twelve champagne glasses I couldn't help bursting into tears.

Bob brought me up short. "Stop this bullshit crying on stage!" he said. "It's not you who has to cry; the public has to cry—snap out of it!" It was the best possible cure for me.

I also learned a great lesson from my amazing costar Willem Dafoe, who played six different roles, including my father, my brother, an old general losing his memory, and Ulay. I had always believed performance was real and theater was fake. In performance art, the knife is real, the blood is real. In theater, the knife is fake and the blood is ketchup. Despite this illusion, which I had always associated with a lack of discipline, Willem taught me that getting into a role can be every bit as demanding and real as performance art.

Me with Alex Poots at the Manchester Festival, 2011

With Bob Wilson's brilliance and crucial input from co-producer Alex Poots and Willem, and the incomparable music of Anohni, *The Life and Death of Marina Abramović* was a great success for three years in theaters around the world, starting at the Manchester Festival (where at the premiere, which I had dedicated to Paolo, he failed to show up) and moving to Teatro Real in Madrid, the Single Theatre in Antwerp, the Holland Festival, the Luminato Festival in Toronto, and finally the Park Avenue Armory in New York. And it turned out that Bob Wilson had been completely right about presenting my tragedies in the form of comic opera: only he could have found a way to convey my very peculiar life and make it feel totally universal.

⌣

Earlier I mentioned my Three Marinas idea, but that's for after my death. I also think of myself as three Marinas now, while I'm alive.

There is the warrior one. The spiritual one. And there is the bullshit one.

You've met the warrior and the spiritual ones. The bullshit one is the one I try to keep hidden. This is the poor little Marina who thinks everything she does is wrong, the Marina who's fat, ugly, and unwanted. The one who, when she's sad, consoles herself by watching bad movies, eating whole boxes of chocolates, and putting her head under the pillow to pretend her troubles don't exist.

Bullshit Marina was so much in evidence after my breakup. I was so shrunken emotionally, so wounded. I felt old and ugly, but mainly I felt dumped. I went back to the psychoanalyst and wept uncontrollably. I told her I couldn't eat or sleep. Once again, she prescribed antidepressants—and this time, she told me, I should really take them. The pills made me feel foggy. And a clear consciousness is so important to me, even if it is a consciousness filled with pain. I threw the medicine away.

I was a complete mess. For a long time.

Charlie Griffin, the printer of my photographs and a friend, saw how sad I was and said I should meet his friend Maxi Cohen. Maxi, Charlie told me, was an artist and filmmaker who'd spent the last twenty-five years filming shamans and rituals almost everywhere on the planet. I met with Maxi and asked her: In all your journeys, which shamans have you encountered who might best be able to help me overcome a broken heart? She told me that very recently, in Brazil, she'd met two extraordinary people, Rudá and Denise.

It was November 2010, and I was about to go to São Paulo to show *Back to Simplicity*, my reflection on the tranquility of nature and animals, at Galeria Luciana Brito. After the show, I decided, I would go to Curitiba, which was nearby, to meet the two shamans. I invited another friend, the English curator Mark Sanders, to join me. Having just gone through a divorce, Mark, too, was heartbroken.

I met with Rudá first. He told me that every part of the body is related to certain parts of your inner life—everything to do with the legs, for example, is family—and that every emotional pain turns to physical pain. When I came to him, I couldn't move my left shoulder—it was frozen. This, according to Rudá, was connected to marriage. The only way to help me, he said, was to work back through my physical pain to the emotional pain, which would then leave the body. All the cells of our body, he told me, have a certain memory: it's possible to free the cells of the old, bad memories and to charge the cells with a different memory, such as love for yourself.

As I lay on a mat, he massaged one of my legs for two hours, and then the other leg for two hours more. He didn't touch the rest of my body, and this wasn't the kind of massage I was used to. It was more like acupressure, bearing down on certain points, and the physical pain was unbearable. At that moment it seemed I'd never felt that kind of physical pain in my life. He said, "Just scream it out"—and I screamed like a lion in the middle of this forest in Curitiba. And each time I screamed he said, "Oh, very good, very good; this one is even better." I screamed till I felt completely out of it.

After four hours of this, I went back to the little place where I was staying and lay down, exhausted. For the rest of the day I couldn't move.

The next day I went back, and once again he went to work on my legs. Only this time, my pain was emotional rather than physical. I remembered terribly unjust things my mother had done to me, things I didn't even know were in my brain. It was like a movie playing in my head. I wept and wept, uncontrollably.

The next day Rudá worked on different parts of my body. Then he came to my left shoulder.

The pain was even beyond the pain from my legs. Again I screamed like a lioness; again Rudá complimented me on my screaming. And again I collapsed at the end of the day.

The following day he worked on the shoulder once more, and as with my legs, this time the pain was emotional. Every terrible moment with Paolo ran through my mind, and I wept until I couldn't

Working with my shamans, Rudá Iandé and Denise Maia, Curitiba, Brazil, 2013

weep anymore. Rudá sang to my shoulder, brushed it gently with a feather, and held it with his hand until it relaxed. And my shoulder folded softly, like the wing of a bird.

Then came the fifth day. I wondered, *What is he going to do now?* So he said, "Now begins the healing process. Because now you are free from the pain of the old memories—your cells are ready to make new ones. Now you have to learn to love yourself.

"I can't do this for you," he said. "You have to do it yourself. You must give love to yourself—your cells' memory must be filled with love. That's all you have to do."

And he told me to take off my dress.

I was completely naked, but there was nothing erotic about it. The shaman just held me, for ten or fifteen minutes, breathing very quietly. Then his wife, a large and voluptuous woman in a flowered dress, came into the hut.

Rudá is all about the exorcism of pain, and his wife, Denise, is all about the happiness of life. Her job, Rudá told me, was to teach me to enjoy my own body, to have real pleasure in lovemaking. And then he left the hut.

Denise and I sat on the dirt, and I told her everything. I told her that Paolo had been the only man in my life for fourteen years, that I'd never even thought of anybody else. I told her how terrible it was when he left me, how unjust. And the last, worst, thing: how awful it was to feel that I was getting old alone. And I couldn't help it: as I talked about all this again, I began to cry again. But as I wept, Denise just smiled. She beamed with perfect happiness.

Then this big woman in the flowered dress jumped to her feet. "Look at me!" she commanded. And she pulled her dress over her head, and she was completely naked. "Look at how beautiful I am!" Denise said. "I am a goddess!"

She pulled one enormous breast up to her mouth and kissed it. Then she kissed the other one. She pulled one knee up, then the other, and kissed each one. Anything on her body she could kiss, she kissed. I stared at her in amazement. This was better than psychotherapy.

This was better than anything. This was the most beautiful fucking human being I'd ever seen in my life. And in that instant, all my misery drained away.

Denise was also an oracle. One day she sat on the ground with a plate full of stones and shells in front of her. As I looked at the plate, she closed her eyes and began telling me things. "You know, you are not from this planet," she said. "Your DNA is galactic. You came to Earth from a very faraway galaxy, for a purpose."

She had my full attention. I asked her what my purpose was. She was silent for a while.

Then she said, "Your purpose is to help humans to transcend pain."

I was speechless.

The day before I left, Rudá made a big fire in the forest. He asked me to take off all my clothes, to get on all fours, facing the fire, and to roar with all my might into the fire. I did this for a long time, and my whole body filled with strength. Every molecule in me felt filled with power. When I finished, I felt I could do anything and face any obstacle. I was free.

And then, not long afterward, I got kissed. At the moment when I felt sure I would never again experience the electricity of my entire body being overcome with love. And I knew at that moment that I had been wrong.

⌒

In 2012, PAC Milan, that city's huge exhibition space for contemporary art, invited me to create a show: the subject was up to me. The invitation came at an interesting moment: I was planning to produce an entire new body of work, and to introduce the Abramović Method for the first time. For the new work I wanted to build more transitory objects, using crystals, and Luciana Brito, my São Paulo gallerist, helped find the money to sponsor my trip to the crystal mines of Brazil. Just as important, though, these funds would also cover my research into places of power in that country and allow me to seek out people there who possessed certain kinds of energy that the rational mind cannot understand.

We decided to document my trip with a Brazilian film crew, and Paula Garcia, a talented Brazilian performance artist I'd met at Luciana's gallery, volunteered to research people and places I should visit, and to create an itinerary. Later, the footage from this trip would become a film called *The Space In Between: Marina Abramović and Brazil.*

I arrived in São Paulo with my group—Serge, the performance artist and choreographer Lynsey Peisinger, Marco Anelli, and Youssef Nabil, a young Egyptian artist from Paris—and met with the film crew, headed by Marco del Fiol, whom I liked at once. Our first stop was Abadiânia, where, we hoped, we were to meet the world-famous healer John of God.

With Paula Garcia and Lynsey Peisinger, New York, 2014

Abadiânia was a very strange place: a tiny village of three streets, where everyone was dressed in white. In the center of the village was the John of God Casa. People from all walks of life—you'd see a rich woman from Texas next to a poor Colombian family—had come from all over the world to seek the healer's help.

To film John of God I needed his permission, and he told our producers Jasmin and Minom Pinto, that the only way he could grant permission was to ask the spirits. We waited a full ten days for the spirits to say yes or no. Then one morning I heard that the spirits were okay with me, and we began filming.

John of God performed two types of operations, spiritual and physical. In the former, he sends spirits into your dreams to heal you. And in the physical procedures, performed without any anesthesia, he cuts into the body—eyes, breasts, stomachs—with much blood, but no pain. We filmed a number of these operations. John of God charges nothing for them, and some of his cures have been miraculous.

We moved on from Abadiânia, filming along the way. In Cachoeira, Recôncavo Baiano, I met a 108-year-old woman who was extraordinarily energetic. What is the most important thing in life? I asked her. "How to enter, and how to exit," she said. "And to have friends and family who love you."

I also spent a lot of time in the rain forest, among waterfalls, rushing rivers, and magnificent rock formations. Marco took some wonderful photographs of me: we called the series *Places of Power.* We went to Vale do Amanhecer in Distrito Federal, where we visited me-

Waterfall, from the series *Places of Power,* Brazil, 2013

diums who practice a kind of complex religious syncretism through prayer and ritual; I participated in ayahuasca rituals in Chapada Diamantina.

While the rest of the company returned home, Paula and I and the film crew went to the mines, where I bought large pieces of crystal to incorporate in my transitory objects. By now I had developed two kinds of objects, for human and nonhuman use. The two copper chairs at the Okazaki Mindscape Museum in Japan, one for people to sit in and one seatless and fifty feet high, were an early example of this. My idea about the transitory objects was to make the invisible visible. When I introduced the chairs for human and nonhuman use, I fully expected the sitter to see his or her own spirit.

For the exhibition at PAC Milan, in March 2012, I had created three types of transitory objects for sitting, standing, and lying down. This was the first time I would use the Abramović Method to prepare the public for their participation. I invited Lynsey Peisinger and the dancer and choreographer Rebecca Davis to assist me. We worked with groups of twenty-five participants every two hours. Upon entering, the participants were asked to put all their belongings, including cell phones, watches, and computers, into lockers, and put on white lab coats and noise-canceling headphones. (This was the first time we used the lockers, which later became a crucial component of the Method.)

Lynsey, Rebecca, and I then guided the participants in a warm-up exercise meant to wake up the senses by moving and stretching the body and massaging the eyes, ears, and mouth, and then transitioned the groups to sit, stand, and lie on each of the objects for thirty minutes. Thus the participants became performers, and the rest of the public could watch them with binoculars, able to take precise note of the tiniest details about them: their slightest movements, their facial expressions, the texture of their skin over a two-hour period. The public was both participating in and witnessing a performance that we were creating together. More and more, I was removing myself from the work.

The Abramović Method at Padiglione d'Arte Contemporanea, Milan, 2012

One day in the early spring of 2013, the phone rang in my office and Giuliano picked it up. I saw a look of amazement pass over his face. *"It's Lady Gaga,"* he mouthed to me.

They'd never met, but since they're both Italian, the conversation seemed to go on for half an hour, with lots of screaming and laughter. After Giuliano hung up, he reported to me that she loved my work and wanted to do a workshop with me as soon as possible. She wanted me to be her teacher.

I'd known ever since she visited the MoMA show that she was a fan. We decided first to have lunch at my apartment, just the two of us, with Giuliano doing the cooking. Gaga arrived at my door alone and very humble. There were tears in her eyes as she embraced me.

Giuliano made a beautiful meal, which she hardly touched. Instead we talked and talked about her life, and why she felt she needed this workshop. "I'm young, and there are three teachers I want to learn from," she told me. "Bob Wilson, Jeff Koons, and you."

We decided on a four-day workshop at my upstate house, and we set the date and the time. Gaga volunteered to have the workshop filmed, so the clip could be used for the Kickstarter campaign I was planning for the institute. I wanted to hire the visionary architect and writer Rem Koolhaas to make plans for my building in Hudson, and the plans would cost over a half million dollars. I would need all the help I could get.

I prepared for the workshop by going to Walmart and buying a nurse's uniform—white pants and white shirt, very good cotton—for $14.99. Then I went to a John Deere tractor store and bought a pair of overalls for $29.99. I also purchased a bottle of organic almond oil, a large bar of scentless soap, and a wooden comb. I laid out all these things in her room at Star House, and, with Paula, awaited Lady Gaga's arrival.

She showed up on the appointed day at precisely six A.M., all business. No makeup, no wig. She went right to her room, put her phone and computer away, put on the overalls, came downstairs, and said, "Let's start."

As the photographer Terry Richardson's two-person crew began filming, I told Gaga the ground rules: For the next four days there was to be no food and no talking. She could drink water only. And she would do the exercises I gave her to the best of her ability.

The Abramović Method practiced by Lady Gaga, New York, 2013

Her best was very good. She did every exercise I assigned her, from the first (a three-hour slow-motion walk) to the last (finding her way back to the house from the middle of the woods while wearing a blindfold) with complete precision and seriousness. Not speaking or eating or using a computer for four days was not a problem for her.

That last exercise worried me. Not only was she blindfolded, but the forest was full of thorns, poison ivy, and Lyme disease—bearing ticks. And not only did she find her way out, but in the middle of the exercise, in the midst of thick bushes, she took off all her clothes and completed the walk naked.

Later on, when Gaga received the Young Artist Award from Americans for the Arts, she said that the workshop with me was the best rehab she'd ever had.

After the Lady Gaga workshop, the newly formed MAI office devoted its full energy to our Kickstarter campaign, headed by Siena Oristaglio. This was really at the beginning of Kickstarter, and it was as new to me as it was to the rest of the world. I remember reading in *Time* how it all began: The three young founders wanted to throw a benefit for a sick friend, but didn't have any money. They wanted to raise $1,000, but within a few hours of putting their appeal on the Internet, they got $5,000.

This was so fascinating to me. Everything, I realized, was in the sincerity and clarity of the presentation. And so when I decided to make a Kickstarter video to tell people why I needed money for MAI, I invited my two Brazilian shamans, Rudá and Denise, to my upstate house and asked their advice.

They told me the best thing I could do would be to seclude myself completely for six days in my little hut by the river and just watch the stream, without eating, speaking, reading, or writing. Every day, they said, they would bring me water to drink from the main house.

After six days of sitting in silence and watching the river, I came out and made the video in a single take. The message was direct and clear. I was asking help from Kickstarter for money to pay the architect Rem Koolhaas and Shohei Shigematsu and their New York firm, Office for Metropolitan Architecture (OMA), to make drawings for the building in Hudson that I'd bought five years earlier and donated to MAI, a nonprofit organization.

I said that when I first bought the building in 2008, I was looking for a place to store my transitory objects, which were very expensive to store in New York City. In Hudson, close to my upstate house, I had found that very old theater building, built in 1929, which seemed ideal. As did Hudson itself, which was just two hours from Manhattan, and close to Dia:Beacon, MassMoca, Bard College, Cornell, and Williams College.

When I saw the interior of this big old abandoned theater, I suddenly realized I no longer wanted to use it for storage. Instead I had a vision that it could become a center for long-durational, immaterial works. In my mind, the only architects I wanted to work with were Rem and Shohei. Koolhaas was not only a great architect but a writer and a philosopher. In one of his most famous books, *Delirious New York*, he wrote, "The city is an addictive machine from which there is no escape."

Rem and Shohei were interested in creating a specific place, radically simple and severe, both for long-durational performances and for the public to learn what performance art is. When visitors entered

MAI, their first action would be to sign a contract and give their word of honor that they would stay for six hours and not interrupt any activities with early departure. It's a simple exchange: visitors give their time; MAI gives them experience.

Our Kickstarter campaign began.

The way it works is that you set up a specific time period, thirty days maximum, for raising the funds you need. The public can give any amount from $1 to $10,000, and in return, you have to give them rewards. For our campaign, I decided, the rewards for the larger gifts should be immaterial. For pledging $1,000 or more, for example, a donor would get to spend one hour on Skype looking into my eyes. If you pledged $5,000 or more, I would workshop your project in any medium via webcam. Alternately, you could have a movie night with me at my place in New York, watching one of my favorite films and discussing it with me afterward over coffee and ice cream.

The biggest reward of all, for pledging $10,000 or more, was no reward and no mention of your name.

We set our goal as $600,000: the Kickstarter rule was that if we raised anything less in the thirty-day period—even if it was $599,000—we would have to give it all back. If we raised more, on the other hand, we could keep it. We wound up with $620,000—in large part due to Lady Gaga posting the video of her workshop online. Her forty-five million young followers on social media paid close attention. Of course the immediate focus was on her nudity. But the strange beauty of what she was doing in the exercises was even more interesting to the kids who were watching. *What is performance art?* they wondered. *And what is this institute that this strange woman Abramović is talking about?*

The video drew many thousands of young people to our Facebook page, and it soon would attract many of these same young people to my museum events. These were kids who wouldn't come to a museum for any other reason. I was so grateful to Lady Gaga for bringing them to my work.

Every day we reached out to new masses of people, seeking support. Throughout the campaign, we created a number of online events, videos, and content to help boost the effort: for example, Gaga doing the Method, Pippin Barr's Digital Institute, me doing a Reddit Ask Me Anything. With each of these releases, we wrote to press and other possibly interested groups to spread the word. We coordinated all our efforts onto our social-media platforms: Facebook, Twitter, Instagram, and Tumblr.

At the same time, my team wrote to my contacts, asking for their individual support, whether in the form of donations or help spreading the word.

There were a lot of disappointments—some people who I thought would really help a lot gave little. On the other hand, many people I didn't know at all—in Poland, New Zealand, Greece, Turkey, China, Norway, and so many other places—gave so much. And this was thrilling. For me, Kickstarter was a thermometer, measuring how passionate people were about starting this institute for immaterial art, and in the end, 4,600 people were passionate enough to give money. And I set about giving them all something back.

I had one year to bestow my rewards, and for a year, I worked very, very hard at it. I hugged several hundred people in a single day outside London's Serpentine Galleries, and on another day, at Kickstarter headquarters in Brooklyn.

Digital rendering of the Marina Abramović Institute, 2012

Top: Audience of my final lecture for *Terra Comunal*, SESC, São Paulo, 2015;
bottom: As One (performance, 7 minutes), Athens, 2016

And then, after the plans were made and paid for, we found out that to build the institute the way we wanted would cost $31 million.

This was a big problem. For one thing, my work doesn't sell for much. And I quickly found out that rich people weren't exactly lining up around the block to invest in immaterial art. In May 2014, MAI received an invitation from Richard Branson and the philanthropy collective Ignite Change to give a presentation on the institute on Necker Island, Branson's Caribbean retreat. Siena accompanied me, and we encountered a very diverse group of people. The most fascinating were Branson himself and Chris Anderson, the curator of TED, and his wife, Jacqueline Novogratz. My talk was enthusiastically received. In it, I said I had two wishes: for Richard Branson to give me a one-way ticket to outer space on Virgin Galactic and for Chris Anderson to give me a TED talk. Richard didn't comment on the space trip, but Chris came up to me and told me I could do a TED talk in 2015, a year devoted to the theme of taking risks. He thought I would fit perfectly.

The Necker Island visit was exciting, but no commitments to fund the institute came out of it. I started having lunches with billionaires. I would bring Koolhaas's beautiful plans with me and use all my persuasive powers, and I kept hitting a wall. Soon I got exhausted. And discouraged.

Then I met Thanos Argyropoulos. At the Onassis Cultural Center in Athens, he heard me give one of my lectures on my utopian plans for the institute and became very enthusiastic about helping me. Thanos was a London School of Economics graduate who knew everything about investments and banking, which for me and Serge was unknown territory. We were very happy to welcome him to our team.

On the set of *Seven Deaths* with Thanos Argyropoulos, 2016

Thanos started looking at the numbers, and in three hours he discovered that if I kept putting my own money into the institute at the present rate—I was putting all the proceeds from the sale of my works into MAI; I had five people working Kickstarter, handling press and social media, programming, and development—I would be bankrupt in three months. This was a real emergency.

In the meantime we found asbestos in the Hudson building. It had to be removed if the building was to be used, and the removal would cost another $700,000. The money simply wasn't there. Thanos suggested we close the building for a while and look for other options.

I felt like huge rocks had been lifted from my shoulders. And just like that, the entire concept of my institute morphed: Why not (we thought) make MAI *itself* immaterial—and nomadic? Suddenly we had a new motto: "Don't come to us—we'll come to you." Institutions would call us, and they would pay for us to go there. In a flash, our whole financial model shifted: overhead vanished; red ink turned to black.

We developed a program to bring the Abramović Method to cultural institutions around the world as well as to curate and commission durational works by local and international performance artists. We wrote a new mission statement to reflect the change in our focus: "MAI explores, supports, and presents performance. MAI encourages collaboration between the arts, science, and the humanities. MAI will serve as the legacy of Marina Abramović."

I had finally created my institute, and I dedicated it: *To Human Beings.*

In the summer of 2013, while Sean and I were in Oslo for a show of my work, the collector Christian Ringnes asked me to make a sculpture for a big new sculpture park he was sponsoring in the city. I told him that I don't believe in sculptures in parks—I think nature is perfect without any art. But I went to the location anyway to see if it would give me any ideas. While Sean and Christian and I were strolling around the park with Gillespie and Kim Bradstrup, my gallerists in Oslo, we came to a little hill. It was from this point, Christian said, that we believe Edvard Munch painted *The Scream*. When he said that, I immediately thought of something.

Earlier that day, I'd visited the Munch Museum, where I saw people standing in front of *The Scream*, taking selfies with their mouths open. But—after all, it was a museum—nobody was actually screaming. Now I told Christian my idea: to make an exact measurement of the frame of Munch's painting, to re-create the frame in iron, and to place it exactly at that spot in the park—it was called the Ekeberg Hill—where all the citizens of Oslo would be invited to experience *The Scream* in a new way by standing in front of the empty frame and screaming into the void.

It was a gloomy, rainy day in Oslo. I invited the small group with me to scream and to see how we felt. After we'd screamed and screamed I started working to realize the idea. The empty iron frame was installed on the hill, and I created a video, also titled *The Scream*, inspired by and dedicated to Edvard Munch. Over the period of a month, Lynsey Peisinger and I filmed 270 people screaming through the empty frame.

Before they screamed Lynsey had to prepare them, right there in the park, with body movement and breathing exercises. Norwegian people can be very stoic: they don't show their emotions easily. Some of them admitted they'd never screamed in their life. But after Lynsey's preparation, when they stood in front of the frame, it was like opening a volcano of emotions. During the filming the police came many times, because the screams were echoing through the city below, and people were reporting rapes.

The empty frame remains in the park for the performance to continue.

On the last day of filming, after we'd finished our work, Christian invited us on his boat to have dinner and watch the sunset over the fjord. It was a beautiful late-August evening—the sky was a brilliant orange-red. The Scandinavian autumn was already in the air.

Meeting with Petter Skavlan to discuss the *Seven Deaths* project, Athens, 2016

Christian had invited five friends that he wanted me to meet: one of them was a tall, distinguished-looking man named Petter Skavlan. When I asked him what he did, he said he was a screenwriter for European and Hollywood movies. The previous year, *Kon-Tiki*, a movie he'd written, had been nominated for an Oscar for Best Foreign Language Film.

In a flash I remembered something I'd had in the back of my mind for so many years, the idea I'd thought of in the brutal gold-mining pit of Serra Pelada, *How to Die*. It was such a strong idea, I thought; I'd really never given up on it. Excitedly, I told Petter about my concept of juxtaposing the deaths of seven opera heroines (all sung by Maria Callas, of course) with documentary footage of actual deaths. Petter, whose mind was razor-sharp, got it instantly. And he said, "Why don't you make it simpler? Just make a script out of the seven opera deaths?"

From that moment we started talking about how to really make this project. Callas was my inspiration. By that time I'd read all the biographies of her and watched her extraordinary work on film. I felt such a powerful identification with her. Like me, she was a Sagittarius; like me, she had a terrible mother. We bore a physical similarity to each other. And though I had survived heartbreak, she died from a broken heart. In most operas, at the end, the heroine dies from love.

And Petter knew the list of their deaths as well as I did: KNIFING in *Carmen*; JUMPING in *Tosca*; STRANGULATION in *Otello*; BURNING in *Norma*; SUFFOCATION in *Aida*; HARA-KIRI in *Madame Butterfly*; CONSUMPTION in *La Traviata*. Right there on the boat, we imagined the piece: I would be filmed standing simply, without any makeup, in front of a white screen, telling the story of each opera in less than ten sentences. After each description there would be a cut to me enacting the opera death. In Callas's mind, the man killing her onstage was always Aristotle Onassis; in my mind, Willem Dafoe was the only man who could play my killer in each of the seven acts.

I envisioned seven video installations, one for each death, all seven to be shown sequentially. In addition, Petter suggested filming a feature documentary called *Living Seven Deaths*, the chronicle of the making of *Seven Deaths*, along with the story of how the piece relates to Maria Callas's life. The glorious sound of Callas's voice would fill every death scene.

Since then we've been working toward the realization of these two big pieces. In my dream, seven different film directors will direct the videos, and Riccardo Tisci will make all the costumes. The process is long, and just recently I wrote something that I hope will not be prophetic: *Make a film that is longer than the time you have left to live.*

Left: Portrait of Maria Callas by Cecil Beaton, 1957; *right:* my homage to Maria, 2011

At the same time, I was thinking about mounting my upcoming exhibition in the Serpentine Galleries, which I'd been invited to do the previous year. The general idea was to show unseen works, things few people knew I'd done in previous years; the curators, Julia Peyton-Jones and Hans-Ulrich Obrist, were very excited about this notion, but I wanted to do something bigger. So I returned to my shamans once more to prepare mentally and physically.

Early one morning, in the middle of the Brazilian jungle, I decided to take a swim in a beautiful waterfall. Afterward I sat on the edge of the rocks to dry in the morning sun—and out of nowhere, a very clear thought struck me: that I should not show any work in the gallery; that—even more radically than at PAC Milan—the gallery should be completely empty. That the public would come in and I would take them gently by the hand and bring them to a wall in the gallery, just to look at the blank space in front of them. That the public would become the performing body instead of me.

On arrival at the exhibition, visitors would literally and metaphorically leave their baggage behind in lockers, putting away their bags, jackets, electronic equipment, watches, cameras, phones. The show would have no rules, no formula—just the artist, the audience, and a few simple props in the empty white space. This was the best way I could think of to demonstrate immaterial art.

I would be present in the gallery from ten A.M. to six P.M., six days a week. The plan was for the exhibition to last sixty-four days, and so I would be there for a total of 512 hours. And *512 Hours* became the name of the show.

I knew I would need a collaborator for this very demanding work, and once again I found the best possible collaborator in Lynsey Peisinger. Lynsey and I had already worked very closely for three years on *The Life and Death of Marina Abramović*, as well as on the PAC Milan show and *The Scream*. She knew the Abramović Method well by now, and she also brought so many of her own ideas to it. I knew that in Lynsey I'd found somebody I could completely trust to continue my legacy. She herself selected and trained eighty-four facilitators for the new show.

512 Hours opened on June 11, 2014, and the work was exhausting in every possible way. To begin with, we asked visitors to wear noise-canceling headphones; any communication with them had to be nonverbal. Lynsey and the facilitators were dealing with every conceivable kind of energy from the public, a complex and difficult task. They would lead the visitors to different rooms in the gallery, where they would go through various exercises: just looking at the wall, counting grains of rice and lentils, doing a slow-motion walk, lying on a cot with eyes closed, standing on a platform.

Lynsey and I kept a diary during the exhibition, each of us recording an entry at the end of each day and putting it on the gallery website and social media. For me, the most powerful experience was watching the public standing on the platform. It was just a simple wooden platform, five inches off the ground. But when a person stands on such a platform with many others, everything changes, in them and around them.

The exhibition drew a huge variety of people from different social groups, races, religions. Many of them were people who generally don't go to art galleries, but they came for this experience: you'd see a science-fiction writer next to a Bangladeshi housewife next to a whole family with many children next to an English farmer next to an art critic—all of them standing completely still, eyes closed, in total silence. There was something in those moments that made me feel all of my work, over my whole career, had been worth it. In *512 Hours*, I found proof of the transformative power of performance. I also understood that this was the time to transfer my own experience to everyone else—and that the only way to do this was by letting people see and feel these things for themselves.

Over the course of the exhibition, I saw so many people undergo

512 Hours (performance, 512 hours), Serpentine Gallery, London, 2014

so many experiences, but one stood out: a twelve-year-old boy who came every day after school just to stand on the platform with his eyes closed for a long time—he wasn't interested in any other part of the show. His name was Oscar. When I asked him what drew him to this exercise, he said, "I'm not so good at school, but when I stand on the platform, then go home and stand in my room with my eyes closed, everything is okay."

These are some of the video diary transcripts from the show:

Day 1: I told them to close their eyes and breathe slowly. I told them that with their eyes closed, they see more, feel more, sense more, hear more. I also told them to reach a sense of peacefulness. To feel the energy of others and their own energy. To stand on the platform with closed eyes and feel the environment.

Day 8: The most important thing I noticed today was that only in stillness can we recognize movement.

Day 16: It was the worst day we ever had to date. The energies were fragmented. There was no center. Whenever I created an energy space, it was dissipated after a few minutes. It was endless work—like a house of cards, we could not build anything.

Day 32: Halfway. At the beginning there was only an idea. When the idea becomes reality, we have more experience. That gives us clarity. The public is in the position of observer, also participant. Then observer again. And the roles shift all day long. This is completely different from any other show.

Day 40: I believe that the line between real life and life at the Serpentine is blurred. Even when I leave here, it makes no difference: I'm still in the same space in my mind. So I've decided not to resist. There is no separation between me, the spectators, and the work. It's all one thing.

Last day (Day 64): It was an important journey. I know this work is not ending now, but the beginning of something big and different. It's about humanity, humbleness, and collectivity. It is very simple. Maybe together we can change consciousness and transform the world. And we can start doing this anywhere.

⌒

512 Hours began a year of nonstop activity. Soon after the Serpentine event, I had a show, *White Space*, at Lisson Gallery in London. The exhibition consisted of an immersive sound environment by that title from 1972, as well as several other works from my early career, some never seen before. While I was in London, Alex Poots invited me to dinner, telling me he had someone special he wanted me to meet: Igor Levit, the twenty-seven-year-old Russian-German pianist. And he *was* special—not only did he play magnificently, but he was full of life (and great Jewish jokes). It was a wonderful evening, with lots of laughter, but Alex also asked me to design a method for an audience to listen to one of the most difficult pieces of classical music—and one of Igor's great showpieces—the *Goldberg Variations*. I was immediately intrigued by the challenge of bringing classical music—which I believe to be the most immaterial of arts—to a contemporary audience in a completely new way.

Promotional photo for *Goldberg*, with pianist
Igor Levit, New York, 2015

The following months were thrilling and exhausting. I began preparing a combined retrospective and MAI exhibition for SESC, the Brazilian cultural organization. Lynsey, Paula Garcia, and I traveled to São Paulo to select local artists and to commission new long durational performances from them. I took them into the Brazilian countryside and conducted a *Cleaning the House* workshop to prepare them to perform for the duration of the exhibition, two months total. In the end, eighteen Brazilian performance artists created a fascinating variety of pieces. This was a huge achievement for them, and also for MAI as it was the first time we had programmed performance work and had created something that big together. The exhibition would be called *Terra Comunal* (*Common Ground*), a title based on my experiences in Brazil in places of power, among waterfalls, trees, rivers, insects, plants, and people with special energy. The piece was all about time and space, new forms of interaction, and creating a sense of community.

After more than a year spent preparing the retrospective and the exhibition for a mid-March opening, I flew to Vancouver to deliver my TED talk, "An art made of trust, vulnerability, and connection." I spoke about the development of my work and how bringing the public into it was opening new paths toward exploring human consciousness. I was overwhelmed by the response and by the talk's online impact afterward: to date we've had over a million views.

But, after all of this travel and work, I was completely overwhelmed.

Projects were stacked up for the months ahead. I had created a site-specific sound installation called *Ten Thousand Stars* for the Venice Biennale that summer as part of the exhibition *Proportio,* organized by Axel Vervoordt, which involved recording my voice speaking the names of ten thousand stars in our galaxy. It took me thirty-six hours, but it was ready for the opening in early May.

Around this time, Riccardo Tisci had also asked me to art-direct Givenchy's first show in New York—on September 11. Creating a look and a feel for the show that would at once honor the solemnity of the 9/11 anniversary and display Riccardo's simple and elegant designs to their best advantage was a formidable challenge. I wrote him a letter:

Dear Riccardo,

When you asked me to work with you on this show, I felt honored but I also felt a great responsibility.

The 11th of September is the saddest day in recent American history. As the artistic director, I want to create something respectful and humble. The location of the show, Pier 26, is significant because of its position and clear view on the Freedom Tower. Constructing the set from recycled materials and debris means that it could be constructed and deconstructed without any waste.

Our choice of music, from six different cultures and religions, has the power to unite people without discrimination.

This event that we are creating together is about forgiveness, inclusivity, new life, hope, and above all, love.

Love,
Marina

The Contract, with Riccardo Tisci, black-and-white print, 2011

Then there was Australia. In June I was to fly to Tasmania, where the Museum of Old and New Art in Hobart would mount a combined retrospective and demonstration of my Method. I would be present for the opening, and for ten days afterward. Immediately after that, Lynsey and I were to bring a twelve-day version of the Method to the John Kaldor Foundation in Sydney, where, using a series of simple props and exercises—similar to what we did for the Serpentine show—we would once again make the public the subject.

Is it any wonder that as early as March, during the SESC project in

São Paulo, I began to have heart palpitations? I was having panic attacks, imagining I had a brain tumor. I saw myself suffering a stroke, winding up in a wheelchair. I was feeling horrible—and feeling even worse when I flew from Brazil to the Venice Biennale. And then to Tasmania. And then to Sydney. One night, while I was having dinner there with Giuliano, I knew I had to see a doctor. He took my blood pressure: it was 211 over 216—heart-attack territory.

The medicine the doctor prescribed lowered my blood pressure, but I kept feeling worse. My ankles and the rest of my body were swollen and heavy. The Givenchy show and Igor's *Goldberg Variations* at the Park Avenue Armory still lay ahead. It would be very long before I could take any kind of break.

I powered through it somehow, even at the busiest times. My team and I worked like crazy on the Givency show, and our efforts were rewarded. The September 11 event, on a soft, warm, cloudless evening, was perfect. Appropriately for the solemn occasion, Pier 26 was decorated humbly with industrial-looking sheds, wood boxes, and rough benches. As the crowd filed in, the air filled with the deep sound of Tibetan chanting, and performers atop the sheds moved with stately slowness: one waving tree branches, one holding her hand under a faucet of running water, two embracing, one climbing a ladder. After a half-hour a gong sounded, and the models began to file out in Riccardo's amazing, elegant clothes to the sound of music from various world cultures: Jewish and Muslim hymns, traditional Balkan throat-singing performed by Svetlana Spajić, and an operatic rendition of "Ave Maria."

I immediately went on to develop a concept for *Goldberg* and enlisted the brilliant lighting director Urs Schoenebaum. After placing their watches, cell phones, and computers in lockers, the audience would enter the semi-darkened Armory, receive noise-canceling headphones, and recline in lawn chairs. At the sound of a gong, the public would put on the headphones and relax. Then, for the next thirty minutes, as the space went completely dark (except for thin, horizon-like strips of white lighting on the side walls), a movable platform holding Igor seated at a grand piano would move with majestic slowness and in complete silence along a track from the back of the Armory to the front, near the audience. When the platform reached the front, it would stop—and then another gong would sound and the audience would remove their headphones, and Igor would begin to play the *Goldberg Variations*. (The piano's keyboard would also be lit by a strip of light, so Igor and the audience could see his hands.) Over the eighty-two minutes of the piece, the platform would revolve, again slowly and silently, completing exactly one revolution by the end.

All was perfection. And backstage, my whole body was in shingles. Finally, after *Goldberg*, I called Dr. Linda, who advised me to consult Dr. Radha Gopalan, a heart-transplant specialist who also practiced alternative medicine. Radha, who came from Sri Lanka, believed in combining eastern and western medical traditions: he had studied acupuncture and other forms of natural healing. The first thing he advised me to do was to throw out all my medications and start from the beginning.

Dr. Gopalan's second piece of advice was to go to Kalari Kovilakom, an Ayurvedic retreat in the southern tip of India, for one month. I had done Ayurvedic retreats before, but not since before *The Artist Is Present*, and this was the most radical place I'd ever been to—a cross between a monastery, a sanatorium, and a minimum-security prison. A sign on the entrance read, "Please leave your world here."

Artist Portrait with a Candle from the series *Places of Power,* Brazil, 2013

For thirty days, I barely spoke. I never opened a suitcase—each day I was given three freshly washed sets of pajamas. For thirty days I ate ghee and meditated. I underwent hours of intensive massage daily. I never looked at a computer or a smartphone. E-mail was a thing of the past. And after thirty days, I was healed.

I couldn't come directly back to civilization after this experience: my body, now completely relaxed, wasn't prepared for the transition. So I went to a beach resort on the Indian Ocean, a place full of happy families where I knew absolutely no one and could glory in my solitude. And one afternoon as I walked along a deserted beach, I decided to soak myself in the surf.

I took off my clothes and waded in. The waves were enormous, and the water was jade-blue, sparkling with sunlight. The ocean was so gigantic. Sometimes I just need to feel life, with every one of my pores open. When I came out of the water, I felt completely energized. I felt luminous. Then I got dressed again and walked into the forest just above the beach. As I moved deeper into the woods, the noise of the surf faded, and all at once I could sense beings all around me: everything was life.

PHOTO CREDITS

INTERIOR: pp. 43 and 52: Nebojsa Cankovic; p. 61: Dickenson V. Alley, Copyrighted work available under Creative Commons Attribution only license CC BY 4.0, Courtesy Wellcome Library, London; pp. 66, 67, and 76: Courtesy Marina Abramović Archives and Sean Kelly Gallery, New York; p. 86: Jaap de Graaf, Courtesy Marina Abramović Archives and Sean Kelly Gallery, New York; p. 97: © Giovanna dal Magro, Courtesy Marina Abramović Archives and Giovanna Dal Magro; p. 100: Jaap de Graaff; p. 101: Elmar Thomas; p. 105: Hans G. Haberl; p. 117: Courtesy Marina Abramović Archives and Sean Kelly Gallery, New York; p. 159: Gerard P. Pas, Courtesy Gerard P. Pas; pp. 214 and 219: Courtesy Marina Abramović Archives and Sean Kelly Gallery, New York; p. 228: Courtesy Marina Abramović Archives and LIMA; pp. 232 and 238: Courtesy Marina Abramović Archives and Sean Kelly Gallery, New York; p. 245: S. Anzaic; p. 257: Courtesy Marina Abramović Archives and Sean Kelly Gallery, New York; p. 260: Alessia Bulgari; p. 265: Attilio Maranzano, Courtesy Marina Abramović Archives and Sean Kelly Gallery, New York; pp. 271, 272, and 273: © Attilio Maranzano, Courtesy Marina Abramović Archives and Sean Kelly Gallery, New York; p. 280: (*left*) Courtesy Bildarchiv; Preussischer Kulturbesitz/Walter Vogel, (*right*) Attilio Maranzano; p. 283: (*left*) Peter Hassmann, Courtesy Valie Export, (*right*) Kathryn Carr; p. 296: Courtesy Marina Abramović Archives and Sean Kelly Gallery, New York; p. 302: Larry Busacca, Courtesy Larry Busacca/ Getty Images; pp. 305 and 306: Courtesy Marina Abramović Archives and Sean Kelly Gallery, New York; p. 310: Marco Anelli © 2010; p. 311: Alessandro Natale; pp. 312, 318, 320, and 331: Marco Anelli ©

2010; p. 336: Martin Godwin; p. 340: Courtesy Casa Redonda; p. 346: (*top grid*) © 24 ORE Cultura S.r.l., © Fabrizio Vatieri, © Laura Ferrari, (*bottom*) © 24 ORE Cultura S.r.l., © Laura Ferrari; p. 348: Courtesy Marina Abramović Archives and MAI; p. 351: Courtesy OMA and MAI; p. 352: (*top*) Victor Takayama for FLAGCX, 2015, Courtesy MAI, (*bottom*) Panos Kokkinias, 2016, Courtesy NEON and MAI; p. 357: (*left*) © The Cecil Beaton Studio Archive at Sotheby's, (*right*) René Habermacher; p. 360: Marco Anelli © 2014, Courtesy Marina Abramović Archives and Serpentine Gallery, London; p. 362: Marco Anelli © 2015, Courtesy The Park Avenue Armory; p. 364: Courtesy Marina Abramović Archives and Sean Kelly Gallery, New York; p. 366: Courtesy Marina Abramović Archives and Luciana Brito Gallery, São Paulo; INSERT 1: p. 3: (*bottom*) Marco Anelli © 2010; p. 5: (*bottom*) Alessia Bulgari; p. 6: Courtesy Marina Abramović Archives and LIMA; p. 7: Attilio Maranzano; p. 8: Courtesy Marina Abramović Archives and Sean Kelly Gallery, New York; INSERT 2: p. 1: Courtesy Marina Abramović Archives and Art Bärtschi & Cie, Geneva; p. 2: Omid Hashimi and Tim Hailand, 2011; p. 3: (*top*) © dpa picture alliance archive / Alamy Stock Photo, (*bottom*) © Patrick McMullan Courtesy Sean Kelly Gallery, New York; p. 4: (*top*) Brigitte Lacombe; p. 5: (*bottom*) Marco Anelli © 2014, Courtesy Marina Abramović Archives and Serpentine Gallery, London; p. 6: (*top*) Courtesy Marina Abramović Archives and Sean Kelly Gallery, New York, (*bottom*) Annie Leibovitz, Courtesy *Vanity Fair*; p. 7: (*top*) Courtesy of SundanceTV LLC/ JC Dhien, (*bottom*) Rahi Rezvani; p. 8: (*top*) Marco Del Fiol, Courtesy Givenchy, (*bottom*) James Ewing, Courtesy The Park Avenue Armory